The Bible
and the Comic Vision

The Bible
and the Comic Vision

J. William Whedbee

Fortress Press
Minneapolis

THE BIBLE AND THE COMIC VISION

First Fortress Press edition 2002

Copyright © 1998 Cambridge University Press. Reprinted with permission.

ISBN 0-8006-3486-1

Cover design: Jessica Thoreson
Cover art: Berruguete, Alonso (1486-1561). Job Choir. Cathedral, Toledo, Spain. Copyright Scala / Art Resource, NY. Used by permission.

Library of Congress has catalogued the hardcover edition as follows:

Whedbee, J. William
The Bible and the comic vision / J. William Whedbee
p. cm.
Includes bibliographical references and indexes.
ISBN 0 521 49507 5
1. Wit and humor in the Bible. 2. Bible. O.T.—Criticism, interpretation, etc.
I. Title.
BS1199.W58 W44 1998
    220.6–dc21   97–20970
                                                                  CIP

The paper used in this publication meets the minimum requirements of American National Standard for Information Sciences—Permanence of Paper for Printed Library Materials, ANSI Z329.48-1984.

Manufactured in the U.S.A.

07   06   05   04   03   02   1   2   3   4   5   6   7   8   9   10

CONTENTS

Acknowledgments

This book has taken a long time to be born, and many people have contributed to its birthing. First and foremost I am deeply indebted to my teachers in Hebrew Bible to whom I dedicate this book: Brevard S. Childs, Erhard Gerstenberger, Judah Goldin, David A. Hubbard, William S. La Sor, B. Davie Napier, and Marvin H. Pope. From these "magnificent seven" scholar-teachers, I want to single out David Hubbard for a special note of thanks. David lamentably met an untimely death last year. He was my "first" professor of the Bible, who taught me Greek, Hebrew, and Aramaic, and much else about life and literature. An enchanting storyteller, erudite scholar, and enlightened sage, he was a rare and splendid teacher. Indeed, he was a mentor for all seasons whose greatest gift was perhaps his capacity for friendship.

Other colleagues and friends over the years were always ready and willing to read different parts of my book, offering steady encouragement and gentle criticism. Perhaps more importantly, they persistently albeit patiently kept pushing me to move ahead, especially when my energies flagged and my confidence wavered. How can I thank them? If I counted all the ways, I would fill up too many pages and evoke the displeasure of my editor. At least I can list their names, trusting them to know how and why this book owes so much to their contributions which were both tangible and intangible: Martha Andresen, James Armantage, Eleanor Beach, Athalya Brenner, Elizabeth Brunazzi, Margaret Dornish, Carl Ernst, Stephen and Pauline Erickson, Tamara Eskenazi, Cheryl Exum, Gina Foster, Wolfgang Harnisch, Jerry Irish, Zayn

Kassam, Catherine Keller, Robert Polzin, Mili Quinlan, Kent Richards, David Robertson, Martha and Robert Voelkel, Tracy Wolff, and Steven Young.

Of this larger group, I want to highlight eight individuals whose contributions deserve special and heart-felt gratitude. Martha Andresen not only allowed me to audit her inspiring course in Shakespearean comedy which deepened my insights into the complexity of the comic vision, but she also kindly read the whole manuscript and offered many valuable suggestions. David Robertson heard a very early version of my treatment of Job and comedy, inviting me to include it in an anthology of essays on Job and thus launched the first stage of publication; he also read and commented helpfully on several chapters of the manuscript. Tracy Wolff gave the first half of the manuscript a most discriminating reading which improved both style and content. Stephen Erickson provided stimulation with his philosophical acuity and literary sensibility; perhaps more importantly, his understated humor and ironic wit helped keep me reasonably sane during a sometimes crazy time in my life. Margaret Dornish, my current chair, has been a wonderful colleague of almost thirty years; she unfailingly supported me during all the phases of my project. Zayn Kassam not only helped me get over many obstacles in my computer misadventures, but also gave my entire manuscript the benefit of her unerring editorial eye. Jerry Irish read the whole manuscript and helped me to tidy up some unkempt sentences and to clarify some fuzzy arguments. Finally, I must particularly thank Tamara Eskenazi who believed in the project before I did; Tamara first heard some of my early reflections on the Bible and comedy in a summer school course I taught at Iliff Seminary in 1981. Since then she has read each individual section during the various stages of the book's birthing, always pressing me to deepen my interpretation of the biblical texts and especially urging me to tease out the larger implications of correlating the Bible with the comic vision. The collective efforts of all my readers have significantly strengthened my book, and when I did not follow their counsel my book no doubt is the poorer.

I owe much to my colleague Robert Woods and my administrative assistant Evelyn Khalili, both of whom led me patiently through the labyrinthine world of the word processor so that I never got permanently stuck in cyberspace. Moreover, going above and beyond the call of duty, Robert Woods kindly took time away from his sabbatical to finish the formatting for the whole manuscript. Thanks, too, must go to the Office of Academic Computing at Pomona College for its support.

Pomona College has always provided a warm and congenial atmosphere to conduct my work. College grants and sabbatical leaves have graced my time at Pomona which has been my only institutional home. My different presidents and deans have been supportive and encouraging. And what shall I say about my wonderful students who have been a joy and inspiration to teach? Their papers on various comic themes in the Bible have often made me rethink different issues and on occasion quote directly when their insights begged to be cited and acknowledged. For over thirty years it has been a pleasure to spend time with such imaginative and talented students from whom I have learned so much. At the other end of the spectrum, I am happy also to pay tribute to my older students. Elder Hostel programs have furnished a most stimulating environment to present some of the materials of my book. My older students have shown infectious enthusiasm, eager questioning, and boundless curiosity in listening to lectures on the comedy of the Bible. The wisdom of their years often provided illuminating angles of vision, showing a maturity of insight that only long lives of experience could bring. Here, too, I must acknowledge my debt to my most devoted auditor: Roni Tofield is an irrepressible and amazingly vibrant student whose 86 years of age don't hold her back from an ever fresh approach to our ancient biblical texts. I thank her for the years of auditing which have enlivened my courses and exemplified a model of intellectual passion for my more typical 18–22 year old students.

I am also most grateful to the editorial staff at Cambridge University Press. Alex Wright, the erstwhile religion editor at

Cambridge, first approached me about my project and then accepted it for publication. His successor, Ruth Parr, has continued to be a vital link with Cambridge Press, generously extending to me its expert editorial services. In particular, I am grateful to Andrew Taylor, my copy editor, for his exemplary reading of the manuscript and for saving me from some embarrassing errors. Here, too, I want to thank the anonymous reviewers enlisted by Cambridge Press; they made several constructive criticisms which proved useful in revising the manuscript.

Earlier versions of some chapters have appeared as essays or parts of essays in other publications. Portions of chapter 2 initially were published in "Isaac, Samson, and Saul: Reflections on the Comic and Tragic Visions," co-authored with J. Cheryl Exum (*Semeia* 32 [1984]). An earlier version of chapter 5 appeared under the title, "The Comedy of Job" (*Semeia* 7 [1977]). Chapter 6 was originally published under the title, "Paradox and Parody in the Song of Solomon: Towards a Comic Reading of the Most Sublime Song," in *A Feminist Companion to the Song of Songs*, ed. Athalya Brenner (Sheffield: JSOT Press, 1993). I am grateful to Scholars Press and Sheffield Academic Press for permission to use the material.

Last but not least I am glad for the opportunity to express my deep gratitude to my parents of blessed memory; both my mother and father did not live to see the appearance of my book. Although neither one fully understood why it was taking me so long to finish it, they never swerved in offering encouragement. My son David, now 29 years old and a fledgling scholar himself, was only a little boy of 4 years old when I gave my first lecture on comedy in the Bible. David has always been an unending source of joy, manifesting an exuberant zest for life and especially a good sense of humor – the last perhaps the most important for one whose father finds comedy in the Bible.

Note on translation and transliteration

Translations of the biblical texts are predominantly taken from the *Revised Standard Version* or the *New Revised Standard Version* unless otherwise noted. There are two major exceptions to this general practice: first, in chapter five ("The Comedy of Job") I typically use the translation of Marvin H. Pope, *Job*, The Anchor Bible (New York: Doubleday & Co., 1965); second, in chapter six ("Paradox and Parody in the Song of Solomon") I generally use the *Tanakh: A New Translation of the Holy Scriptures* (The Jewish Publication Society, 1985). In translating the name of Israel's God, I use Yahweh (not LORD). In transliterating the Hebrew, I have omitted the diacritical marks in order to be as "reader-friendly" as possible. I have transliterated mainly to highlight word-plays in the Hebrew which are germane to the argument.

Introduction: an anatomy of comedy in the Bible

Holy Books never laugh, to whatever nations they belong.

(Charles Baudelaire)[1]

IS THERE COMEDY IN THE BIBLE?

Most readers of the Bible would likely echo Baudelaire's argument about "holy books," contending along with many philosophers, theologians, and literary critics that the Bible is not a congenial home for the comic vision. A. N. Whitehead echoes a host of readers past and present when he asserts: "the total absence of humour from the Bible is one of the most singular things in all literatures."[2] It should occasion, therefore, no great surprise that for many the coupling of comedy and the Bible is a contradiction in terms.

Moreover, when one scans the more standard approaches of biblical criticism, comedy receives scant place – at least until the present time.[3] For example, a random glance at a

---

[1] Charles Baudelaire, "On the Essence of Laughter, and, in General, on the Comic in the Plastic Arts," in *Comedy: Meaning and Form*, Robert W. Corrigan, ed. (San Francisco: Chandler Publishing Co., 1965), p. 455.

[2] A. N. Whitehead, cited in *Dialogues*, Lucien Price, ed. (Boston: Little and Brown, 1953), p. 30. I owe this citation to Yehuda T. Radday, "On Missing the Humour in the Bible: An Introduction," in *On Humour and the Comic in the Hebrew Bible*, Yehuda T. Radday and Athalya Brenner, eds. (Sheffield: Sheffield Academic Press, 1990), p. 21 (see also footnote on p. 31).

[3] See, however, the pioneering books of A. J. Baumgartner, *L'Humour Dans l'Ancien Testament* (Lausanne: Grayot, 1896); J. Chotzner, *Hebrew Humor and Other Essays*, (London: Methuen, 1905). These two works are the exceptions that prove the rule, since they have had very little impact on biblical interpretation and are seldom cited.

number of Bible dictionaries reveals that most do not even
have an entry under comedy or humor until the most recent
ones such as *The Interpreter's Dictionary of the Bible, The Anchor
Bible Dictionary,* and *A Dictionary of Biblical Interpretation.*[4]
Standard commentaries reflect a similar paucity of interest in
comic forms in biblical literature, though the situation is
changing notably with books such as Esther and Jonah (see
below). One usually finds, however, only scattered references
to the comic dimensions of texts such as Balaam's talking ass
(Num. 22) or Abraham's negotiations with God on behalf of
the "righteous" in Sodom and Gomorrah (Gen. 18).

The lack of focus on comedy in the Bible is not altogether
surprising: after all, the term "comedy" is Greek in origin,
usually Aristotelian in its literary critical application, and
hence seemingly remote from the more obviously central and
constitutive biblical genres. To be sure, in the long, complex
history of Judaism and Christianity, there were notable exceptions to this prevailing pattern such as we find in medieval
Christianity's display of a comic sensibility in its miracle and
mystery plays, the role of the carnivalesque in such medieval
Christian institutions as "The Feast of Fools,"[5] and Hasidic
Judaism's affirmation of the intimate interplay between
humor and religion. However, centuries of liturgical and
theological use of the Bible have helped to obscure and
largely exclude a vital role for comedy and humor in biblical
literature and religion.

As a consequence, the rich, variegated history of the Bible's
multiple roles in Western culture shows at best ambiguous
encounters between the Bible and comedy – encounters

[4] W. F. Stinespring, "Humor," in *The Interpreter's Dictionary of the Bible,* George Arthur
Buttrick, *et al.,* eds. (New York: Abingdon Press, 1962), pp. 660–662; Gary A.
Herion, *et al.,* "Humor and Wit," in *The Anchor Bible Dictionary,* David Noel
Freedman, ed. (New York: Doubleday, 1992), vol. III, pp. 325–333 (see especially
the section on the "Old Testament," by Edward Greenstein, pp. 330–333); S. E.
Medcalf, "Comedy," in *A Dictionary of Biblical Interpretation,* R. J. Coggins and J. L.
Houlden, eds. (London: SCM Press, 1990), pp. 128–129.

[5] See especially the brilliant analysis of Mikhail Bakhtin, *Rabelais and His World,*
Helene Iswolsky, trans. (Bloomington: Indiana University Press, 1984); note also
the more popular examination in Harvey Cox, *The Feast of Fools: A Theological Essay
on Festivity and Fantasy* (Cambridge, MA: Harvard University Press, 1969).

often strained and hostile, sometimes subtle and nuanced, almost always ambivalent, and occasionally even volatile. Interaction between comedy and biblical religion has swung from one extreme to another. On the one hand, from early on many influential interpreters opposed any significant link between comedy and the Bible, sometimes claiming that such a linkage might be blasphemous.[6] On the other hand, we discover by way of contrast that both Judaism and Christianity could allow a significant place for the comic spirit. For example, on the Jewish side, a festival like Purim and its accompanying text of Esther developed a vibrant carnivalesque tradition involving comic forms and rituals; Jewish humor also emerged as a weapon of an oppressed and marginalized people to help its survival amidst the perilous conditions of exile. The tradition of Christian humor and festivity became especially prominent in the Middle Ages. Of course Dante gave the most memorable expression to the comedy of redemption when he immortalized the Christian biblical and theological vision in his grand Medieval poem which came to be known as *The Divine Comedy*.

Northrop Frye has made the Dantesque view a central aspect of his own approach to the Bible, a vantage point that sees comedy as an overarching category of the Christian tradition:

From the point of view of Christianity . . . tragedy is an episode in that larger scheme of redemption and resurrection to which Dante gave the name of *commedia*. This conception of *commedia* enters drama with the miracle-lay cycles, where such tragedies as the Fall and the crucifixion are episodes of a dramatic scheme in which the divine comedy has the last word.[7]

It is symptomatic of the relative neglect of comedy in biblical studies that few scholars have taken up the challenge of Frye's observation and looked at the potential of comedy as

---

[6] See Radday's salient remarks on differences and similarities between Judaism and Christianity on this hostility toward the presence of comedy in the Bible: Radday and Brenner, *On Humour and the Comic in the Hebrew Bible*, pp. 33–38.

[7] Northrop Frye, "The Argument of Comedy," in *Theories of Comedy*, Paul Lauter, ed. (Garden City, NY: Doubleday, 1964), p. 455.

an illuminating perspective for exploring biblical texts. As I observed earlier, biblical scholars have not totally ignored the possibilities of comic forms, but observations have been few and far among the commentaries. For example, the great German critic Gunkel offered some sharp-eyed remarks on comic episodes in Genesis (see below); one should also single out for special praise Edwin M. Good's pioneering book, *Irony in the Old Testament*, a volume that presents a series of provocative, penetrating interpretations of both comic and tragic irony in the Hebrew Bible.[8] But on the whole comedy as an important interpretive perspective appears infrequently in the standard commentaries, dictionaries, and journals, though recent years have seen the emergence of greater interest.[9] Even when comedy does enter the arena of biblical criticism, its particular focus, form, and function do not receive adequate and systematic representation. The volumes edited by Exum and Radday/Brenner have begun to make amends for the desultory application of comic categories to biblical literature, but a more comprehensive and cohesive exposition is still lacking.[10]

In this book I intend to develop a more adequate anatomy of biblical comedy, an anatomy that is grounded in contemporary literary criticism. As an epigraph for my presentation I cite Baudelaire's provocative assertion, "Holy books never laugh . . ." – an assertion that I have chosen ironically as a backdrop against which to argue a contradictory thesis: the Holy Book we call the Bible revels in a profoundly ambivalent laughter, a divine and human laughter that by turns is both mocking and joyous, subversive and celebrative, and finally a

---

[8] Edwin M. Good, *Irony in the Old Testament* (Philadelphia: Westminster Press, 1965).

[9] See, e.g., J. Cheryl Exum, ed., *Tragedy and Comedy in the Bible* in *Semeia: An Experimental Journal for Biblical Criticism* 32 (1984); Radday and Brenner, eds., *On Humour and the Comic in the Hebrew Bible*; Conrad Hyers, *And God Created Laughter: The Bible as Divine Comedy* (Atlanta: John Knox Press, 1987); Conrad Hyers, *The Comic Vision and the Christian Faith: A Celebration of Life and Laughter* (New York: Pilgrim Press, 1981). Hyers deserves credit for a probing exploration of the vital place of comedy in religious life and literature.

[10] See references in note 3.

laughter that results in an exuberant and transformative comic vision.

I wish further to argue that what gives this comic vision its passion and vital depth is precisely its recognition of the place and power of tragedy, of that vision of the dark, jagged side of human existence which unveils the stark presence of unredeemed death, of unjustified disaster, of unmitigated despair.[11] But tragedy is generally episodic in the overarching movement of the Bible, though no less terrifying in its effects. The comic vision, I submit, can embrace the tragic dimension without eliminating or negating it – let alone explaining or totally healing its destructive effects.[12] Yet comedy cannot be felt in its full force apart from tragedy, nor can comedy be delineated and fully appreciated without tragedy. So it is in general, and so it is, I contend, in the concrete forms of the biblical heritage.

SKETCHING AN ANATOMY OF COMEDY IN THE BIBLE

Comedy has been unpropitious to definers.

(SAMUEL JOHNSON)[13]

Before turning to the Bible and its diverse modes of expressing a comic sense and sensibility, I need briefly to delineate the chief lineaments of the comic vision. At the outset I recall

[11] See the splendid exploration of biblical tragedy in J. Cheryl Exum, *Tragedy and Biblical Narrative: Arrows of the Almighty* (Cambridge: Cambridge University Press, 1992); I wish, too, to express my gratitude to Cheryl Exum for early conversations on this theme which led to our collaborative essay, J. Cheryl Exum and J. William Whedbee, "Isaac, Samson, and Saul: Reflections on the Comic and Tragic Visions," in Exum, *Tragedy and Comedy in the Bible*, pp. 5–40.

[12] Note Wylie Sypher's formulation: "the range of comedy is more embracing than the range of tragedy; and if tragedy occurs at some middle point in ethical life where failure is weighed against man's nobility of spirit, comedy ventures out into the farther extremes of experience in both directions...". See his "The Meanings of Comedy," in *Comedy: An Essay on Comedy, George Meredith and Laughter, Henri Bergson* (Garden City, NY: Doubleday & Co., 1956), p. 213.

[13] Samuel Johnson, *The Rambler*, Number 125 (1751), in Lauter, ed., *Theories of Comedy*, p. 255.

the pithy observation of Samuel Johnson as a cautionary note: "Comedy has been unpropitious to definers."[14] Hence I will not offer a definition or a reductive formula; rather I want to draw out certain recurrent features of comedy, features which appear throughout the ages in classic comic works and thus tie disparate comic forms together in a kind of "family resemblance" (Wittgenstein).[15] Such a delineation will necessarily be eclectic and expansive, obviously demanding due limitation and qualification when assessing specific literary texts. One must be acutely sensitive to the risk of imposing later and perhaps alien schemas on the ancient biblical literature. The persuasiveness of any interpretation of the Bible in terms of a comic vision depends on the degree to which one can argue for comic forms that are congenital and congenial to the biblical texts within their native Hebraic and Near Eastern setting. I would hasten to add, however, that a larger comparative context embracing the relationship between the Bible and its complex, continuous roles within Western culture can also illumine the whole spectrum of biblical and post-biblical texts. Going back and forth between the Bible and its varied dramatic, literary, and religious "afterlives" may open up the possibility for fresh insights into both the original biblical texts and later works which have been influenced by the Bible. In sum, though caution must be exercised against the threat of anachronistic and alien readings, careful attention to the full network of possible intertextual linkages can extend and deepen the range of potential comic resonance within the texts and their multiple contexts and subtexts.

I will focus on the comic vision from four interrelated per-

[14] Wylie Sypher is almost as pithy and offers a general explanation: "If we have no satisfactory definition of laughter, neither do we have any satisfactory definition of comedy. Indeed, most of the theories of laughter and comedy fail precisely because they oversimplify a situation and art more complicated than the tragic situation and art. Comedy seems to be a more pervasive human condition than tragedy . . . Tragedy, not comedy, limits its field of operation and is a more closely regulated form of response to the ambiguities and dilemmas of humanity. The comic action touches experience at more points than tragic action." See "The Meanings of Comedy," p. 206.
[15] Ludwig Wittgenstein, *Philosophical Investigations* (third edn.), G. E. M. Anscombe, trans. (Englewood Cliffs, NJ: Prentice Hall, 1953), p. 32.

spectives: (1) plot-line; (2) characterization of basic types; (3) linguistic and stylistic strategies; (4) functions and intentions.

First, the typical plot-line of comedy begins with a view of a largely harmonious, integrated society, a situation which is challenged or tested in some way as the action unfolds; but comedy conventionally swings upward at the end and reintegrates the hero within her or his rightful society, whereas tragedy typically ends with a fallen hero and a vision of disintegration, alienation, and death. To use Frye's apt image, comedy follows a "U-shaped plot, with action sinking into deep and often potentially tragic complications, and then suddenly turning upward into a happy ending."[16] Thus whatever trials and threats the hero must endure, comedy usually ascends from any momentary darkness and concludes with celebration, joy, and at least the promise of new life, whether in a marriage festival or the birth of a new society. In brief, comedy typically ends in carnival, whereas tragedy ends in catastrophe. Thus comedy contains a "U" in contrast to tragedy's inverted "U." Using this pattern of divergent plotlines, Robertson has offered a stimulating comparative treatment of Exodus 1–15 as comedy over against Euripides' tragedy, *The Bacchae*.[17] Similarly, Trible has invoked Frye's model to explicate the Book of Ruth as "A Human Comedy."[18] Finally, to anticipate my own argument, the U-shaped plot is embedded in the comic vision in Genesis, Exodus, Esther, and especially Job.

Second, we find certain conventional types within comedy. Buffoons, clowns, fools, simpletons, rogues, and tricksters, incarnate the human, all too human, and sometimes subhuman or animal form. For example, the sly serpent of Eden is a seductive trickster who raises uncomfortable questions about God's motivations and serves as an agent of transformation for the primal couple; Jacob and Rebekah appear as

---

[16] Northrop Frye, *Fables of Identity: Studies in Poetic Mythology* (New York: Harcourt, Brace & World, Inc., 1963), p. 25.

[17] David Robertson, *The Old Testament and the Literary Critic* (Philadelphia: Fortress Press, 1977), pp. 16–32. See the discussion below in chapter three.

[18] Phyllis Trible, *God and the Rhetoric of Sexuality* (Philadelphia: Fortress Press, 1978), pp. 166–199.

consummate tricksters in a family of tricksters, whereas Isaac and Esau appear as befuddled simpletons; Balaam the diviner-seer is satirized as a blind fool in contrast to his talking ass that has super-vision (she sees the "angel of the Lord," whereas her master doesn't!);[19] even the mighty Moses reveals some blind spots, receiving a sometimes parodied treatment in his call narratives in Exodus. Thus, whenever great or noble personages appear, they are often satirized and subjected to subtle parody or outright ridicule, thereby undercutting their pretentiousness and reducing them to the common lot of humanity. Foreign kings are favorite targets: the Egyptian Pharaoh in Exodus is savagely satirized as an arrogant imposter and then finally destroyed; King Ahasuerus emerges as a fool who can be easily manipulated both by the wicked Haman and the wise Esther; and the mighty Nebuchadnezzar is reduced to the ridiculous posture of an animal grazing in the fields until he recognizes his proper place of submission to the high God Yahweh.[20] Typically, however, when comedy isolates a figure for ridicule, the ultimate goal is still reintegration into the social group, though not always, as the case of the Egyptian Pharaoh vividly illustrates.

Third, comedy has characteristic linguistic and stylistic habits and strategies. Comedy typically delights in various forms of verbal artifice such as punning or word-play, parody, hyperbole, redundancy, and repetitiousness. Moreover, comedy especially exploits incongruity and irony, high-

---

[19] After I had completed this manuscript my attention was called to David Marcus' new book, *From Balaam to Jonah: Anti-prophetic Satire in the Hebrew Bible* (Atlanta: Scholars Press, 1995), a book which came into my hands too late for appropriate inclusion.

[20] See the fine essay by Athalya Brenner, "Who's Afraid of Feminist Criticism? Who's Afraid of Biblical Humour? The Case of the Obtuse Foreign Ruler in the Hebrew Bible," *Journal for the Study of the Old Testament* 63 (1994), pp. 38–55. It is gratifying to read a comprehensive and compelling analysis of the role of humor in satirizing "the obtuse foreign ruler," an analysis reached independently from mine. In addition to the cases I have dealt with, Brenner adds the unnamed king of Jericho in Joshua 2, Balak and Balaam in Numbers 22–24, Eglon of Moab in Judges 3, Ahab in I Kings 21, and Belshazzar in Daniel 5. Brenner offers penetrating and forceful observations about the subversive power of humor, especially in the hands of marginalized women.

lighting discrepancy, reversal, and surprise. Comedy moves with relish into the realm of the ludicrous and ridiculous. Comedy cannot be reduced to a simplistic equation with the humorous and laughable, though comedy nevertheless often seeks to elicit laughter. The laughter is often complex and ambivalent, ranging from sardonic and subversive to joyous and celebrative. To be sure, mocking, sardonic laughter is more dominant in biblical literature. The laughter is often at someone's expense – laughing *at*, not laughing *with*.[21] This side emerges when the comedy takes the form of parody and satire, serving to deflate pretentious, pompous figures. Comedy celebrates the rhythm of life with its times of festivity and joyous renewal, but it must frequently resort to ridicule in order to bring down the arrogant and boastful who block or threaten the free movement of life. Comedy perennially takes up arms against the forces that stifle life and laughter, though even here its barbed arrows generally only sting, not kill. If satire fails to move on to the genuinely restorative and celebrative, it is questionable whether it still remains in the domain of comedy.[22]

Fourth, and finally, comedy has a multiple range of functions and intentions befitting its complicated forms within literature and life. Paradoxically comedy throughout the ages has oscillated between conservative and subversive tendencies, being used both to maintain the status quo and to undercut prevailing ideologies in the name of revolutionary and utopian goals.[23] Thus one pole of comedy serves to undergird and conserve social norms, using its weapons of satire to inhibit and even destroy forces that threaten the status quo. Such comedy may, nonetheless, follow the pattern of the

[21] See Brenner's discriminating analysis, "On the Semantic Field of Humour," in Yehuda T. Radday and Athalya Brenner, *On Humour and the Comic in the Hebrew Bible*, pp. 51–52 and 57–58.

[22] Cf. the classic treatment offered by Northrop Frye, "The Mythos of Winter: Irony and Satire," in his *Anatomy of Criticism: Four Essays* (New York: Atheneum, 1966), pp. 223–242.

[23] "The ambivalence of comedy reappears in its social meanings, for comedy is both hatred and revel, rebellion and defense, attack and escape. It is revolutionary and conservative. Socially, it is both sympathy and rebellion." So Sypher, "The Meanings of Comedy," p. 242.

U-shaped plot-line with its ineluctable drive through the crises and complications befalling the heroes until the concluding upswing which restores the rightful society and celebrates the victory of life and love. At the other pole comedy reveals its subversive and even revolutionary functions. It takes dead aim at a tyrannical and oppressive society and attempts to subvert it in order to institute a new society built upon traditions that foster liberation and life. Hence such comedy can ultimately be transformative, not just restorative.[24]

This dual thrust of the comic vision – its conservative, restorative tendency and its subversive, revolutionary power – emerges in various ways in the biblical exemplars of comedy. Moreover, these seemingly disparate functions can be manifested in the intrinsic aggressive force of comedy, an aggressiveness that appears in the defense of conservative values or in the promotion of revolutionary aims. To illustrate only the latter case, comedy has contributed to revolutionary impulses in the drive for liberation represented in the dramas of deliverance that form foundational narratives in the Bible. The Book of Exodus, for example, represents a comedy of deliverance that manifests a revolutionary mythos of liberation, revealing both the theme of freedom from bondage and reveling in the festive spirit of a newly liberated society. To anticipate my argument below, the comic vision animates the Exodus story both by dramatizing the subversive power of comedy in its relentless satire of Pharaoh as archetypal oppressor whose arrogance and folly are ruthlessly exposed as Israel's God "makes sport of" the Egyptians (Ex. 10:2) and by celebrating Yahweh's triumph over the Egyptians at the Red Sea (Ex. 15). Though obvious moral and theological

---

[24] See the superb recent exploration of comedy in the poetry of Emily Dickinson, an analysis which especially highlights the disruptive, subversive, and ultimately transformative power of the comic vision: Suzanne Juhasz, Cristanne Miller, and Martha Nell Smith, *Comic Power in Emily Dickinson* (Austin: University of Texas Press, 1993); for example, note the following formulation that resonates very well with my perception into the power of biblical comedy: "If Dickinson's comedy stems from profound discomfort with society as it has been constructed, and her comic strategy destabilizes that construction, . . . then her transformations sketch the outlines of a world that more readily suits her aspirations" (p. 138).

concerns can be raised about Yahweh as a divine warrior who delights in destroying the Egyptians and who will visit his genocidal fury against the Canaanites, certain dimensions of justice and mercy that become part of the liberation rhetoric can supply a self-critique and corrective for the excess of violence.[25] In any event, the Exodus mythos has been a force for revolutionary movements through history. Genuine liberation can sometimes come with the laughter of deliverance and lead to transformation. The Jewish Passover ritual continues to embody and express the comic powers of celebration and transformation in its annual recital of the Exodus story.

In summary, from these different perspectives I will show how the comic vision emerges in key texts in the Hebrew Bible. Moreover, as we shall see, the ability of biblical authors to use humor and comedy as a strategy for survival in the midst of exile and oppression receives ample representation in fundamental texts of the biblical heritage. Biblical comedy contains the power both to subvert and transform political, social, and religious structures.

FINDING A STRATEGY OF PRESENTATION

In the essay that follows I concentrate on exemplary texts rather than attempting an exhaustive cataloguing and analysis of every conceivable comic form in the Bible. Moreover, I deal with the Hebrew Bible as opposed to the Christian Scriptures. There are ample materials for exploration within the Hebrew Bible. More importantly, an examination of the New Testament texts from a comic perspective inevitably opens up radically different vistas that accompany a late Hellenistic and Roman text which is written in Greek and which shares the expanded horizons of the Greco-Roman world. Ultimately, looking at the Christian Bible under the rubric of the comic vision promises fresh insights in how the

---

[25] See the incisive and illuminating remarks by Rolf Knierim in his *magnum opus, The Task of Old Testament Theology: Method and Cases* (Grand Rapids: Wm. B. Eerdmans Publishing Co., 1995), pp. 130–134.

Hebraic biblical vision becomes transformed, but that poses another question and demands another book. Northrop Frye, as indicated above, has suggestively charted one direction in which to move on this question. However, recent work on the place of comic forms in Jesus' role as "cynic sage" within the Gospel traditions, Via's suggestive proposal about the possible impact of classical comedy on Paul and Mark, and O'Leary's fascinating analysis of comic rhetoric in the Apocalypse reveal other intriguing possibilities for future research.[26]

In the present work I have selected six exemplary texts from the Hebrew Bible, isolating and identifying key components of the comic vision and then teasing out implications for understanding the central role of comedy within biblical faith. Two major parts form the body of the book. Part I examines what I call "The Genesis of Comedy – the Comedy of Genesis," exploring in depth and detail the foundational narrative of the first book of the Bible, a text which establishes so many fundamental themes for the Bible. Here the claims for the comprehensive range of the comic vision in Genesis are fully probed, dividing the discussion between the two traditional parts of Genesis: hence chapter one will focus on "The Comedy of Creation" (Gen. 1–11), and chapter two will develop "Domestic Comedy in the Household of Faith: Israel's Fathers and Mothers as Comic Figures" (Gen. 12–50). Part II of the book builds on part I and is titled "Generating Comedy: Biblical Texts and the Drive to Comic Regenera-

---

[26] See the brilliant and suggestive essay by R. Bracht Branham, "Authorizing Humor: Lucian's *Demonax* and Cynic Rhetoric," *Semeia* 64 (1994), Vernon K. Robbins, ed., pp. 33–48; note especially Burton Mack's response in the same issue: "Branham does not apply his insight in the nature of Cynic humor to the chreiai and pronouncement stories of Jesus, but he could. Were he to do so, I am convinced that we would never be able to read them the same way again . . . If we were ever to catch on to the humor, I think our picture of Jesus and his first followers may change as drastically as it did when the pronouncement stories turned into elaborated chreiai" (p. 287). Dan O. Via, Jr., *Kerygma and Comedy in the New Testament* (Philadelphia: Fortress Press, 1975). Stephen D. O'Leary, *Arguing the Apocalypse: A Theory of Millennial Rhetoric* (New York: Oxford University Press, 1994), pp. 201, 212, 222; I discovered this book in the helpful review of Peter Gardella, "Ego and Apocalypse in America," *Religious Studies Review* 21/3 (July 1995), p. 200: "O'Leary makes a good case for reading apocalyptic in terms of the dramatic rhetoric of comedy."

tion"; it will focus on a variety of exemplary texts. Thus chapter three has the rubric, "Liberation and Laughter: Exodus and Esther as Two Comedies of Deliverance." Setting these two famous stories in tandem, I show the comic resonance that connects in vital ways the two dramas of deliverance and their accompanying rituals of Passover and Purim.

The fourth chapter – "Jonah as Joke: A Comedy of Contradiction, Caricature, and Compassion" – represents a powerful embodiment of the comic spirit. Jonah echoes important concerns voiced in Genesis and Exodus, on the one side, and anticipates issues raised by Job, on the other, revealing in its comic narrative ambivalent attitudes about a compassionate creator and his relationship to the world of humans and animals.

My case for the Bible's incarnation of the comic vision receives its most severe test in the Book of Job. Hence the fifth chapter explores the interplay and tension between comedy and tragedy in Job, arguing that ultimately Job transcends its own deeply felt tragic sensibility by an affirmation of comic faith. Here again the title gives the game away: "The Comedy of Job: Creation, Chaos, and Carnival." Examining how the comic spirit inhabits the Book of Job and energizes its comic plot-line, I show how and why Job may be aptly called "the great reservoir of comedy."[27]

Finally, in the sixth chapter, I analyze the comic potential of Israel's most famous love lyrics: "Paradox and Parody in the Song of Solomon: Towards a Comic Reading of the Song of Songs." The Song's revelation of a comic vision offers an "answer to Job"[28] (which it immediately follows in the Jewish canon), but also stretches back to Genesis and resonates with the story of the primal couple of Eden. A short conclusion rounds out the volume, summing up the comic trajectory and tracing out its larger arc in biblical literature.

---

[27] Christopher Fry, "Comedy," in Robert W. Corrigan, ed., *Comedy*, pp. 15–17.
[28] I am obviously echoing here Jung's famous *Answer to Job* (Cleveland: The World Publishing Co., 1960). I refer also to Tamara C. Eskenazi's unpublished paper on "Song of Songs as An Answer to Job," presented at the national meeting of the Society of Biblical Literature, San Francisco, 1981.

The genesis of comedy – the comedy of Genesis

The play on the word "genesis" in the title of part I contains both a claim and a challenge: a *claim* in that I wish to argue that just as the book of Genesis holds pride of place as the fundamental story of beginnings in Western culture, so it is also a dominant generative source of comedy in Western literature; a *challenge* in that I hope such a bold claim will entice, lure, provoke the reader at least to entertain the possibility that a close reading of Genesis will reveal significant comic forms which in fact help to energize the inner dynamic of the book as a whole. Both claim and challenge hold a promise that disclosure of the multifaceted comedy of Genesis will open new vistas and thereby illumine traditional themes of Genesis such as chaos and creation, blessing and curse, good and evil, promise and fulfillment.

Although various interpreters have suggested the possibility of comic episodes and humorous incidents in Genesis, one rarely finds anyone who would argue for a comprehensive interpretation of the book within a comic vision. Yet in light of a capacious view of comedy, I think that Genesis emerges as a vital incarnation of the comic vision. Of course, I am not completely alone in holding this opinion: only recently Daniel Russ among others has proposed that not only can the Bible be legitimately interpreted as the "genesis of comedy," but the book of Genesis "may be said to be the proto-comedy of the Bible."[1] I

---

[1] Daniel Russ, "The Bible as Genesis of Comedy," in *The Terrain of Comedy*, Louise Cowan, ed. (Dallas: The Dallas Institute of Humanities and Culture, 1984), p. 43.

want to take up Russ' suggestion and argue the case for the "comedy of Genesis."[2]

Genesis is conventionally divided into two major sections, usually labelled "Primeval History" (Gen. 1–11) and "Patriarchal History" (Gen. 12–50). Rarely have scholars identified the first part of the story as comic (later dramatists and novelists are quite another matter!); in fact, interpreters have most commonly and consistently rendered the opposite verdict, thus invoking tragedy to describe the Genesis version of the origins of human evil and its grim consequences. This has been particularly true of Christian interpretations which reflect theological premises rooted in such characteristic Christian doctrines as the fall and original sin. Epitomizing such central teachings, Milton gives a most compelling dramatic presentation of the tragic view in his famous epic poem, *Paradise Lost.* This imagery and ideology of the "fall" pervades not only the more explicit theological representations, but also marks secular literature as well, whether in novels, plays, or poems. Of course Jewish interpreters have generally resisted this Christian reading,[3] but claims for a tragic fall continue to burden even more modern literary-critical analyses of the opening chapters of Genesis.

Fortunately, greater interpretive space is gradually being opened up for fresh readings of the primeval story, space in which the comic potential is beginning to surface from its opaque depths. To be sure, notes of pain, hard labor, alienation, and death are sounded in these stories of cosmic and

---

[2] Novelists and poets have often found comedy in Genesis. For example, after I had finished an earlier draft of this chapter, I was delighted to come across W. J. A. Power's new book, *Once upon a Time: A Humorous Re-telling of the Genesis Stories* (Nashville: Abingdon Press, 1992). Here, too, I want to mention the fresh, humorous poetic rendering offered by B. D. Napier, *Come Sweet Death: A Quintet from Genesis* (Philadelphia and Boston: United Church Press, 1967); I was privileged to hear these pieces in their original oral form when Professor Napier delivered them to appreciative audiences at Yale University. Finally, I need at least to pay homage to what is perhaps the grandest novelistic rendition of Genesis ever written: Thomas Mann, *Joseph und Seine Brüder* (Berlin: S. Fischer Verlag AG, 1975), a novel that contains many fine moments of Mann's ironic humor.

[3] Jonathan Magonet, *A Rabbi's Bible* (London: SCM Press, 1991); see especially his chapter, "Leaving the Garden: Did They Fall or Were They Pushed," pp. 111–122.

human beginnings, but other notes of humor, wit, and comic revel are audible as well. I am above all concerned with listening intently to all the notes of this overture to the biblical symphony, concentrating on discerning afresh the sounds of comedy, however subtle, muffled, and indistinct they may be on first hearing. Those who have ears to hear, let them hear!

CHAPTER 1

The comedy of creation (Genesis 1–11)

Creation itself is in the nature of a cosmic joke.
(Marcel Gutwirth)[4]

The world must be peopled.
(Shakespeare, *The Tempest*)

But God be with the Clown
Who ponders this tremendous scene
This whole Experiment with Green -
As if it were his own!
(Emily Dickinson)[5]

In its present form Genesis 1–11 unfolds as a series of narratives stitched together by intertwining genealogies. Whatever the exact processes of origin and development (which are all but impossible to identify), biblical scholars usually argue that the composition includes two sources or strata most commonly referred to as the Yahwist ("J") and the Priestly writer ("P"). One can therefore discern at least two distinct voices, often presented in counterpoint, sounding dissonant notes. Moving from a magisterial opening panorama of the creation of a fundamentally good cosmos (Gen. 1–2), the narrators then proceed to introduce the complexities and contradictions of earliest civilization as humanity moves from the idyllic garden world of pastoral myth to the crowded, tension-filled scene of urban culture. It is above all a narrative that

[4] Marcel Gutwirth, *Laughing Matter: An Essay on the Comic* (Ithaca and London: Cornell University Press, 1993), p. 165.
[5] *The Complete Poems of Emily Dickinson*, Thomas Johnson, ed. (Boston: Little, Brown, & Co, 1960), p. 577.

revels in aetiologies, featuring the mythical origins of cosmic and communal structures and focusing especially on divine-human relationships, sexual and familial bonds, ethnic and nationalistic concerns – all set within the complex interplay of good and evil.

As I have observed, it is tragedy – at least since Milton's epic achievement – that has been most commonly invoked to describe the major movement of the cycle of tales in Genesis 1–11. Frye gives forceful expression to what in fact is an ancient, widely accepted view – at least in Christian eyes: "In seeing the archetypal human tragedy in the story of Adam, Milton was, of course, in agreement with the whole Judaeo-Christian cultural tradition . . ."[6] Frye continues in his argument to apply the archetypal power of the Genesis Fall story to subsequent biblical narratives: "In the Bible the tragic fall of Adam is followed by its historical repetition, the fall of Israel into Egyptian bondage, which is, so to speak, its ironic confirmation."[7]

One could adduce myriad examples that represent multiple variations on Frye's Miltonic take on the biblical tradition, but his assertions suffice to highlight the tragic mold into which the opening chapters of Genesis have been cast. That Christian theology has been a dominant force in shaping the interpretive grid for Genesis 1–11 is clear.

A closer look at the Genesis stories themselves shows how distant they are from the language and imagery of fall (which represents minimally a precipitous descent from higher to lower) and original sin (which in Augustine's influential reading becomes a "sexually transmitted disease" passed along the seminal tract). Recently from the margins of the more dominant tradition voices of dissent have emerged, offering the possibility of new readings.[8] Various interpreters

---

[6] Northrop Frye, *Anatomy of Criticism: Four Essays* (New York: Atheneum, 1966), p. 213. A minority of scholars, however, also find comedy in the Fall story; e.g., see the suggestive analysis by K. W. Grandsen, "Milton, Dryden, and the Comedy of the Fall," *Essays in Criticism* 26 (1976), pp. 116–133.

[7] N. Frye, *Anatomy of Criticism*, p. 213.

[8] David Rosenberg and Harold Bloom, *The Book of J* (New York: Grove Weidenfeld, 1990), pp. 175–192; Leslie Brisman, *The Voice of Jacob: On the Composition of Genesis* (Bloomington: Indiana University Press, 1990), pp. 1–8; Sean McEvenue,

have pointed the way to what might be a more illuminating and incisive angle of vision which opens up in turn the possibility for a comic reading of Genesis 1–11. Even Frye, for instance, in his more recent work has described "the story of the fall of man in Genesis" as "originally . . . one of the sardonic folktales of the Near East that explain how man once had immortality nearly within his grasp, but was cheated out of it by frightened or malicious deities."[9]

THE CONTEXT OF CREATION AND THE PRECONDITIONS FOR COMEDY

Although one normally does not expect to note any resonance between the comic vision and the priestly creation account in Genesis 1, one can nonetheless locate there preconditions highly conducive for the emergence of comic forms and motifs. First, Genesis 1 provides a hospitable context for comedy in its central themes – creation of order out of chaos, the triumph of light over darkness, and especially the affirmation of the essential goodness of creation. The repetition of the keyword "good" depicts vividly God's estimate of his creative works: what emerges in God's eyes is a fundamentally good world, a well-ordered cosmos pulsating with divinely endowed powers of reproduction, regeneration, and renewal.[10] Perhaps the Renaissance image of the "green world" captures best the power of the good creation, a world ripe with the burgeoning powers of generation and growth,

Interpreting the Pentateuch (Collegeville, MN: The Liturgical Press, 1990), p. 65; James Barr, *The Garden of Eden and the Hope of Immortality* (Minneapolis: Fortress Press, 1993), pp. 12–14.

[9] Northrop Frye, *The Great Code: The Bible and Literature* (New York: Harcourt Brace Jovanovich, 1982), p. 109.

[10] Barry Sanders notes the lack of the qualifying "good" on the second day of creation, an absence that the rabbis also observed. Following a midrash that focused on the weeping of the waters caused by the separation, Sanders wants to overgeneralize a dour, dark view of the Creator which represents a microcosm of the creation. Such an interpretation offers insight into the complex vitality of the text, but it oversimplifies the picture and thus distorts the prevailing emphasis which affirms the basic goodness of creation – including the work of separation of the waters. See Sanders, *Sudden Glory: Laughter as Subversive History* (Boston: Beacon Press, 1995), pp. 55–57.

a world therefore rich with the potential for the manifestation of the comic spirit that revels in new life as it comes and comes and comes again. "The account," asserts Russ, "unmistakeably indicates that [God] created a world pregnant with comic overtones."[11]

Second, the presence of incongruity often provides a precondition for comedy. The most striking source of incongruity in the biblical creation account is the paradoxical relationship between divine creator and human creature. Radical dissimilarity between God and humanity is conjoined with a powerful affirmation of similarity: the human creatures are made in the image and likeness of their creator (1:27), yet they are not fully divine. They are both like and unlike God in significant and surprising ways, opening space for incongruous and ironic development (cf. also 3:22). The combination of anomalous affinity and sharp difference gives rise to the ambivalent patterns of attraction and alienation between fundamentally unequal yet symbiotically dependent partners in the divine-human relationship. Indeed, one can argue that it is precisely the interplay and tension between two unequal sets of players that affords the opportunity for the playing out of both comic and tragic possibilities in this thickly interwoven tale of primal beginnings. Humanity is like God, but cannot – and must not – be too much like God. The very temptation to be like God motivates diverse responses from the human creatures, responses that are fraught with both comic and tragic dimensions.

Third, if there be a single dominant theme programmatically announced in Genesis 1 and then subtly reiterated, amplified, and sometimes subverted in the remaining chapters, it would appear in what we can aptly call the first commandment given to humanity: "God blessed them . . . and said . . ., 'Be fruitful and multiply, and fill the earth and subdue it; and have dominion over the fish of the sea and over the birds of the air and over every living thing that moves upon the earth'" (1:28). This commandment set under the

---

[11] Russ, "The Bible as Genesis of Comedy," p. 44.

sign of divine blessing establishes the fundamental pattern for humanity to exercise its divinely imaged role as surrogates for God in the creation: continued life requires multiplication which becomes the indispensable basis for mastery. Thus re-creation or reproduction of the human species becomes the means for constituting and perpetuating the human community and ensuring its dominion over the earth and its creatures.

However, the plot thickens in the process of enacting this commandment. For God to be God, he must have both the power to create and then to sustain his creation which means survival by multiplication. But such multiplication must retain some semblance of order, thus requiring from God's perspective the element of mastery or dominion. His delegation of such authority to a human surrogate, paradoxically identical in image, but unequal in power, to master the earth and its creatures opens the door for abuse and alienation because of the fundamental inequality of the partners. What happens when the junior partner wants to become a full partner? In the arousal of that desire one can locate the possibility for both comic and tragic responses.

This double commandment of multiplication and mastery animates not only the rest of the primeval story (see its reiteration in 8:17 and 9:1–2), but also motivates the patriarchal story in Genesis (see, e.g., 17:2–6; 35:11; 48:16). Coupled with this key commandment – and its multiple variations – is the recurrent generational formula (*toledoth*, "begettings," "generations"), long recognized as the most crucial and revealing skeletal frame of the book. It forms typically the lead-off caption or headline for a following unit, whether a narrative or genealogy proper (2:4a; 5:1; 6:9; 10:1; 11:10,27; 25:12,19; 36:1,9; 37:2). Highlighting the most basic framework of human existence – the movement from birth to death – this generational formula epitomizes the process of fulfillment of the first commandment: generation of new life through multiple begettings and births becomes the way of a viable future for the human community, a community linked by the fragile chain of birth and death. As Fokkelman succinctly puts it, "this

image of concatenation reveals the overriding concern of the
entire book: life-survival-offspring-fertility-continuity."[12] In a
word, fertility becomes the energizing power of Genesis, and
fertility normally evokes festivity. Although fertility and festivity do not automatically constitute comedy *per se*, they often
form a dynamic dyad in comic narratives and represent one
significant precondition for the comic vision.[13] Indeed, in
fulfillment of this theme, we often expect comedy to celebrate
marriages and births. To see how and why comedy revels in
such celebrations, it behooves us to explore the concrete texts
of Genesis.

PRIMAL PLOTS, PUNS, AND PARODIES
(GENESIS 1–11)

In my view, the comic perspective of the primeval story in
Genesis reveals itself particularly in what I call "primal plots,
puns and parodies," a combination that contains more dominant comic tones within the sometimes tragic movement of
the text. Moreover, the protagonists of these little dramas will
also reveal comic facets, especially in various forms of trickster roles.

The plots of these stories revolve around the different
kinds of fulfillment of what I have called the first commandment (1:28), an imperative that Clines has aptly described
as an "announcement," that is, an advance signal about the
emplotment of the book.[14] The variations on this plot
announcement and its pattern of fulfillment give much of
the tension and incongruity to the pace of the narrative.
Our primal ancestors have great success in multiplying, but
often some of their number contradict or subvert the
process of multiplication and mastery by acts of murder and

---

[12] J. P. Fokkelman, "Genesis," in *The Literary Guide to the Bible*, Robert Alter and Frank
    Kermode, eds. (Cambridge, MA: Harvard University Press, 1987), p. 41.
[13] See Chester J. Barber, *Shakespeare's Festive Comedy: A Study of Dramatic Form and Its
    Relation to Social Custom* (Princeton: Princeton University Press, 1959) for a bril-
    liant exposition of the role of festivity in comedy.
[14] David J. A. Clines, *What Does Eve Do to Help? and Other Readerly Questions to the Old
    Testament* (Sheffield: Sheffield Academic Press, 1990), p. 50.

vengeance (4); by acts of miscegenation between divine beings and beautiful women, sexual encounters which produce a race of giants and provoke a divine limitation on human life-span (6:1–4); by acts of evil sufficient to warrant a great flood (6:5ff), the aftermath of which leads to an expanded reiteration of the commandment to multiply and master (9:1ff). In the wake of the flood, the descendants of Noah do obey the mandate to multiply and fill the earth, but the question of mastery becomes confused and complicated by the creation of the institution of slaves and masters in Noah's curses and blessings of his sons (9:25–27), by the founding of the first kingdom under the leadership of the hunter-warrior Nimrod (10:8–11), and by the mad-cap scene of Babel and the babblers (11). So the theme of multiplication and mastery does course its variegated way through these old tales, but often in twisted and tortuous forms. In sum, the emplotment of the primeval story often takes incongruous turns that draw it into the orbit of comedy as the narrators spin out the elaborate cosmic joke God has played on the human race.[15]

The garden of Eden: paradise lost and knowledge gained

The tale of the Garden of Eden is the Bible's first fully human story, as the spotlight shifts from the realm of the magisterial, monological Creator God (Gen. 1) to the action of the anthropomorphic, earth-centered God named Yahweh who becomes vitally involved with the earthlings of Eden (Gen. 2–3). It is indeed a story of loss – as Milton's epic bears eloquent witness – but it is paradoxically also a story of gain. Often told and re-told in tones tragic, the story also contains richly comic themes, a possibility only recently proposed. A close reading deconstructs the rather monolithic view so inscribed in the more normative tradition, yielding instead multiple interpretive options that include comedy. In my

---

[15] See the marvelous adaptations of biblical images of God as a "cosmic joker" in John Lowe, *Jump at the Sun: Zora Neale Hurston's Cosmic Comedy* (Chicago: University of Illinois Press, 1994), pp. 78–79, 146, 157, 188, 239.

judgment, the comedy especially reveals itself in the intricate, subtle interplay of primal plots, puns, and parodies, a combination that displays striking illustrations of comic irony and incongruity as well as celebrative affirmation of the resilience of life.

The narrative contains a variety of plot trajectories ranging from the more traditional tragic form to a more complicated bitter-sweet comic mode. Labels for the competing plots are legion, variously identifying Genesis 2–3 as a domestic tragedy like *Paradise Lost* or a trial featuring a "universal legal process" (Westermann) or "a love story gone awry" (Trible) or "children's literature" recounting a "seriocomic mishap" (Bloom).[16] A recapitulation of the major movement of the story allows us to begin to glimpse the fissures and gaps that reveal the presence of a strong comic undercurrent in this famous fable of human beginnings.

The story is set within an idyllic, harmonious pastoral world and gives pride of place to the creation of the first human (who like God is initially alone). It then unfolds with a flowing narration of the significant dimensions of the garden: the planting of a luxuriant garden filled with wonderful trees; the description of the Edenic river dividing into four tributaries; the placement of the human in the garden as its tiller coupled with a strange, intrusive prohibition not to eat the fruit of one particular tree; the forming and naming of animals as potential helpers for the human and their subsequent disqualification as appropriate helpers; the mysterious creation of the first woman who is a fitting helper for man and whose very designation (*'ishah*) resonates with her origins from man (*'ish*); a surprising aetiology of marriage in which the man leaves his family for his wife's; and a lovely image of the couple's innocent, idyllic nakedness. Without any advance warning the narrator suddenly introduces the sly serpent who holds with the woman "the first theological

[16] Claus Westermann, *Genesis: A Practical Commentary*, David E. Green, trans. (Grand Rapids: Wm. B. Eerdmans Publishing Co., 1987), p. 24; Trible, *God and The Rhetoric of Sexuality*, p. 72; Rosenberg and Bloom, *The Book of J*, p. 185.

conversation *about* God"[17] and who seductively leads her along the path from temptation to transgression of the divine commmandment not to eat from the forbidden tree; the transgressive act triggers a chain of fateful transformations in the world of the primal couple: awareness of nakedness marked by a sense of shame and vulnerability followed by divine discovery, interrogation, and punishment by the overlord who issues a series of oracles that represent aetiologies of present conditions involving especially the serpent, the woman, and the man. Finally, the tale contains a mitigation of the harsh sentences, featuring a new name for the woman (Eve=*havah*="life") who thereby becomes "the mother of all living" (*hay*); provision of new clothing for the humans suggestive of a divine gesture of solicitous care as well as designating them as civilized human beings differentiated from both gods and animals; a surprising and ironic acknowledgment that the humans in the very act of seizing proscribed knowledge have stepped across the divide between humanity and divinity to become "like the gods, knowing good and evil." But the hard-won knowledge comes at a high price: ostensibly because of divine jealousy, too much likeness to the gods evokes the divine decision to expel the couple from the garden in order to block the way to the tree of life whose fruit must not be eaten lest the humans live forever.

The movement of the story shows how far it stands from a plot featuring a tragic fall, a fall absolute, catastrophic, and programmatic in its theological and historical effects. Such a trajectory represents a particular kind of Christian projection of Lucifer's fall from heaven (see Isa. 14:12 and especially its later reinterpretation in terms of the fall of Satan and his angels), reading the fate of the primal pair in light of the satanic fall.[18] In contrast to this largely Christian version, Adam and Eve in the Genesis rendition indeed suffer losses,

---

[17] Dietrich Bonhoeffer, *Creation and Fall: A Theological Interpretation of Genesis 1–3*, John C. Fletcher, trans. (London: SCM Press, 1959), p. 70.

[18] Jeffrey Burton Russell, *Satan: The Early Christian Tradition* (Ithaca: Cornell University Press, 1981), pp. 130–131.

but losses countered by significant gains; curses are balanced by blessings in disguise. The knowledge of good and evil is a most ambiguous possession. Thus pain and death are curiously intertwined with divine-like knowledge; newly won enlightenment and wisdom bespeak both the prospect of death and the promise of new life. After all, the woman receives her new name as life bearer only after the disclosure that humans will return to the dust of their origins.

In sum, the emplotment of the garden story reflects a pattern of incongruous twists and turns which hardly follow the trajectory of fall: more fundamentally the plot represents a tale of metamorphosis marked by a series of fateful transformations which various agents produce. The transformations reflect a new map of the cosmos, highlighting the complexity of the conditions of cosmic and communal existence. The themes and tones of the story-telling create the climate for bitter-sweet comedy, not terrifying tragedy. Thus McEvenue rightly avers that Genesis 3 is "characterized by a dramatic subtlety which one associates more easily with comedy than with tragedy."[19]

The comic tone comes out in the pattern of pivotal puns which both concentrate and energize major moments in the story line. Although puns may represent in Freud's estimation the lowest form of verbal humor, they play a powerful role not only in the garden narrative but throughout Genesis.[20] With characteristic verve Bloom revels in the narrator's pleasure in punning: "J's narratives have a Shakespearean exuberance of invention and her language brims with ceaseless wordplay . . ."[21] In the Garden story, the puns are primal and pivotal, condensing and inscribing in dazzling verbal play crucial aetiologies that vividly depict the relational realities of the original creation and its condi-

---

[19] McEvenue, *Interpreting the Pentateuch*, p. 65.
[20] The Genesis narrators would agree with the claim of Beckett's *Murphy*, "In the beginning was the pun." Cited in Jonathan Culler's essay, "The Call of the Phoneme: Introduction," in his edited volume, *On Puns: The Foundation of Letters* (Oxford: Basil Blackwell, 1988), p. 16.
[21] Rosenberg and Bloom, *The Book of J*, pp. 318–319.

tions. They represent a form of etymological doubling, a kind of parody in miniature which results in a verbal resonance across word fields.

First, Adam is Adam because he is scraped and shaped from the soil (*'adamah*), thus being in his primal condition a true son of the soil, and only possessing vitality by virtue of the divine breath of life (*neshmat ḥayyim*) which makes him a living being (*nephesh ḥayyah*). The first human is a strange compound of dirt and breath, an animated, inspirited "earth creature"[22] who is inextricably and incongruously linked both to dust and deity.

Second, reversing the usual procedure of males coming from females, Yahweh surgically separates the first woman from Adam who names her "woman" (*'ishah*) because she was taken from "man" (*'ish*). Hence one becomes two, and the pun forms the tie that binds the two in a new oneness in the act of sexual intercourse or in the birth of the child ("they become one flesh"). Presenting two seeming equals who perfectly correspond to one another, the stage is set to explore the profound paradox of identity and difference.

Third, nakedness is suggestively coupled with slyness and shrewdness in a pun that makes the pivotal transition from the description of primal nakedness of the original pair to the intellectual acuity of the serpent: "the man and his wife were both naked (*'arummim*) . . . and the serpent was more shrewd (*'arom*) than any other wild animal that Yahweh God had made" (2:25; 3:1). The ironic connection between innocent albeit vulnerable nakedness and the knowing, sly serpent is subtly drawn.

Fourth, and forming a kind of climax in the pattern of puns, is the man's naming of Eve (*ḥavah*) who becomes the "mother of all living" (*'em-kol-ḥay*) whose very name therefore reverberates with *life*, hence expressing the primal drive to people the world and ensure survival and continuity for humanity. If puns are jokes embedded in inventive word-play, then this final pun in the garden story is most suggestive: the

[22] Trible, *God and the Rhetoric of Sexuality*, p. 80.

divinely threatened death ("in the day you eat thereof, you will surely die") does not immediately occur but is delayed and, in fact, even cheated by the promised continuation of life in Mother Eve whose name guarantees life. Is the joke on God or on humanity? In any event, woman receives a honorific title and indispensable role as life-bearer and preserver; the Adamic naming of woman as Eve in the face of death dramatizes human defiance and the will to live. As usual the eloquent von Rad captures the melody of life presented in this climactic pun:

> One must see the man's naming of the woman as an act of faith, certainly not faith in promises that lie hidden, veiled in the penalties, but rather an embracing of life, which as a great miracle and mystery is maintained and carried by the motherhood of woman over hardship and death . . . Man could regard life in spite of all the punishment as maintained and not forfeited. This life, which over and beyond the death of the individual is passed on by mothers, he now takes and blesses even though it is threatened by death. Who can express the pain, love, and defiance contained in these words?[23]

Can one not find the elemental rhythm of comedy signaled in this primal pun with its stress on the primacy of life? What an amazing and ironic twist on this tale of death and life which embeds in woman's proper name her exalted status as "mother of all living!" Here is perhaps the deepest element of what Langer calls the "comic rhythm," that is, "the rhythm of 'felt life' . . . the essential comic feeling, which is the sentient aspect of organic unity, growth, and self-preservation."[24] In woman's crucial role as mother we have the way by which the first commandment – "be fruitful and multiply" – is to be fulfilled, a way intimately connected with the rhythm of comedy. Eve's name, juxtaposed next to the announcement of the "dust-to-dust cycle" of human existence (3:19, 20), becomes the sign that the comedy of life and love will continue.

That Eve as mother names her sons "Cain" (Gen. 4:1) and

---

[23] Gerhard von Rad, *Genesis: A Commentary,* John H. Marks, trans. (Philadelphia: The Westminster Press, 1956), p. 93.

[24] Susanne Langer, "The Comic Rhythm," in Corrigan, ed., *Comedy,* p. 140.

"Seth" (4:25) not only shows her assuming Adam's earlier role as namer, but testifies specifically to her function as fertile bearer of new life. Moreover, that her two sons' names frame the narrative of the murder of the unfortunate Abel helps to confirm the narrative's dominant emphasis on life: yes, the tale bespeaks full awareness of death inscribed in the bloodied body of an innocent victim, but it depicts also the commitment of the human community to the preservation and perpetuation of life. That people begin to call on the name of Yahweh immediately on the heels of Seth's birth dramatically bears witness to the affirmation of a deity who continues to bring life in the midst of death (4:25).

Interpreters usually do not detect the presence of parody in the Garden story, yet a closer reading of the tale – especially over against the sublime, solemn, priestly version in Genesis 1 – discloses other possibilities. In fact, whatever the original chronological sequence of the two creation narratives, I would characterize the garden story in the present ordering of the text as a "parodic double" of the first creation account. Such "parodic-travestying literature," argues Bakhtin, "introduces the permanent corrective of laughter, of a critique on the one-sided seriousness of the lofty direct word, the corrective of reality that is always richer, more fundamental, and most importantly too contradictory and heteroglot to be fit into a high and straightforward genre."[25]

First, as Brisman has suggested, the Yahwist narrator has again and again counterpointed and ironically subverted the sombre lines of the priestly version.[26] Indeed, to Brisman, "the all-too-human Yava" engages in a variety of "second thoughts" in revising key efforts in his creative work.[27] Put even more bluntly, Yahweh appears as a kind of "bungler"[28] at getting creation right, whose motto might read, "If at first you don't

---

[25] M. M. Bakhtin, *The Dialogic Imagination: Four Essays*, Michael Holquist, ed., and Caryl Emerson and Michael Holquist, trans. (Austin: University of Texas Press, 1981), p. 55.

[26] Brisman idiosyncratically calls the Yahwist narrator "Jacob" and a composite version of the Elohist and the Priestly writer "Eisaac." See Brisman, *The Voice of Jacob*, p. xv. [27] *Ibid.*, pp. 2–3. [28] Rosenberg and Bloom, *The Book of J*, p. 183.

succeed, then try, try again." For example, the newly created
Adam is judged to be inadequate because incomplete: "It is
not good that the human be alone" (2:18) – thus forming an
echoing contrast to the litany of monotonic "good" in Genesis
1 where the creator affirms all things as good. Yahweh then
proceeds to form all the animals and birds, even allowing the
human to name them and thereby fix their character and
destiny; but "for the human was not found a helper as his
partner" (2:20). The suspense and tension mount as the long
parade of animals moves past the lonely man. Yahweh finally
gets it right, producing the first woman from the man in an
incongruous reversal of natural birth. An enthusiastic
response from the man recognizes and revels in the intimate
affinity of the newly gendered couple: "this at last is bone of
my bone, and flesh of my flesh; this one shall be called woman
(*'ishah*), for out of man (*'ish*) this one was taken" (2:23). The
striking pun enclosed in the poetic lines not only captures the
heightened sense of belonging between man and woman, but
parodically corresponds to the priestly poem on the creation
of the god-like, yet gendered humans: "So God created
humankind in his image, in the image of God he created
them; male and female he created them" (1:27).

The contrast between the two versions of the humans' creation and the complementary, if not contradictory, pictures of
the creator's *modus operandi* could hardly be more pointed:
the calm, methodical, self-congratulatory creator of Genesis
1 sharply differs from the hasty, haphazard potter-planter god
in the garden, who gets the job done but seems to operate by
trial and error. The contrast is striking and even provocative,
not overtly favoring one image over the other, but dramatizing difference by juxtaposing a precise, measured report side-
by-side with a colorful, lively, humorous tale.[29] Over against
the majestic, transcendent deity whose speech automatically

[29] See Jack Miles' fascinating study of God as the major character of the Hebrew
Bible; e.g., note the following assessment of the God that we meet in the opening
chapters of Genesis: "God – lofty, unwavering, and sincere in his creative actions
– has become as the Lord God intimate, volatile, and prone to dark regrets and
darker equivocations. The Lord God is God. There are not two protagonists in
this text, only one. But this one protagonist has two strikingly distinct personalities." Jack Miles, *God: A Biography* (New York: Alfred A. Knopf, 1995), p. 38.

and effortlessly materializes itself in a clearly demarcated, orderly creation we see a God who "gets his hands dirty" and who makes mistakes.[30] "A revisionist at heart," concludes Brisman, "he sees what he did at first was somewhat flawed and must be corrected."[31]

Still another contrast comes in the close of the two different creation accounts. The priestly version concludes with the image of the Creator's rest on the seventh day and the aetiology of the sabbath, whereas the Yahwist finishes with an aetiology of marriage with its surprising reversal of expectation in having the man leave his father and mother and cling to his wife, thus becoming again the one flesh of the primal union (2:24). Brisman offers a compelling observation on the comic sensibility of this reunion:

Whether one regards [the Yahwist's] memorable line as representation of sexual desire or as a rationale for domestic loyalty, the wonder of the line is related to the sense that we are sharing not a first ritual but a first domestic joke. Jacob's [i.e., the Yahwist's] story is like that of Aristophanes in Plato's *Symposium*, where a divided spherical self leaves the halves forever in sexual quest for repair of the cleavage.[32]

Moreover, the reversal of roles – in which the man leaves his parental household for his wife – contains a shift in cultural orientation and expectation that typically has the wife leave her parents for her husband. Incongruous turns and reversed perspectives continually emerge from beneath the textual surface, complicating the storyline and evoking a sense of discrepancy.

Although rarely mentioned again in the Hebrew Bible, Genesis 3 represents one of the most influential texts in post-biblical interpretation, a text that unfortunately has become the seed-bed for the tragic construal of the loss of paradise as well as for an egregiously misogynistic portrayal of the fate of Eve and all her daughters.[33] As we have already suggested, however, there is another way of reading the text, a way that

---

[30] Brisman, *The Voice of Jacob*, p. 4.   [31] *Ibid.*, pp. 4–5.   [32] *Ibid.*, pp. 6–7.

[33] See Carol Meyers, *Discovering Eve: Ancient Israelite Women in Context* (New York: Oxford University Press, 1988), pp. 3–23; for a comprehensive survey of the images of Eve, see John A. Phillips, *Eve: The History of an Idea* (San Francisco: Harper & Row, 1984).

both corrects more blatant misreadings and leads to more balanced and nuanced interpretations.

Rather than invoke the Christian theological categories of fall and original sin, we do better to trace the trajectory of the text along a track we may name "temptation, transgression, and transformation." What concerns the text, in particular, is an exploration of the aetiologies of present human existence, an exploration that presents primal themes in narrative form and thus poses the existential dilemmas of humanity in the form of a tale of our common ancestors, archetypal man and woman. The narrative especially activates the polyphonous play of "the dialogic imagination,"[34] allowing many competing voices to emerge in what constitutes the first dialogue in the Bible. Indeed, it is striking to note how much Genesis 3 is dominated by dialogue, the moments of speech articulating key questions of human existence – all revolving around the issues of fundamental relationships. Dialogue dramatizes the psychological dimensions of the tale, injecting discordant notes of ambiguity, contradiction, and disputed meaning. It is a masterful narrative which especially features the power and presence of the first woman, the pivotal character in the movement of the Edenic drama.

Parody enters the narrative at virtually every level, whether in the characterizations of God, serpent, man or woman, or in strategic plays on language and theme.[35] For example, the serpent, so often identified by later tradition with Satan, is simply portrayed as the most clever of any of God's wild creatures, but is a talking animal who puzzlingly steps forward in the ambiguous role of God's opponent (a "devil's advocate"?) and the humans' helper. In particular, he assumes the guise of a trickster, "a character having the capacity to transform situations and overturn the status quo."[36] In any event, the serpent addresses the woman, not the man, and quickly

[34] Bakhtin, *The Dialogic Imagination.*
[35] For the most discriminating recent study of the complex phenomenon of parody, see Margaret A. Rose, *Parody: Ancient, Modern, and Post-Modern* (Cambridge: Cambridge University Press, 1993).
[36] Susan Niditch, "Genesis," in *The Women's Bible Commentary,* Carol A. Newsom and Sharon H. Ringe, eds. (Louisville: Westminster/John Knox Press, 1992), p. 14.

demonstrates his subtlety and seductiveness. The topic centers on what God said or didn't say concerning the trees in the garden, particularly the tree of the knowledge of good and evil. This is the first of several different renditions of the scope and significance of the first prohibition in the Bible (2:17). Already double-voiced words of polyphony and parody come to the fore. Indeed, the serpent appears as a kind of skilled parodist, who slyly voices a loaded question that provokes the woman to quote the earlier divine speech, though in fact she misquotes it. She exaggerates by expanding the restrictiveness of the original commandment: "You shall not eat of the fruit of the tree . . . *nor shall you touch it,* or you shall die" (emphasis mine) (3:3). Does she add this little touch to tighten up and thus strengthen the prohibition or does her slight emendation bespeak resentment? Whatever the case, the serpent immediately retorts, "You will not die; for God knows that when you eat of it your eyes will be opened, and you will be like God(s), knowing good and evil" (3:4). By directly contradicting God's warning and claiming to disclose the hidden motivation for the prohibition – divine jealousy of special powers – the serpent both subverts divine authority and casts a shadow of suspicion on the supposed beneficence of the creator.

Having heard the serpent's arguments, the woman allows other senses to take over and decides to take the forbidden fruit: "So when the woman saw that the tree was good for food, and that it was a delight to the eyes, and that the tree was desirable to make one wise, she took of its fruit and ate; and she also gave some to her husband who was with her, and he ate" (3:6). Repetition of key words from preceding texts shows a keen-eared and sharp-eyed parodist at work. First, one cannot help but hear an echo of the priestly creation account, parodying the repeated litany, "God saw that it was good." This language has been transferred to the mouth of the woman, who like God, knows a good thing when she sees it. Second, the terms employed to describe all the trees in the garden (2:9) are taken up and focused on the one forbidden tree, thus shifting the frame of reference from the general to the particular, albeit in an ironic application to the tabooed tree. Hence such language as "pleasant (*neḥmad*) to the eyes" and "good for food" is now reiterated in altered form to describe the process of reflection through which the woman passes before she decides to eat the fruit. The subtle changes are suggestive: the phrase, "good for food," now appears first in contrast to the earlier account; then the tree's physical beauty is noted (substituting another Hebrew term, *ta'awah* ("delightful") for *neḥmad* ("pleasant"); and finally, *neḥmad* reappears, but now is applied to the desirability of the tree for its wisdom. The partial repetitions and small but significant alterations, refocusing the general qualities of "every tree" on the one forbidden tree, suggest a form of parody that takes up good qualities in order ironically to make the forbidden tree all the more alluring. The resulting series of images coupled with the cogent logic of the serpent constitutes for the woman a compelling argument, leading her to disobey the original divine commandment – all in the name of securing fruit whose good attributes have become all too inviting. The serpent seductively insinuates his persuasive words into the internal psychological disposition of the woman so that what appears intrinsically and unambiguously desirable answers apparently to hidden desire. In brief, the fruit of the tree was delectable to the taste, delightful to behold, and desirable for its wisdom – a triad of enticing qualities which the woman cannot resist: "she took of its fruit and ate; and gave to her husband, who was with her, and he ate" (3:6).

Throughout the narrative the man emerges as a compliant, pliable figure who is "even comical"[37] in his passivity. The silence of the text on his failure to resist is telling, a gap that has provoked many commentators like Augustine and Milton to come up with ingenious rationalizations for the man's behavior. In contrast, the woman stands out as an active, independent, decisive figure; she hardly is the evil temptress so popular in the dominant misogynistic tradition.[38] What accounts for this reversal in perspective and presentation

[37] *Ibid.*
[38] For this reversal of perspective, see especially Trible, *God and the Rhetoric of Sexuality*, p. 113; Meyers, *Discovering Eve*, p. 91; Illana Pardes, *Countertraditions in the Bible: A Feminist Approach* (Cambridge, MA: Harvard University Press, 1992), pp. 37–54.

when one moves from more conventional portrayals of man and woman in Genesis 2 (where the woman is utterly passive and the man is active) to the strikingly different mode of Genesis 3? Is this once again the way of parody, inverting and subverting the relationship between the sexes that usually prevails in androcentric society? Does this portrayal of woman's role of active initiator reflect a more egalitarian relationship which may have its historical and sociological prototype in pre-monarchical Israel?[39] Does this livelier woman emerge because the author is a woman?[40] Is the massive and sometimes monstrous misogynistic misreading of text not only to be attributed to patriarchal bias but also to the lack of a sense of humor on the part of the great majority of readers?[41] Obviously these questions evoke radically different responses, but they at least illumine the polyphonic richness and ambiguity of the first great dialogue in biblical literature.

The plot thickens even more as we listen to the central dialogue in the narrative: the encounter between Yahweh and the transgressing trio of God's earth-bound creatures who have aspired in different ways to become like the gods. The scene of discovery is one of the most powerful set-pieces of Genesis. The deity is depicted as taking a leisurely stroll in his garden estate at the time of the cool evening breezes, while the human caretakers cower amidst the magical, mysterious trees, waiting anxiously to be discovered in their hiding place. The serpent also is lurking close at hand, since God will address in due time this other upstart creature of the field. Yahweh's first question, "Where are you?", is addressed to the man, who responds forthrightly: "I heard the sound of you in the garden, and I was afraid, because I was naked; and I hid myself" (3:10). But the second set of questions ("Who told you that you were naked? Have you eaten from the tree of which I commanded you not to eat?") evokes a classic self-excusing response that blames the woman and then implicitly the deity: "The woman whom you gave to be with me, she gave me fruit from the tree, and I ate" (3:11–12). Yahweh

---

[39] Meyers, *Discovering Eve*, pp. 120–121.
[40] Rosenberg and Bloom, *The Book of J*, p. 178.   [41] *Ibid.*

then asks the woman, "What is this that you have done?" (3:13a), to which the woman responds, "The serpent tricked me, and I ate" (3:13b). All in all it is a comical scene, where God as a stern parent confronts his erring children with simple "Where, Who, What" questions which they answer by resorting to a transparently lame, yet laughable strategy of "buck-passing." The multiple repetitions of the key verb "eat" heighten the comic effect.

Yahweh is quick to react to his transgressive creatures, issuing a series of oracles addressed in reverse hierarchical order to serpent, woman, and man. Breaking the prose style of the surrounding narrative, the oracles are poetic in style and constitute the center-piece of the whole tale of trickery and transgression. The oracles express in elevated language fundamental transformations in human and animal social order (3:14–19). Typically, the speeches have been equated with the judicial sentences handed down by the presiding judge in a trial, but one wonders whether this is the most compelling designation. God as offended parent who chastizes his disobedient children is a more apt image. The pattern, "because you have done x" (3:14 and 17), inscribes in a cause-effect sequence the consequences of creaturely action. The calamitous and dire punishments often emphasized in later theological literature are just not here, but rather fundamental and recurrent life and death rhythms of human communities are simply described. To be sure, strife, toil, sweat, and pain are part of the cycles of post-edenic human existence, whose ambiguous presence stands out all the more against the portrayal of an easier, more idyllic time. For example, the woman's role as mother is now burdened by pain, and her desire for primal oneness (cf. 2:24) leads to masculine domination in the sexual union (3:16). Man's affinity with the soil is reaffirmed, but the soil is now cursed and resists man's sweat-stained labor (3:17–19). Death is now both feared and greeted with relief when the man returns to his original condition, "a dust-to-dust cycle of human life and death"[42] inscribed in proverbial speech: "you are dust, and to

---

[42] *Ibid.*, p. 185.

dust you shall return" (3:19b). The language of curse is not applied directly to humans, but only to the serpent and the soil (3:14, 17), both of which are now alienated from the humans, the woman and her seed ever seeking to subdue the serpent and the man ever seeking to subdue the soil. The woman figures prominently in all three oracles, serving as a kind of mediatorial agent, positioned in relationship to the serpent, on the one hand, and the man, on the other (3:15–17). In short, these poetic oracles comprise a piece of wisdom lore, composed now as poetic oracles, telling life like it is.

Employing Bakhtin's suggestive language, we can read this more complex representation of life in ancient Israel as a "parodic double" of the mandate to multiply and master in Genesis 1:28,[43] a kind of bittersweet commentary on the specific strategy for fulfilling the first commandment. As Shakespeare reminds us in *The Tempest*, "the world must be peopled" – but at what price? Yes, the humans will come together to procreate and multiply, but the sexual desire of the woman for the man will lead to masculine domination (3:16). Though historically this inequality may have been limited originally to sexual union,[44] it has been extended to justify all sorts of female subjection to males. In any event, the potential equality and mutuality of the male-female bond depicted in Genesis 1:27 receives a harsh twist, a cruel parody of the original idyllic quality of the drive for primal union (2:24). Moreover, mastery of the animals is also reiterated, but now we find a sharpened sense of enmity and conflict symbolized in the battle between the serpent's seed and the woman's offspring. What a stunning inversion of the original conditions of creation! Comic play in the form of a parodic revision illumines and enlivens the contradictory position the humans hold in the uncertain relationship with animals and gods, though the resulting humor harbors a bite and sting.

Yet the narrative does not find closure, and what follows the series of divine oracles is perhaps even more unexpected and

---

[43] Bakhtin, *The Dialogic Imagination*, p. 53.
[44] Meyers, *Discovering Eve*, pp. 114–117.

surprising. First, immediately in the wake of the inexorable movement of humans' death when they return to their dusty origins, the narrator reports the second naming of woman – which in fact is the first proper naming, since she becomes only now a fully formed character in the narrative.[45] "The man named his wife Eve (*ḥavah*) because she was the mother of all living (*'em-kol-ḥay*) (3:20), housing in her very name her power as mother of new life, an act of trust in the future, which both registers defiance in the face of death and offers eloquent testimony to the stubborn drive to perpetuate life.

Second, God provides for his willful creatures a new set of clothing, a merciful gesture that not only masks human nakedness and shields human vulnerability, but further distinguishes the humans as creatures set apart from gods and animals. Blissful, unabashed, open-bodied nakedness now is covered up, except as recovered in erotic encounter as celebrated in the Song of Songs.

Third, and perhaps the most startling action of the deity, is his acknowledgment of their newly acquired divine likeness: "See, the man has become like one of us, knowing good and evil; and now, he might reach out his hand and take from the tree of life, and eat, and live forever" (3:22). So the serpent on some level was right all along. What an ironic twist on the major story line, lending credence to the view that some sort of divine jealousy about holding on to its special prerogatives is present. It offers, too, a glimpse of the possibility of immortality at the very beginnings of the biblical story.[46] Moreover, parody, that double-voiced gesture which intensifies ambiguity, is again at work: what the serpent had initially said about the underlying motivation is now reiterated by Yahweh, creating that echoing effect which complicates the issues, compromises the character of God, and thus provokes God to expel humanity from Eden lest the couple eat from

---

[45] See the illuminating interpretation of the characterization of Eve in Mieke Bal's formidable analysis, "Sexuality, Sin, and Sorrow: The Emergence of the Female Character," in *Lethal Love: Feminist Literary Readings of Biblical Love Stories* (Bloomington: Indiana University Press, 1987), pp. 104–130; note also the convincing critique, in Pardes, *Countertraditions in the Bible*, p. 41.

[46] See Barr's fresh analysis of this issue in his discriminating study, *The Garden of Eden and the Hope of Immortality*.

the tree of life and gain immortality. Once more the text discloses a "parodic double" of the divinely imaged humanity of Genesis 1 in which the priestly writer speaks in the voice of the pluralized divine council ("let us make humankind in our image, according to our likeness . . ." – 1:26), a voice which affirms a positive sense of identity. In Genesis 3, however, Yahweh speaks similarly in the plural, but this time begrudgingly stressing the humans' illicit grab for "god-likeness," and using it as a justification for making the tree of life another taboo. Yahweh declares the tree off-limits and even places armed guards at the entrance of the garden. As Brisman pointedly describes the utter incongruity of the situation, the Priestly Writer says in essence to the humans, "Be like, be like," to which the uncanny Yahwist sardonically retorts, "Be not too like."[47] Indeed, one can assert that much of the biblical drama becomes consumed with the tension between these two poles in the complex relationship between humans and god(s). But for now the problem is solved by simply cutting off access to the tree of life.

In sum, the Garden Story contains more dominant comic notes than the traditional and largely Christian tragic reading would suggest. Whether viewed from the perspective of plotline, parodied speech, forceful puns, or character portrayal, the scenes are marked by comic and humorous touches. The human pair, notably the woman, shows curiosity, courage, and adventurous experimentation which verge more toward humor and comedy than grim-faced tragedy. Even – or especially – God is caricatured as a rather ambiguous character whose volatile, jealous nature provokes his divinely imaged human creatures to take all too human (and divine) steps, a characterization marked by sardonic wit, punning play, and comic irony.

Blood(y) brothers: what's in a name? (Genesis 4)

Cain and his descendants dominate the first story of life outside of Eden, but Cain's blood brothers make decisive

---

[47] Brisman, *The Voice of Jacob*, p. 8.

appearances at the beginning and end of the story. Above all the story features "first murderers," a tale of homicide and inexorable cycles of vengeance, yet enframed by the birth of new lives. If there be a beginning of human sin, it is surely best found here.[48] The story does not initially present itself as revealing notable comic traits and a sadly tragic face appears, though in the literary after-life of the text "the changes of Cain" disclose both tragic and comic characterizations, especially from the fertile imagination of the Medieval Period.[49]

If a comic touch be present in any form, it may appear in the pattern of puns which figure suggestively at beginning and end as well as in the middle. The story opens with the accent on the coming of new life: Adam has sexual intercourse with Eve and she conceives and gives birth to a son whom she triumphantly names Cain (*qayin*), since "I have created [*qaniti*] a man [equally together] with the Lord" (4:1).[50] Cut off from access to the tree of life and aware of threatened death in the future, the woman participates boldly in the creation of life, thus fulfilling her role as "mother of all living" and perhaps even claiming special, god-like powers as a co-creator with Yahweh.[51] It is an exultant claim, registering defiance in the face of death and reveling in her function as mother-creator. Eve therefore continues the active, assertive, self-initiating role that marked her in the earlier narrative, assuming now the powerful prerogative of creator and namer.

Abel (*hebel*, "breath, vapor") is born next, but his name is not explicitly punned. However, if names be markers and makers of identity, his name does not bode well for him, since

---

[48] Meyers, *Discovering Eve*, p. 87.
[49] See the comprehensive, compelling study by Richard J. Quinones, *The Changes of Cain: Violence and the Lost Brother in Cain and Abel Literature* (Princeton: Princeton University Press, 1991). Quinones focuses on the root sense of the Cain-Abel story as a "tragedy of differentiation" (pp. 9–12), tracing the story through its highly varied permutations in the corpus of Western literature. He singles out the comic adaptations of the story in the mystery plays of the Medieval Period; see especially his discussion of the *Mactatio Abel* of the Townley cycle which he calls "vibrant comedy" where "at times, the upstart comic audacity of Cain is dramatically brilliant . . ." (p. 57).
[50] Cassuto, cited in Pardes, *Countertraditions in the Bible*, p. 40.   [51] *Ibid.*, p. 44.

"vapor" is by nature evanescent and short-lived (cf. Ecclesiastes where *hebel* is the key word). Abel becomes the innocent, but seemingly insubstantial brother who is paradoxically favored by Yahweh but whose vapor-like life is snuffed out by his envious and murderous brother.

The second significant pun on a personal name comes at the end of the narrative, when Seth is born. Eve once again acts as namer, but this time she is more constrained and chastened perhaps as a result of the loss of her second son, calling her third born, Seth ("appoint"), playing on the name with the words, "God has appointed (*shat*) for me another child instead of Abel, because Cain killed him" (4:25).[52] So at beginning and end we find an inscription of life written with varying degrees of divine involvement but wrought also with the creative powers of woman. Between these two acts of birthing and naming comes the story of the "first murderers" and hence the bloody foundation of the first city and its mixed blessings for human civilization. Fraught with ambiguity and ambivalence, this tale of first births and first deaths contains grim-faced, macabre images of murder set paradoxically in the midst of ongoing life, of erotic desire in the service of good and evil, of angry, aggressive action in the grip of envy and murderous instincts, and of divine punishment mitigated by merciful signs of grace and protection.

Yet one also perhaps hears the sardonic laughter of parody, as we discern once again the echo of double-voices that play especially upon the language and themes of the earlier garden story. God continues to be a most ambiguous charac-

---

[52] I follow here once again Pardes' insightful interpretation of the significance of Eve's naming of her second son (see her *Countertraditions in the Bible*, pp.51–53). Note, too, her comment: "My contention is . . . that the tragedy which befalls Eve's son is meant, among other things, as a retributive deflation of her hubris. The son who was the object of her (pro)creative pride turns out to be the destroyer of her creation" (p. 53). Her interpretation is most compelling, dramatizing the deeply tragic dimension of the Cain-Abel-Seth story. But as I will argue especially in conjunction with Job, tragedy may be conjoined intimately with the redemptive capacity of comedy. Indeed, one can make the case that this initial sibling rivalry of the Bible which tragically ends in fratricide is later counterpointed by the story of Joseph and his brothers where a murderous plot of brothers against brother ends up as a story of reconciliation and restoration.

ter, whose seemingly arbitrary preference for Abel's offering over Cain's begins the chain of jealousy and resentment that culminates in the elimination of the one brother and the exile of the other. No explanation is offered for the seemingly unmotivated divine favoritism, and various surmises from history, sociology, psychology, or theology are speculative and usually unsatisfactory attempts to explain and justify the mysterious, uncanny actions and motives of the deity. Yahweh's preference, however, engenders conflict within Cain, who is forced to choose whether or not to do the "good" (*tob*): "If you do well (*tetib*), will you not be accepted? And if you do not do well, sin is lurking at the door; its desire is for you, but you must master it" (4:7). The words "desire" and "master," first addressed to the woman in the garden (3:16), are now picked up and applied to the personified voice of sin whose ravenous desire for Cain must be mastered. Can we not call this a parody of erotic desire, replaying in another relationship the ambivalent connection between desire and domination (3:16)? In a brilliant stroke, the narrator has moved from the external playing out of the mastery of erotic desire between man and woman to the internal problem of mastering the murderous desire to destroy another human being. The resonance in the repetition of the language of desire and mastery is indeed striking: initially the theme was concentrated in the ambiguous erotics between the primal couple, but now it is located in the internal psyche where contending forces rage within and find deadly expression in the first homicide. Possession or mastery of the one by the other is at stake: the first for the perpetuation of life, the second for the perpetration of death. The drama of life and death becomes centered on the continued birthings and namings by the mother of all living over against the deadly rivalries between brothers. "Civilization and Its Discontents"[53] is born in this process of living and dying and the begetting of new life.

---

[53] Sigmund Freud, *Civilization and Its Discontents*, James Strachey, trans. and ed. (New York: W. W. Norton & Co., 1961).

Cain succumbs to sin's desire for him, and he murders his brother. The ensuing dialogue between Yahweh and Cain dramatizes the ambiguity in the characterization of Cain, an ambiguity that has evoked the numerous "changes of Cain" in the western tradition.[54] Partially repeating in style and substance the interrogative sequence of the garden scene, the divine questions lead once more to accusation and punishment:

Yahweh said to Cain, 'Where is your brother Abel?' He said, 'I do not know; am I my brother's keeper?' And Yahweh said, 'What have you done? Listen; your brother's blood is crying out to me from the ground! And now you are cursed from the ground . . . When you till the ground, it will no longer yield to you its strength; you will be a fugitive and wanderer on the earth.' Cain said to Yahweh, 'My punishment is greater than I can bear! Today you have driven me away from the soil, and I shall be hidden from your face; I shall be a fugitive and wanderer on the earth, and anyone who meets me may kill me' (4:9–14).

Cain displays not a little *ḥuspah* in this exchange, first sarcastically countering the question with a rhetorical question, "Am I my brother's keeper?" and then lamenting his own fate with a cry for help. His lament surprisingly elicits an act of mercy from Yahweh who not only spares the life of the murderer but gives him a protective mark to ward off any human attacker: "Then Yahweh said to him, 'Not so! Whoever kills Cain will suffer a seven-fold vengeance.' And Yahweh put a mark on Cain, so that no one who came upon him would kill him. Then Cain went away from the presence of Yahweh, and settled in the land of Nod, east of Eden" (4:15–16).

It is the image of the defiant, unrepentant Cain that caused Romantic interpreters to cast him in the role of the "tragic rebel" eternally doomed to endure his fateful destiny as history's archetypal wanderer, ever seeking a place of rest and refuge, and then paradoxically settling in the "land of wandering" (*Nod*).[55] Once again the narrator crystallizes the fate

---

[54] See Quinones, *The Changes of Cain.*
[55] *Ibid.*, pp. 87–108.

of a character by creating a powerful pun: divinely decreed to be a "wanderer" (*nad*), he lives in a land called "wandering" (*Nod*). In fact, this compelling pun is central and constitutive for the narrative, positioned approximately in the middle-point. It serves both to climax the theme of murder and exile and to create the context for the birth of Cain's son and the emergence of civilization. Founding the first city – "named Enoch after his son Enoch" (4:17) – is Cain's attempt to deal with the problem of nomadic existence, of the incongruous destiny of dwelling in a land of wandering. But can a wanderer ever settle down? To Radday, this dilemma inherent in Cain's whole career catches and carries the meaning of the ancient tale and reveals a form of subtle humor, caricaturing the first city builder.[56] Whether physical or psychological wandering is intended, this little pun stresses how Cain can never find a permanent habitation and home – even if he founds a city; he must embody and experience the contradiction of one who founds a city, yet paradoxically never can find rest in it. Moreover, the history behind this foundation of civilization marks it as a site of perennial restlessness and unresolved tension. Once again the humor proves to be vicious, taking savage delight in showing the fundamental contradictoriness and restlessness of human existence. Divinely destined to wander, Cain determines to settle down and found a city – but he does it in the land of wandering. Whether tragic villain or comic fool, Cain takes the first faltering steps on the stage of human history as a Janus-faced figure whose only constancy is ceaseless change and incessant instability, living out his fate as fugitive and wanderer east of Eden.

Giants on the earth (Genesis 6:1–4)

Genesis 6:1–4 is one of the strangest texts in the Bible – and in my view one of the most celebrated pieces of parodied mythology we possess from antiquity. Usually it is contextually

---

[56] Radday, "Humour in Names," in Radday and Brenner, eds., *On Humour and the Comic in the Hebrew Bible*, pp. 86–89.

linked with the following flood story and interpreted as evidence to justify the massive eradication of human and animal life, but it is truer to the episodic flow of the primeval story to look at this seemingly anomalous text on its own merits before blurring its rich significance by connecting it too quickly to the ensuing flood story.

From very early the text's rather blatant but conventional mythological motif – divine intercourse with beautiful human women to produce giants on the earth – evoked forced but ingenious explanations of the "sons of gods" as angels or humans, thus attempting to protect the integrity of the monotheistic ideal.[57] In light of other signs of divine plurality in this string of stories (cf. 1:26; 3:22; 11:7), there is no compelling reason to eliminate or suppress the polytheistic imagery. Moreover, though probably fragmentary and somewhat isolated, the episode has thematic resonance with stories before and after: most notably, for example, with the perilous but persistent attempts to blur the lines of distinction between humanity and divinity. Usually the attempts come from the human side (Gen. 3 and 11), but here the motivation and desire come from divine beings (the mysterious "sons of God"), adding a depth (or height) dimension that suggestively complicates and enlivens the representation of the relations between gods and humans. What we have is a truncated version of an older and fuller descent myth where divine beings are responsible for the rape of women and the resulting violation of the earth.[58] Once more "women" are instrumental in the transition to human and historical time, serving as sexual objects to be taken by stronger divinities, and fulfilling a perverse and parodied destiny as Eve's daughters to become "mothers of living." But here the illicit desire comes directly from the divine sphere, and masculine divin-

---

[57] See the comprehensive presentation in Claus Westermann, *Genesis* (third edn.) (Neukirchen-Vluyn: Neukirchener Verlag, 1983), vol. I, pp. 491–517.

[58] See the insightful delineation of this myth by Philip R. Davies, "Women, Men, Gods, Sex and Power: The Birth of a Biblical Myth," in *A Feminist Companion to Genesis*, Athalya Brenner, ed. (Sheffield: Sheffield University Press, 1993), pp. 194–203.

ities possess innocent women. Sometimes the sons of God run amok, taking beautiful women and siring a race of giants, a transgression that prompts Yahweh to limit the human life-span to 120 years (6:3).

What a bitingly humorous mockery of the action and reaction of divine beings! First, we have a parody of the multiplication and mastery theme of Genesis 1:27–28: the humans are beginning "to multiply on the face of the ground" (6:1), but the sons of god want to get in on the action and seduce the alluring daughters, taking "women for themselves of all whom they chose" (6:2), hence exercising a perverse form of mastery over women.

Second, echoing the divine concern that the humans might become too much like the gods (3:22; cf. also 11:4–6), the narrator shows that the divine beings also are not immune from erotic desire when they "see" that the daughters "were fair" (*tob*) (6:2a). One can note too the possible parody of the action of the creator in Genesis 1 when "God saw" his creative handiwork and pronounced it "good" (*tob*). Indeed, one could parodically paraphrase this ludicrous mismatch by calling to mind the earlier language of desire attributed to Eve ("the woman saw that the tree was good . . . and she took . . . and ate"): the sons of god saw that the daughters were good and they took as many as they chose.[59]

Third, we have a parody of the sublime priestly affirmation: "So God created humankind in his image" (1:27), but now the creation of partly divine offspring results from divine-human intercourse. I find it rather strange and unjustified that many translators use the word "marry" to describe the divine seizure of women for sexual purposes; the more accurate translation in this context would seem to be "rape." Why use a euphemistic word like "marry" in an attempt to dignify the actions of the divine beings? What is involved is "an act of

---

[59] Note the parallels to the action of "seeing" and "taking" in Gen. 12:1 off and I Sam. 11, an action that also evokes divine intervention; to be sure, human males are the perpetrators in these other biblical tales, whereas here divine beings are involved. Cf. Westermann, *Genesis*, pp. 495–496.

aggression made possible by a superior force,"[60] a description that would seem to suggest rape. What is ironic is that the divine perpetrators of this mongrelization of humanity are not explicitly condemned (contrast the punishment of the sons of God in Ps. 82). Once again humanity is judged and found wanting, thus receiving Yahweh's punishment of a limited life-span of 120 years; once again the line of demarcation between gods and humans is re-drawn and mortality becomes the human lot.

Finally, does one not find a parody of the heroic ideal in the aetiology of the concluding verse? "The *Nephilim* [fallen ones, giants] were on the earth in those days – and also afterward – when the sons of God entered the daughters of humans, who bore children to them. These were the heroes of old, warriors of renown" (6:4). The descriptive, reportorial style, so lacking in harsh condemnatory language, enhances the parody and shows a kind of "wry appreciation" of the ancient mythic heroes.[61]

Although we can raise questions about the actions of uncontrolled divinities who let their sexual desires get out of hand, we should not miss the mocking humor. The "gods," too, "may be crazy," but then that is only a way of affirming how much the gods are also bound up in the "comedy of errors" that the Bible calls creation. The degree of tolerance for – and even delight in – irreverent parody of sacred themes adds a lusty, lustrous tone to the divine-human comedy of Genesis.

"Boating for Beginners": the comic adventures of Noah and his sons in the time of the great flood (Genesis 6–9)

At least from the time of the Medieval *Wakefield Mystery Plays*, dramatists and readers have found the biblical flood story an ever-flowing fountain of comic characters, motifs, and scenes.

---

[60] Westermann, *Genesis: A Practical Commentary*, p. 44.
[61] The phrase is Bloom's; see Rosenberg and Bloom, *The Book of J*, p. 189.

In the contemporary world we have enjoyed not only the comic renditions of Noah and the flood from Bill Cosby and Woody Allen, but also the outrageously humorous treatments of the great flood by Julian Barnes in his *The History of the World in Ten and One-Half Chapters*[62] and Jeanette Winterson's equally hilarious novel, *Boating for Beginners.*[63] Last but not least such literary critics as Bloom and Brisman[64] find comic moments and motifs in the original biblical story, especially in the version usually attributed to the Yahwist (J). Hence from varied quarters, we can observe ample precedent for discovering the presence of the comic vision in this hugely popular tale about Noah and his three sons.

As a point of entry we can detect once again pivotal puns placed strategically at the beginning and end of the Noah traditions.[65] All but hidden away in the so-called priestly genealogy of Genesis 5 a Yahwistic fragment appears, presenting a popular etymology on Noah's name that gives a striking preview of the cluster of Noah tales that stretch from Genesis 6:5 to Genesis 9:28. Indeed, Thompson describes Genesis 5:29 as "a prophecy about Noah which, with consummate ironic humor both introduces the Noah story to come and links that story to the garden story and to Yahweh's curses."[66] Breaking up the stiffly formal style of the genealogy ("When X lived Y years, he became the father of a son"), a naming formula appears that shines a spotlight on Lamech's first-born son: "He named him *Noah*, saying, 'This one shall bring us relief or comfort (*ynḥm*) out of the soil (*'adamah*) that Yahweh has cursed'" (5:29).

The language of this popular etymological play (*noaḥ//naḥam*) will ripple through the text, moving back-

---

[62] Julian Barnes, *The History of the World in Ten and One-Half Chapters* (New York: Random House, 1990).

[63] Jeanette Winterson, *Boating for Beginners* (London: Methuen London Ltd., 1985).

[64] Rosenberg and Bloom, *The Book of J*, p. 190: "I begin to feel redundant in my insistence that J is a comic writer when we come to the story of Noah and his sons." Also note Brisman, *The Voice of Jacob*, pp. 18, 21.

[65] See Brisman, *The Voice of Jacob*, p. 18.

[66] Thomas L. Thompson, *The Origin Tradition of Ancient Israel: I. The Literary Formation of Genesis and Exodus 1–23* (Sheffield: Sheffield Academic Press, 1987), p. 29.

wards and forwards in the primeval story and carrying both
the past and the future. The echoes of paradise lost – "the soil
(*'adamah*) that Yahweh has cursed" (5:29; cf. 3:17,19; 4:11) –
resound through the narrative and are picked up again in the
post-flood tradition of Noah's image as "a man of the soil"
(*'adamah*) who is the first to plant a vineyard (9:20). Noah's
name with its multiple plays on the roots *noaḥ* ("rest") and
naḥam ("comfort, relief") serves a proleptic or even prophetic
function in the plot, intimating key moments in the movement of the story. Embedded in the name Noah is his double
image as not only the survivor of the flood but the first
viticulturalist who brings "relief" (*naḥam*) by planting a vineyard and discovering the gift of wine. Twice we are told that
Yahweh "regretted" (still another meaning of *naḥam*) making
humans (6:6, 7). Then we hear a palindrome on Noah's name
in the expression of divine mercy: "Noah found favor (*ḥen*) in
the eyes of Yahweh" (6:8). When the waters subside the ark
comes to a rest (*tanaḥ*) on the mountains of Ararat (8:4).
Finally, a glimmer of hope appears in the image of a "resting-
place" (*manoaḥ*) (8:9) which the first dove fails to find but
which Noah and his ark ultimately find after the flood waters
have subsided. In sum, the plays on the pair of key roots
(*naḥam, noaḥ*) range from "relief" (5:29) to "regret" (6:6,7) to
"favor" (6:8) to "rest" (8:4) to "resting-place" (8:9), creating
an echo effect that reverberates throughout the narrative.[67]

The story also contains delightful anthropomorphic – possibly satirical – touches in the portrayal of Yahweh. First, the
language of the first creation account is reprised to describe
God's action of seeing, but with the opposite result: no longer
is creation evaluated as "good" but is now viewed as "evil"
(6:5). In reaction, God not only "regrets" (6:6,7) but "is

---

[67] After finishing this description of the punning in the Noah story, I came across a
stunningly artful rendition from the elegant pen of Avivah Gottlieb Zornberg: "At
this point [i.e., Gen. 6:6], God, with a terrible humor, quotes the word-play on
Noah's name, subtly transforming the meanings and indulging in a positive flurry
of puns. The root *nahem*, "comfort," which held out hope of comfort or relief, now
denotes "regret," a radical revision of the entire Adam project." See her fascinating book, *Genesis: The Beginning of Desire* (Philadelphia: The Jewish Publication
Society, 1995), p. 38.

grieved to his heart" (6:6) to observe what has happened to his handiwork. Then he carefully "shuts" Noah into the ark with his own hands before the flood waters come. After the deluge is over, God "smells" the savory odors of the massive pyre of burnt offerings and promises never to curse the ground because of humankind and destroy every living creature as he has done (8:21). What emerges is a rather capricious, yet solicitous deity who first regrets ever having created humans and then after the mass destruction is sated with the fragrance of the bountiful barbecue of slaughtered animals, promising never to do it again. What heightens the effect of this promise is not merely the emphasis on the olfactory pleasure of the deity but the bizarre logic of the argument: "Yahweh said in his heart, 'I will never again curse the soil because of humanity, for the imagination of the human heart is evil from youth; now will I never again destroy every living creature as I have done'" (8:21). Here God once more shows himself as a creator who is not afraid to make mistakes – and most astoundingly, to admit it.[68] In this portrayal Yahweh appears as "an almost whimsical deity turning to a spring-time mood,"[69] a deity who can spin off a brief, but beautiful poem that guarantees the cyclical movement of seasons and times: "As long as the earth endures, seedtime and harvest, cold and heat, summer and winter, day and night, shall not cease" (8:22).

That some interpreters locate a climax here in the Yahwist version of the flood story is not surprising: yet what a strange "happy ending" of a story which features a monstrous flood that wipes out the first creation, but a catastrophe which does not fundamentally change the inclination or imagination of that same evil human heart, cited at the outset as God's primary reason for unleashing the destructive flood (cf. 6:5 and 8:21). God's guarantee of unceasing seasons is coupled with the acknowledgment that the human creature is seriously flawed, yet mass destruction seemingly has failed to resolve the basic problem; hence one might as well accommodate one's self to the situation and get on with it. Parody

[68] McEvenue, *Interpreting the Pentateuch*, p. 66.
[69] Brisman, *The Voice of Jacob*, p. 23.

of the deity's action, however, at least injects a note of whimsy, offering the "corrective of laughter" (Bakhtin) to an otherwise sombre, seemingly senseless event that could be read as a tragedy of avalanche proportions.

Yet in the final form of the text, the story does not conclude with Genesis 8:22, but continues with the Priestly Writer's reiteration of the first commandment of Genesis 1:28, repeating and thus renewing the mandate to multiply and master, albeit with some striking changes: "God blessed Noah and his sons, and said to them, 'Be fruitful and multiply, and fill the earth. The fear and dread of you shall rest [in every living creature], into your hands they are delivered. Every moving thing that lives shall be food for you; and just as I gave you the green plants, I give you everything'" (9:1–3). Since God has apparently developed a smell and taste for animal flesh, he accords the same privilege to humans. This functions as an aetiology for the transition from vegetarianism to carnivorousness. Only two limits are now imposed: an injunction against eating the blood with the flesh, and a requirement of a life for a life (9:4–6). The divine image stamped upon humans defines human life as sacred and humans as a protected species. The passage concludes with a restatement of the command to multiply, thus forming an *inclusio* (9:7).

The next section focuses with all due priestly seriousness on the institution of a covenant with Noah and his descendants. The covenant guarantees again that there will be no new flood to destroy the earth, designating the rainbow as the "sign of the covenant" (see Gen. 9:8–17). This distinctly priestly text affords a striking contrast between the rather staid Priestly Author(s) and the Yahwist who emerges as a comic writer of the first rank.

The first vineyard: a drunken father, a leering son, and a cursed descendant (Genesis 9:18–28)

The image of Noah the first wine producer is only loosely joined with his greater claim to fame, his role as the survivor of the great flood; yet juxtaposing the two stories in sequential order offers still another sample of comic incongruity:

who would expect the vaunted Noah – the most righteous person of his generation – to end up a drunkard who is alienated from one of his sons (and grandsons)? The tradition of Noah as viticulturalist attaches itself perhaps even more closely with the popular word-play on Noah's name as the one destined to "bring us relief from our work and the toil of our hands out of the soil that Yahweh has cursed" (5:29). As the discoverer of wine Noah provides a partial antidote to the struggle with the cursed soil in the post-edenic world. To be sure, like the fruit of the forbidden tree, the fruit of the vine is both delicious and dangerous since Noah, "the righteous and blameless one of his generation," becomes history's first drunkard when he is overcome by consuming too much of a good thing. No specific blame, however, is attached to his inebriation as such; but drunkenness leads to nakedness, and nakedness leads to some sort of a violation of a sexual taboo. It is uncertain exactly what Ham perpetrated against his sotted, naked father: we simply read that Ham "saw the nakedness of his father, and told his brothers outside" (9:22). "Show and tell" was not fully appreciated in those days, but perhaps the text implies that more than seeing and telling was involved.

In contrast to Ham's action, the two other sons demonstrate proper respect by walking backwards into the tent to cover their father's nakedness with faces turned away and eyes averted (9:23), an action that Bloom finds "hilariously respectful."[70] Whether one may perceive hilarity here probably depends on the eye of the beholder, but it does seem to depict the playing-out of a primal scene rooted deeply in ancient taboos and conventions (cf. Lev. 18 for a possible religio-historical background). At any rate, Ham's behavior was clearly not acceptable to Noah, who awakens from his drunken stupor and "knows" what "his youngest son had done to him" (9:24). A sexual violation of an incestuous nature seems to be involved, an act euphemistically disguised by the verb "see."

---

[70] Rosenberg and Bloom, *The Book of J*, p. 190.

Whatever the exact nature of the violation, Noah proceeds surprisingly to level a curse against Canaan, Ham's son, condemning him to abject slavery to his brothers. Noah then pronounces blessings on Shem and Japheth (9:26–27). Why the puzzling shift from Ham, the alleged perpetrator, to Canaan, the target of the curse? The commentators propose long and learned explanations, none of which fully satisfies. Perhaps the easiest answer is some combination of an editorial attempt at harmonization and the age-old nexus between father and son in a crime-punishment sequence. That the narrator finally names Canaan as the recipient of the curse of enslavement is ironically right since Canaan emerges as the chief rival for Shem's divinely favored descendant, Israel. Suffice it to say that the strange story resonates with the preceding primal tales with their themes of "nakedness" (cf. 2:25; 3:7, 10, 11), illegitimate sexual practices (cf. 6:1–4), complications implicit in the process of multiplication and mastery (cf. 1:28; 3:16; 9:1–3), and the primal patterns of blessing and curse (cf. 1:28; 3:14, 17; 4:11; 5:29), though now for the first time placing into a human mouth the power of blessing and curse. Historians usually connect the events with the legitimation of Israelite claims of superiority over the Canaanites, thus attempting to provide justification for the conquest and the enslavement of the indigenous Canaanite inhabitants. What seems to be involved is a piece of rather vicious ethnic stereotyping which uses sexual innuendo as a way of subverting a rival ethnic group's claims for the possession of the land. Later analogues for this phenomenon appear in the descriptions of the sexual practices of the males of Sodom and Gomorrah (Gen. 18,19) and the incestuous acts of Lot's daughters which give the popular views of the origins of Moab and Ammon (Gen. 19). Often such stories project a kind of virulent "ethnic humor" focused on the supposed perverse sexual practices of rival groups.

In Noah's declarations, the final twist is not simply to counterpose the cursed Canaanites and the blessed Semites (ostensibly, the Israelites), but to bless the "Japhethites" as well: "May God make space (*yephet*) for Japheth, and let him

live in the tents of Shem; and let Canaan be his slave" (9:27).
Historians debate who these descendants of Japheth might
be, often proposing the Philistines as likely candidates.
Bloom suggests that "perhaps J's humorous thrust is that even
the Philistines were less sexually depraved than the
Canaanites!"[71] What gives this possible "humorous thrust" in
the narrative even greater vigor is the use once again of a climactic pun to make the point stand out in more vivid relief;
hence as I have indicated in the translation, the narrator
spins off a word-play on the name Japheth who, true to his
name, will be spacious. Moreover, the repetition of the
refrain, "Let Canaan be his slave" (9:27b; cf. 9:25, 26), concludes the series of pronouncements, highlighting the problematic process of the multiplication and mastery among the
peoples of the earth.

Babel and babble: on tall towers and twisted tongues (Genesis 11)

Sandwiched between two versions of the genealogies of Shem
comes the final tale of the primeval account, conventionally
called the "Tower of Babel." The tale is truly legendary, filled
with fabulous motifs and fantastic lore, all rooted in the soil
of Near Eastern traditions. It contains one of the classic puns
of Genesis, a play on the name of Babel that becomes a prime
symbol of the irreducible multiplicity of language and of the
deep-seated linguistic confusion that marks the human
scene. The pun also epitomizes one of the most artfully constructed parodies in Genesis, a parody in which a bemused
deity contemplates from far and near the feverish, foolish
attempts of humans to storm the heavens and win a name for
themselves. The combination of pun and parody creates a
fitting comic climax to the primal story of human beginnings.

Fokkelman offers an ingenious and insightful analysis of
the story that gives full recognition to the role of chiasm and
paronomasia.[72] His analysis demonstrates convincingly the

---

[71] *Ibid.*
[72] J. P. Fokkelman, *Narrative Art in Genesis: Specimens of Stylistic and Structural Analysis* (second edn.) (Sheffield: JSOT Press, 1991), pp. 11–45.

degree of self-conscious artistry at work in the narrative. Both the outer framework (vss. 1 and 9) as well as the inner correspondences of the two halves (vss. 2–4 and 5–8) reveal adroit crafting, belying the different attempts to argue for the disunity of the narrative and to dismember it into fragmented earlier versions.

For my purpose the pattern of punning and parodying shows how well the story fits into the dominantly comic movement of the whole primeval narrative. Beginning in Genesis 3 and then continuing in Genesis 6:1–4, the thematic trajectory of human attempts to transgress limits and thus to threaten God extends into this last tale. Once more, but now on a collective scale, humanity strives to rival the gods: "Come, let us build ourselves a city, and a tower with its top in the heavens, and let us make a name (*shem*) for ourselves" (11:4). Like the primal couple in the garden, humans want to be like the gods – or at least nearer to the gods. Once again God and his heavenly cohorts react with jealousy to the threat posed by collective human action: "Look, they are one people, and they have one language; and this is only the beginning of what they will do; nothing that they propose to do will now be impossible for them" (11:6). The decision comes in plural form, revealing again the polytheistic background of the old tale (see also 1:26; 3:22), and showing the divine displeasure in the overweening ambition of humankind: "Come, let us go down and confuse their language there, so that they will not understand one another's language" (11:7). Confusing the once unified language becomes the prelude to scattering the unified human community, stifling any illicit human attempt to bridge the gap between earth and heaven, between humanity and divinity.

The aetiological conclusion, expressing in popular wordplay the origins of Babylon, gives the punning punch-line for the whole narrative: "Therefore he called it Babel, because there Yahweh 'babbled' (*balal*) the language of all the earth" (11:9). The key issue in the text is "the battle for the proper name between YHWH and the sons of Shem" who want above all "to make a name (*shem*) for themselves."[73] Yahweh's act of naming prevails. Ironically, therefore, the people do acquire a name, but it is not the kind of name that they sought. They construct a site only to abandon it when Yahweh turns construction into confusion, thus "deconstructing" the one language, denominating the site "Babel" ("confusion," "babbling"), and dispersing the babblers over the face of the earth.

We encounter here parody of a high order. Indeed we can label the text a "parodic double" of the positive or at least neutrally descriptive account of the origins of Babel in the preceding chapter (cf. 10:10: "the beginning of [Nimrod's] kingdom was Babel . . ."). Over against all seemingly independent, heroic human attempts to found great kingdoms and build great cities and towers and hence become like the gods, the narrator supplies the corrective of parody, satirizing all grandiose efforts to reach the heavens and to rival the gods.

Northrop Frye goes so far as to call the "Tower of Babel" story a "demonic parody" of Jacob's ladder and its metaphorical relatives, the latter serving as positive images of contact and communication between earth and heaven. "The demonic tower," according to Frye, "signifies the aspect of history known as imperialism, the human effort to unite human resources by force that organizes larger and larger social units, and eventually exalts some king into a world ruler, a parody representative of God."[74]

Similarly the famous mock funeral lament in Isaiah 14 offers a biting satire on the presumption and folly of the Babylonian king who also tried unsuccessfully to storm the heavens: "You said in your heart, 'I will ascend to heaven//I will raise my throne above the stars of God//I will sit on the mount of assembly on the heights of Zaphon//I will ascend to the tops of the clouds//I will make myself like the Most

---

[73] Jacques Derrida, *The Post Card: From Socrates to Freud and Beyond*, Alan Bass, trans. (Chicago: University of Chicago Press, 1987), p. 165.

[74] Northrop Frye, *Words of Power: Being a Second Study of the Bible and Literature* (New York: Harcourt Brace Jovanovich, 1990), p. 163.

High'" (Isa. 14:13–14). The trajectory from Genesis 11 to Isaiah 14 highlights the characteristic biblical representation of the folly of such presumptuous, grandiose gestures, but it does so in different ways: Isaiah uses ironically a funeral lament, whereas the Genesis narrator resorts to a skillfully wrought parody of a foundation myth. The difference in tone between the two texts is striking: Isaiah's taunt, mocking and savagely satiric, is marked by gleeful delight over the fall of a hated tyrannical king and his empire, but the Genesis parody strikes a more playful tone and pictures Yahweh as needing to make one of his periodic descents in reaction to a mock threat by the humans to gain fame by building a tall tower into the heavens. The fame inheres in the name the Babel builders want to make for themselves, but all they end up doing is provoking the deity to give them an infamous name, "Babel" (="babble, bafflement") and then to scatter the "sons of Shem" (="Name") over the earth.

Whether or not the narrator also parodies Yahweh by portraying him as "an antithetical imp or sublime mischief-maker"[75] is debatable, but it is an enticing possibility. After all, Yahweh's scattering the peoples is an ironic fulfillment of his original mandate to "fill the earth," and his confusing human languages is a quaint way of representing the realities of multiple languages. The divine reaction in Genesis 11 hardly strikes one as a grim, harsh punishment as commentators have sometimes argued; for that kind of savage treatment we must turn to the sarcasm of Isaiah's taunt-song on the fall of the Babylonian king. In contrast, the Genesis version of Babylon's founding is comic, a humorous story of Babel and babble, a playful tale of tall towers and twisted tongues.

CONCLUSION: THE COMEDY OF CREATION IN THE PRIMEVAL STORY

Set against the backdrop of the originally "good" creation (Gen. 1–2), the complex thematic trajectories in the episodic

---

[75] Rosenberg and Bloom, *The Book of J*, p. 192.

movement of the narrative run along a dominantly comic track where the emplotment of the story especially features incongruous and partial fulfillments of the commandment to multiply and master (1:28; 9:1ff). This first commandment is a positive mandate set under the sign and seal of blessing, yet its process of fulfillment often yields contradictory and counter-productive tendencies and results. For example, the erotic drives and desires necessary for multiplication often get enmeshed in troubled and troubling relationships: the desire of the woman leads to masculine domination in the sexual union (3:16); the desire of the ravenous beast called sin masters Cain and results in the murder of his brother (4:7); the lust of the "sons of God" drives them to seize beautiful women, producing the mixed progeny of giants and causing Yahweh to limit the human life-span (6:1–4); Ham "sees" his father's nakedness and tells his two brothers, intimating some kind of illicit, incestuous action, a deed that elicits Noah's curse of Ham's son Canaan (9:20–28). Hence sexual imagery, whether implicit or explicit, permeates the narratives, highlighting the rebellious revels of humans (and divinities). The humans are created in the image of God; not surprisingly they want to be like God(s), but their feverish attempts generate divine suspicion and jealousy (cf. 3:22; 6:3; 11:6) and prompt various punitive reactions. Transgressive actions, however, cut both ways: though the humans again and again overstep the boundaries that mark off the divine sphere, the divinities do so as well when they take beautiful women and copulate with them to produce giants (6:1–4). Moreover, the humans may be created in the divine image, yet paradoxically "every inclination of the imaginings of their hearts was only evil continually" (6:5), a judgment marked by divine regret about his human creatures and resulting in the divine decision to wipe out all life except for the survivors in Noah's ark; yet after the flood is over, God whimsically acknowledges that the destruction of life on a massive scale did not correct the basic problem, since the human imagination is still evil from youth (8:21). Repopulation leads to a final stand of a unified human race on "a plain in the land of

Shinar" where they again aspire to a form of cohabitation with the gods by building "a tower with its top in the heavens" (11:1–4). Yahweh once again intervenes to thwart their efforts, scrambling their languages and scattering them across the face of the earth. In sum, Yahweh emerges as a rather capricious, whimsical deity who is satirized as a sometimes unthinking tyrant who can be both life-giving and death-dealing; he is a God who can become jealous when his human creatures made in his image want to be too much like the gods, yet he can be appeased by a sweet-smelling sacrifice after having unleashed a devastating flood and then promise never to do it again.

Intertwined within this plot-line of programmatic announcements, aborted projects, and incomplete fulfillments, are strategically placed puns which encapsulate a basic point in an explosive word-play which often both condenses meaning and anticipates action to come. The string of such primal and pivotal puns is striking indeed: *'Adam/'adamah* ("soil") (2:7); *'ish* ("man")/*'ishah* ("woman") (2:23); *ḥavah* ("Eve")/*ḥay* ("living") (3:20); *Cain/qaniti* ("produced, created") (4:1); *Noaḥ* ("rest")/*naḥam* ("relief") (5:29); *Japheth/yepheth* ("make space") (9:27); *Babel/balal* ("confuse") (11:9). These puns energize the narrative and often form climactic "punch-lines," emerging as little jokes embedded in linguistic play, jokes that convey forcefully the humor and wit of Israel's ancient story-tellers.

Finally, as I have suggested, parody plays a notable role in the primeval story, often infusing "the necessary corrective of laughter" (Bakhtin). For instance, at the beginning the story of creation in Genesis 2–3 forms a kind of "parodic double" of the preceding creation account. At the close of the primeval cycle, the Babel/babble story offers a wonderful combination of punning and parodying. Such examples of parody help relieve the sometimes deadly serious tones of the primeval narratives, injecting the power of humor at key points and infusing the energy of fresh life in the midst of death and dying. The interwoven threads of life and death form a tapestry of bright and dark colors. Created in the image of God, the audacious, daring humans feel and imagine their way into the complex knowledge of good and evil, thus becoming "like the gods" – yet not quite! Destined to die, Eve's daughters perpetuate themselves as mothers of living, co-creating with God new offspring and thus extending the chain of life. Yet as Cain's descendants, humans wander restlessly across the "land of wandering" (*Nod*), attempting vainly to find a home by founding cities and building towers. As Noah's descendants they are survivors who will live out their sojourns under the vicissitudes of both curse and blessing. As citizens of Babel they are fated to babble onward in their scattered existence. Hence human beings as God's last and best creative efforts are strangely mixed products, creatures of incongruity and paradox, apt candidates for comic artistry.

Even God can become a comical creator – at least the narrator is not afraid to use caricature and satire to depict the deity. Solemn and sovereign in the grandeur of some creative moments (particularly in Genesis 1), he can also be capricious, whimsical, jealous, petulant – and yet unexpectedly merciful and gracious even in his most destructive moods. He is a deity capable of "after-thoughts" and "second thoughts," a divinity who therefore can admit to mistakes and try – sometimes awkwardly, sometimes disastrously – to rectify them. For example, recall the process of the creation of man and woman in Genesis 2 – or remember the God of the Flood Story. In the latter case he is a God who can snuff out the lives of human beings as well as beasts and birds because he recoils from the realization that the imagination of his divinely imaged creatures is continually evil, but who then acknowledges after the flood that the massive destruction did not fundamentally alter human susceptibilities toward evil (8:21). This rather damaging admission comes in response to the savory smell of a huge holocaust of burnt-offerings, but this "gracious" god concludes his promise never to do it again with a lovely little poem that pledges that the earth will always endure and times and seasons will not cease (8:22). One is inclined to say, "Isn't that just like Yahweh?"

In the midst of what has turned into a spectacular "cosmic joke" God still does not give up on the human race. After the final scattering of the peoples in the wake of the incident at Babel, one is not led to lament the loss of unity in the human race or in human language; after all, the genealogy does resume, the very repetition of which preserves the identities of the sons of Shem ("name"). The forward drive of the narrative concentrates on the powerful forces of renewal: neither the first commandment is totally abrogated nor is the original goodness of creation completely lost. The continuation of Shem's line into the descendants of Terah awakens new expectations which are further heightened by the surprising mention of wives who are even named. Tension mounts – and a new plot-line emerges – when we learn that Sarai, Abram's wife, "is barren; she had no child" (11:30). What destiny awaits this childless couple who make it half-way from Ur of the Chaldees to Canaan in the company of father Terah, but who stop in Haran where Terah dies?

CHAPTER 2

Domestic comedy in the household of faith: Israel's fathers and mothers as comic figures (Genesis 12–50)

PROMISES, PROMISES . . .

Interpreters have found the soil of the patriarchal story fertile ground for the growth of comic readings, though a consensus is nowhere in sight. However, when one sets aside dominantly historical and theological concerns and approaches the biblical literature as ancient story-telling of a high and sophisticated order, the patriarchal narratives yield a splendid, sustained vision of comedy that is impressive both in its revels and revelations.

THE FIRST HEBREW FAMILY: ABRAHAM, SARAH, AND ISAAC

Look to Abraham your father and to Sarah who bore you; for he was but one when I called him, but I blessed him and made him many.

(ISAIAH 51:2)

As the incredible is promised [Abraham], he laughs; and the age of Isaac ("laughter") begins. This is the age of feasts, of bounty and trust and infinite possibility. But, significantly, to laugh is to make a choice; laughter is two-faced: 'here for mockery, there for joy.'

(ZORNBERG)[1]

The little clue about Sarah's infertility tucked into the folds of the genealogy at the end of Genesis 11 adumbrates the dominant problem of the Abraham cycle: if Sarah can't con-

---

[1] Zornberg, *Genesis*, pp. 112–113.

ceive, how is the Abrahamic line to be perpetuated and hence fulfill the earlier mandate to be fruitful and multiply – not to mention the promise of numerous progeny which is later announced? In any event, what stands as a breach in the genealogical line of Genesis 11 becomes a bridge to the subsequent family stories.

This all too typical tale of a childless couple is abruptly interrupted by the imperious divine call to Abram: "Go from your country and your kindred and your father's house to the land that I will show you. I will make of you a great nation, and I will bless you, and make your name great, so that you will be a blessing. I will bless those who will bless you, and the one who curses you I will curse; and in you all the families of the earth shall be blessed" (12:1–3). This call, offering in pregnant form the emplotment of Abram's story, only intensifies the problem of childlessness: How is the manifold blessing promised to Abram to be realized if he has no legitimate heir? The divine promises ultimately involving numerous descendants and the permanent possession of land stand in obvious tension with the delay and deferral of fulfillment. In my view, the gap between promises and their fulfillment creates the context and conditions for the emergence of comedy. As we will see, comedy loves to exploit the incongruity between promises and their partial or failed fulfillment.

The plot becomes concentrated on the anxiety over the lack of fulfillment, centered chiefly on the issues of childlessness and landlessness: seed and soil become increasingly connected as the elderly couple struggle to overcome Sarai's barrenness as well as their clan's alienness in the land of their sojournings. Genealogy once again gets tightly entwined with geography (the itinerary is a pervasive genre): land is to be had by inheritance, but inheritance demands a legal heir, which in turn demands both legitimate children and legitimate title to the land.

It is the drama of the unfulfilled situation that prepares the stage for the many memorable scenes in which the major characters of Genesis play their differing roles within the domestic setting. God will continue to perform his functions

as the uncanny, unpredictable creator who oscillates between
his sometimes contrary poses as high and holy transcendent
power and intimately involved anthropomorphic personality.
As a persona who appears both as singular and plural
being(s), God plays multiple parts in this high and low
comedy of faith.

The major thematic trajectory – promise and fulfillment –
reveals the vagaries of human response to the divine
demands, ranging from instantaneous obedience to vacillation, doubt, manipulation, and blatant disobedience. All the
players – whether men or women, gods or angels – perform
varied roles, and the narrators' skills in complex, colorful
characterization are impressive indeed.

Following Yahweh's command to Abram to go from his
original land to a new land (12:1–3), the narrator reports
Abram's immediate compliance: "So Abram went" (12:4). As
hero of the faithful, Abram's first significant action – migration from Haran to Canaan – demonstrates what possibly is
the most notable hallmark tradition accords to this first
Hebrew patriarch: his unflinching faith and obedience. After
reaching the promised land, Abram receives fresh assurance
from Yahweh: "To your seed I will give this land" (12:7), a
promise which he acknowledges by building an altar to the
God who had appeared to him (12:7). Moving on to Bethel,
Abram builds another altar and again invokes the name of
Yahweh (12:8). All in all at the outset of the story Abram
demonstrates repeatedly the appropriateness of his reputation for faithfulness, a trait celebrated by all three religions
that find in him a founder-figure.

A closer reading, however, belies this rather traditional,
simplistic depiction of Abram as model of faith. His reputation for obedience is initially compromised in that he takes
Lot with him, thus failing in fact to leave behind his kindred,
though partially mitigating his apparent disobedience is that
he possibly considers "Lot to be his surrogate son."[2] The case

---

[2] L. A. Turner, "Lot as Jekyll and Hyde: A Reading of Genesis 18–19," in *The Bible
in Three Dimensions: Essays in Celebration of Forty Years of Biblical Studies in the
University of Sheffield,* David J. A. Clines, Stephen E. Fowl, Stanley E. Porter, eds.
(Sheffield: Sheffield Academic Press, 1990), p. 86.

becomes even more complicated at the first sign of trouble, which opens space for contradictory and even comical behavior. A severe famine strikes Canaan, and Abram promptly goes to Egypt, the proverbial bread-basket of the ancient world. Such a temporary migration is not necessarily problematic, but one does wonder about Abram's ability to rely on Yahweh who has earlier pledged his providential protection and provision. What further compromises Abram's position after his arrival in Egypt is his decidedly unheroic strategy of having Sarai lie about her wifely status and pretend instead that she is his sister, a strategy of cowardice and prevarication designed to protect Abram and earn him a rich reward in the bargain. The hoax works initially, and Pharaoh inducts Sarai into the royal harem (12:14–16). How Sarai is to fulfill her role as Abram's wife and thus bear the promised offspring Abram doesn't seem to consider. Is it the case that Abram already has given up on the barren Sarai as a potential mother of an heir, thus making her expendable?[3] The presence of Lot, his nephew and possibly adopted son, might show that Abram has already taken measures to insure that he has an heir. In any event, Sarai becomes a pawn in the male world, a bargaining chip in an immigrant alien's attempt to save his own skin and make his way successfully in the world. Abram gives his wife away and only gets her back when Yahweh intervenes and afflicts Pharaoh and his house with great plagues. Discovering the truth, Pharaoh castigates Abram and expels him and his entourage from Egypt.

Commentators have typically subtitled this puzzling narrative "the endangerment of the matriarch," especially focusing on questions of its connections with the parallel stories in Genesis 20 and 26.[4] Germane to a comic interpretation is the narrator's mode of characterizing Abram in this domestic drama. The basic obedience of Abram conditions us to

---

[3] *Ibid.* See also Clines' illuminating treatment in "The Ancestor in Danger," in *What Does Eve Do to Help ?*, p.70.

[4] I find Clines most convincing in his challenging article which significantly advances our discussion of Gen. 12, 20, 26; see "The Ancestor in Danger" (note Clines' reversal of the usual nomenclature), in *What Does Eve Do to Help ?*, pp. 67–84.

expect him to be an exemplary man of faith, but we are instead confronted by an apparent coward and liar who is much more concerned with danger to himself rather than fear for his wife's welfare – let alone regard for the inviolate nature of the marital bond. It is only Yahweh's timely intervention – and ironically Pharaoh's sensibility – that save the day and restore Sarai to her legitimate husband.

For an alleged paragon of faithfulness, Abram has behaved strangely. To be sure, one can cast him into the role of a "trickster," appealing to a widespread anthropological model, and thereby partially mitigating his behavior or at least clarifying it.[5] On this reading, Abram and Sarai emerge as marginal figures who are "underdogs" on foreign soil and who simply resort to whatever means necessary for survival and success. As Niditch argues, the wife-sister scam is another variation on the switch in sexual roles comparable to the bed-trick later played on Jacob. In my judgment, this interpretation is illuminating, but may be enriched and deepened by connecting it with the comic play of ironic reversal. Hence the "pioneer of faith" leaves the promised land as soon as a difficulty arises; he then compounds his lapse with deception. Even Pharaoh appears in a more favorable light than Abram, stepping forward as a defender of the sanctity of marriage: "What is this that you have done to me? Why did you not tell me that she was your wife? Why did you say, 'She is my sister,' so that I took her for my wife?" (12:18–19). Yet Abram is not punished, but merely expelled from Egypt "with his wife and all that he had" (12:20). Abram is thereby blessed with material goods, hence paradoxically fulfilling the initial promise of blessing for himself, though hardly serving as an instrument of blessing for the Egyptians.[6] Abram is able to keep the rewards of his lie, a point that is reinforced with the repetition of the phrase, "his wife and all that he had" in the very next verse. In brief, just when Abram seems caught in an impossible situation, Yahweh steps in both to protect wife and

---

[5] Susan Niditch, *Underdogs and Tricksters: A Prelude to Biblical Folklore* (San Francisco: Harper & Row, 1987), pp. 44–50.

[6] Clines, "What Happens in Genesis," in *What Does Eve Do to Help?*, p. 57.

husband and to allow Abram to keep his goods; Pharaoh as the innocent but injured party can only rebuke his would-be brother-in-law and send him back to Canaan. Such ironic role reversals, scheming use of sexuality, and rewards obtained through deception are all staples of comic narratives in every age.

Returning to the land of Canaan, Abram is immediately confronted with another crisis – this time involving his nephew Lot who suddenly pops back into the picture. Apparently as a result of Abram's Egyptian misadventure, both Abram and Lot have secured vast numbers of livestock "so that the land could not support both of them living together" (13:6), a state of affairs that causes an outbreak of strife between their herders. Abram reverts here to his role as magnanimous patriarch and peace-maker, offering Lot first choice of the land. For the first time, Lot assumes a more active part in the story: he now chooses what seems to be the best land, and his choice reveals his most dominant character trait. He emerges as a person who chooses the easy way, making what apppears to be the most obvious choice: "Lot looked about him, and saw that the plain of the Jordan was well watered everywhere like the garden of Yahweh [shades of Eden?], like the land of Egypt [intimating that Lot preferred life in Egypt?] . . . So Lot chose for himself all the plain of Jordan, and Lot journeyed eastward" (13:10–11).

Apart from Lot's possible role as Abram's heir, he seems to function dramatically in the story as a parodic counterpart to Abram: linked to him genealogically, but increasingly separated from him geographically, nationally, and even morally. As relative of Abram, Lot has prerogatives and privileges (note also his special treatment in Genesis 18–19); however, as legendary progenitor of the Moabites and Ammonites, close neighbors of the Israelites, Lot appears often in an ambiguous, compromised position. Choosing the fertile "garden of Yahweh" despite the known wickedness of Sodom and Gomorrah, he will be almost destroyed. Usually passive, weak, compliant, and equivocating, Lot is pampered and protected by both uncle Abram and Yahweh God. The use of parody and satire serves to subvert Lot (and implicitly his ancestors), showing the sharp-edged quality that comedy can sometimes manifest.[7]

In contrast to Lot's characterization, Abram is typically portrayed in exemplary fashion – apart from his questionable behavior in relationship to his wife. First, he is a peace-maker, emerging as a prototype for the dominant pattern displayed by the patriarchs in conflict situations. He chooses negotiation over war whenever possible, peaceful resolution of differences rather than martial action. Second, Abram is reaffirmed for settling in Canaan, receiving from Yahweh fresh assurance of the promise that "this land is your land": "Raise your eyes now, and look from the place where you are, northward and southward and eastward and westward; for all the land that you see I will give to you and to your offspring forever . . . Rise up, and walk through the length and the breadth of the land, for I will give it to you" (13:14–15, 17). Looking over the land and walking through it become possible ways of laying claim to the promised land. The capstone for his settlement in the land is building an altar in Mamre (13:18), an ancient technique of attesting to possession of land. In sum, using Lot as "parodic-double" and foil, the narrator casts Abram in a dominantly favorable light once he returns to the land of Canaan.

Genesis 14 stands out as an island amidst the sea of surrounding narratives, a story whose strangeness in genre, theme, and characterization heightens the sense of its out-of-placeness. In sharp contrast to all the other stories about Abram, our first Hebrew patriarch appears here as a great warrior and deliverer, more comparable to the judges or the early kings than to his more dominant role – let alone to the other patriarchs. Usually isolated by interpreters and relegated to the realm of late, largely alien additions to Genesis, the chapter has nonetheless evoked voluminous commentary.

---

[7] Cf. the intriguing analysis of the ambiguity of Lot as a complex character in Turner's essay, "Lot as Jekyll and Hyde," pp. 85–102. Though he mentions irony once, Turner does not find parodic elements in Lot's depiction.

For my purpose, the text's very strangeness and its pronounced difference and discontinuity from its context show its potential for a comic interpretation. Recently, Radday has called the text "a hilarious anti-war parody," excoriating pedantic scholars for missing its "*Situationskomik.*"[8]

In Genesis 14, Abram uncharacteristically dons the mantle of the intrepid warrior-hero, ready, willing, and able to do battle in behalf of a relative in trouble. When he hears that Lot and his family have been seized by the imposing coalition of four mighty kings, he responds with alacrity and daring – the complete antithesis to the coward and liar of Genesis 12. Now he is the sure, savvy warrior who gathers his forces together and pursues the invaders; after dividing his forces at night for tactical reasons, he routs his enemies and chases them beyond Damascus, rescuing Lot and the other prisoners along with all the booty. The utter unreality of the dramatic success of the rescue mission against the overwhelming odds presents a larger-than-life heroic character: a Joshua, Gideon, and David all rolled into a single stunning figure.

The opening scene is itself a picture of incongruity. Set forth in the dry, matter-of-fact style of annalistic report, the narrator conjures up a fantastic scenario with many humorous elements: it is not only the disproportion between the antagonists – four mighty Mesopotamian monarchs allied together against five kinglets of the Jordan Valley – but also the many bizarre names that only make sense as "jokes." Following in the tradition of the rabbis and Benno Jacob, Radday finds much humor in the personal and place names of the narrative (e.g., Bera='King Bad'; Birsha='King Evil'; Shinab='King Rebel'; Shemeber='King Highfalutin').[9] Although one may challenge this or that interpretation of the various names in the whole chapter (as Radday himself is quite aware), the overall impression of a humorous, parodied presentation of names strikes one as correct. The very multiplication of the names also seems to be parody rather than "learned necessity."[10]

---

[8] Radday, "Humour in Names," pp. 85–86.   [9] *Ibid.*, p. 64.
[10] The phrase is von Rad's, *Genesis*, p. 172.

Moreover, the battle report, though probably composite, now follows a classic pattern, moving from war to worship: like other warriors of old, Abram is presented as coupling his martial exploits with ritual acts, duly acknowledging the "creator of heaven and earth," partaking of sacred "bread and wine," receiving the blessing of Melchizedek, priest-king of Salem, and giving him "tithes of all" (14:19–20). Abram here does all things well, embodying and exemplifying a stellar model for Israel's warrior-kings, a hero who demonstrates mastery on the field of battle and praiseworthy piety in worship. Though perhaps possessing a quixotic aura, Abram emerges in this almost fairy-tale text as a magnificent, larger than life warrior worshipper. That some scholars have characterized the story as a "romance" should not be surprising.

The major plotline of the Abram story resumes in Genesis 15, taking up the *leitmotif* of childlessness and landlessness. In fact, the two-fold promise of numerous progeny and permanent possession of land becomes intimately interconnected in this classic chapter and forged into a unity. This interrelated thematic trajectory will find a beginning of fulfillment in Genesis 21 with the birth of the long-anticipated son and a partial, strongly ironic fulfillment in the purchase of a burial-plot for Sarah in Genesis 23. What is accentuated between these poles are the delays, deferrals, and deviations in the course between promise and fulfillment. The various complications in the plot-line are laced with comic threads.

The first dialogue between Abram and Yahweh is recorded in Genesis 15, a dialogue that puts in pointed form the particular difficulty of the Abram-Sarai story: the couple continue to be childless, with Sarai especially bearing the shameful label of barrenness. The chapter begins on a mysterious note of visionary revelation:

The word of Yahweh came to Abram in a vision, 'Do not be afraid, Abram, I am your shield; your reward shall be very great.' But Abram said, 'O Yahweh God, what will you give me, for I continue childless, and the heir of my house is Eliezer of Damascus?' And

Abram said, 'You have given me no offspring, and so a slave born in my house is to be my heir.' But the word of Yahweh came to him, 'This man shall not be your heir; no one but your very own issue shall be your heir.' He brought him outside and said, 'Look toward heaven and count the stars, if you are able to count them.' Then he said to him, 'So shall your descendants be.' And he believed Yahweh, and he reckoned it to him as righteousness. Then he said to him, 'I am the Lord who brought you from Ur of the Chaldeans, to give you this land to possess.' But he said, 'O Yahweh God, how am I to know that I shall possess it?' He said to him, 'Bring me a heifer . . . a female goat . . .' (15:1–9a).

I have quoted the first major part of the text to reveal the jarring changes of pace and perspective in this first dialogue between Abram and Yahweh. Abram is not afraid to ask hard questions; Yahweh simply counters Abram's every objection with contradiction (vs. 4) or dramatic gesture – "count the stars, so shall your descendants be" (vs. 5) – or ritual sacrifice coupled with prophetic promises (vss. 9–21). The famous assertion of Abram's "faith" (vs. 6) is overshadowed by the persistent doubts and demands of the skeptical Abram, though the theme of faith still emerges. The interplay and tension between divine word and human response is marked by one inversion after another. Despite the language of faith and solemn revelation, the strong notes of human uncertainty and incredulity stand amidst divine assurance in promissory words and ritualized covenant-making. Yes, faith is registered, covenant made, and promises confirmed, but nothing is solved: such strategies represent delaying tactics that do not get at the root of the problem – Sarai's inability to conceive.

The drama of the unfulfilled promise takes another circuitous turn in the next scene from this problematic marriage. Once more the theme of childlessness is reprised, and hence underscored: "Now Sarai, Abram's wife, bore him no children" (16:1). But this time Sarai has a plan which she proposes to her husband: "You see that Yahweh has prevented me from bearing children; go in to my slave-girl; it may be that I shall obtain children by her" (vs. 2). Sarai's proposal has merit – at least in Abram's eyes, and he takes on a second wife and potential surrogate mother. Hagar conceives and immediately Sarai becomes an object of contempt to her. Sarai reacts with understandable anger, mistreating Hagar and causing her to flee into the wilderness, pregnant, alone, and apparently abandoned.

The angel of Yahweh intercepts the refugee, commanding her to "return to your mistress, and submit to her" (vs. 9), a seemingly cruel imperative which is nonetheless coupled with compensatory oracles: (1) a promise of numerous progeny (vs. 10); (2) a promise of a son whose name – "Ishmael" – bears a punning reminder of God's sensitive hearing of her plight (vs. 11); (3) a characterization of the unfettered freedom of her son who will live unmastered and contentious: "a wild ass of a man with his hand against every one, and everyone's hand against him; . . . he shall live at odds with all his kinsmen" (vs. 12). The oracles are striking variations on the multiplication and mastery theme, whose increasingly complex forms continue to course through the Genesis narratives. Hagar and Ishmael serve as parodic doubles of the first Hebrew family. Just as Isaac will later mirror actions and attributes of his father Abraham, so Ishmael in his prodigious, wild state parodies the character and destiny of his father and his brother. Indeed, Zornberg suggests that "Ishmael . . . represents a parody of Abraham's work in transitional space. But like all parodies, Ishmael comes from his loins, threatens his life . . ."[11] Thus Ishmael and his descendants will always have an ambivalent, tension-ridden relationship with Abraham and his brother's family. Moreover, it is unusual, though not unprecedented, for a foreign woman to receive a promise of a multitude of descendants, a role that puts her in the exalted company of Israel's patriarchs and matriarchs, yet a role that makes Hagar and Ishmael a parody not only of Sarah and Isaac but also anticipates the later story of Abraham's greatest trial (Gen. 22).[12]

[11] Zornberg, *Genesis*, p. 116.
[12] See the fine delineation of the inter-connections between Gen. 16 and 22 in Jon D. Levenson, *The Death and Resurrection of the Beloved Son: The Transformation of Child Sacrifice in Judaism and Christianity* (New Haven: Yale University Press, 1992), p. 94.

Hagar's response to this poignant encounter with God is unprecedented: she uniquely names the God who spoke to her ("You are *el-roi*"), adding once again an enigmatic word-play ("Have I seen [*ra'iti*] after the one who sees me [*ro'i*]?" – vs. 13). Still another pun embeds this action of seeing and living in the place name ("therefore the well was called *Beer-lahai-roi* ['the well of the living one who sees me']" – vs. 14). Here she anticipates the later action of divine and human seeing in Abraham's sacrifice of Isaac, as epitomized in the saying, "On the mount of Yahweh there is vision" (22:14).[13]

In sum, the birth of Ishmael, first son of Abram, begins partially and parodically to fulfill the promise of numerous progeny, yet this son will not be the true heir (Gen. 17:18,19). A son is indeed born to Abram, but he becomes the "wrong" son – in that he fails to hold the position as the legitimate heir; God has heard the plight of Hagar and the name of Ishmael preserves this sense of special divine hearing, but God continues to be curiously deaf to the plight of Sarai. At every key juncture this episode parodies experiences of Israel's fathers and mothers, reiterating promises of multitudes of descendants, showing Yahweh's mercy for a vulnerable mother-to-be, recording pun upon pun of personal and place names; yet it serves only to complicate and retard the major plot-line, delaying and deferring the pivotal fulfillment of the promise. While focusing on the understandable frustration of the aging couple, the story does not solve their fundamental problem – Sarai's childlessness. But the domestic drama continues.

The temporal notations in the story – Abram is eighty-six when Ishmael is born (Gen. 16:16); he is ninety-nine when God next appears to him (Gen. 17:1) – mark the silent passage of time; thirteen years slip by with no events narrated, a chronological gap that accentuates the deferral of significant action. Nothing happens of note in the empty gap of elapsed time. Time's mere passing does serve to heighten the

---

[13] Again, I refer the reader to Levenson's insightful analysis of this theme and the parallels between the stories of Ishmael and Isaac: *The Death and Resurrection of the Beloved Son*, pp. 122–124.

suspense, widening the gap between promise and fulfillment, and rendering even more problematic the ability of God to do what he has pledged.

The next scene in Genesis 17 opens with an awesome theophany: "I am God Almighty; walk before me and be blameless. And I will make my covenant between me and you, and will make you exceedingly numerous" (vss. 1b–2). Once more the *leitmotif* of the Abram stories – the promise of numerous descendants; once more the making of a covenant – the covenant of circumcision. But this time the covenant comes with the addition of three significant new names, each one playing on the incongruity of the promise of children to a childless, over-aged couple. Abram becomes Abraham – "I have made you the father of a multitude" (vs. 5); Sarai becomes Sarah – "I will give you a son by her" (vss. 15, 16); the child will become Isaac ("he laughs") – because "Abraham . . . laughed" (vss. 17,19). Abraham has ample reason for his incredulous laughter: "Can a child be born to a man who is a hundred years old? Can Sarah, who is ninety years old, bear a child?" (vs. 17). Opting instead for a possibility with some rootage in reality, Abraham offers a petition or wish on behalf of his other son, "O that Ishmael might live in your sight!" (17:18). God simply brushes aside Abraham's concerns, reaffirming Sarah's maternal prospects: "No, but Sarah your wife shall bear you a son . . ." (17:19a). Moreover, God does not allow the sound of laughter to die in Abraham's throat, but instead seizes upon the Hebrew verb *yisaq* ("he laughs") and declares that it will be the name of the coming heir: "and you shall call his name Isaac" (17:19b). In so doing, God permanently embeds laughter into the line of Israel's ancestors; Isaac will bear in his very being the sounds of laughter. Thus "God will have the last laugh,"[14] and the joke will be on the doubting father-to-be.

After this first outburst of incredulous laughter and the ensuing dialogue between the skeptical Abraham and the insistent deity, we will hear again and again the echoes of

---

[14] Good, *Irony in the Old Testament*, p. 93.

laughter around this promised child. In fact, the following narrative in Genesis 18 about Sarah's equally incredulous laughter with her even more earthy reaction stands as a perfect complement to the story of Abraham's laugher: it is a case of like husband, like wife. The narrative itself is one of the master strokes of Genesis, pulsating with energy and humor in its narration of a divine visit to an aged couple. To appreciate fully its consummate artistry one should read the whole passage (Gen. 18:1–15), but the dialogue focused on the promised baby captures the comedy of the scene:

They said to him [i.e., Abraham], 'Where is your wife Sarah?' And he said, 'There, in the tent.' Then one said, 'I will surely return to you in due season, and your wife Sarah shall have a son.' And Sarah was listening at the tent entrance behind him. Now Abraham and Sarah were old, advanced in age; it had ceased to be with Sarah after the manner of women. So Sarah laughed to herself, saying, 'After I have grown old, and my husband is old, shall I have pleasure?' Yahweh said to Abraham, 'Why did Sarah laugh and say, "Shall I indeed bear a child, now that I am old?" Is anything too wonderful for Yahweh? At the set time I will return to you, in due season, and Sarah shall have a son.' But Sarah denied, saying, 'I did not laugh'; for she was afraid. He said, 'Oh yes, you did laugh' (18:9–15).

The seemingly preposterous promise of a new baby, the eavesdropping Sarah who is discovered, the divine visitor who feels insulted, the closing *tête-à-tête* between Yahweh and Sarah who attempts vainly to cover up her laughter by lying to her divine guest – all these elements add up to something equivalent to the farce befitting a domestic comedy. That the dialogue breaks off without any clear resolution heightens the suspense and leaves the reader hanging in the balance – not to mention the aging, anxious couple.

Before Abraham and Sarah have their long awaited son, the major storyline is complicated twice more. First, the story of the destruction of Sodom and Gomorrah and the rescue of Lot and his family interrupts the main flow of the narrative, yet it still serves to reinforce the structural and thematic emplotment of the surrounding stories. It not only contains the brilliantly enacted comic scene of Abraham's bargaining with Yahweh for the righteous of Sodom and Gomorrah.[15] It also functions as a kind of parodied replay of such central and characteristic themes as unexpected divine visitors, equivocal human responses marked more by incredulity than faith, and births of national ancestors. Indeed, we seem to find here once again what Bakhtin calls a "parodic double" of the preceding and following tales, a double that highlights by way of contrastive parallelism the complicated path of multiplying the different segments of the larger Abrahamic family and thus fulfilling the divine promise.[16]

Although the story has its horrifying moments (notably the threatened gang-rape of the visitors which Lot tries to avert by offering his two virginal daughters), it also contains its comical scenes. For example, "Lot's ludicrous delay is comically ironic,"[17] a delay that shows that he was not overly convinced by the urgent warning from his divine visitors. Indeed, his own attempt to warn his sons-in-law was not at all convincing, since "he seemed to his sons-in-law to be jesting" (once again an echo of *saḥaq*="jesting, joking"). Although the divine guests continued to urge him to get out, we read that he "lingered" (19:16); finally, they had to lead him by the hand outside the city. A third warning to flee to the hills evokes a ludicrous reply from Lot:

Oh, no, my lords; your servant has found favor with you, and you have shown me great kindness in saving my life; but I cannot flee to the hills, for fear the disaster will overtake me and I die. Look, that city is near enough to flee to, and it is a little one. Let me escape there – is it not a little one? – and my life will be saved!" (19:18–20).

---

[15] Gabriel Josipovici draws our attention to the possible parodic parallel between Gen. 18 and Jud. 6. See his immensely stimulating book, *The Book of God: A Response to the Bible* (New Haven: Yale University Press, 1988), p. 119. Indeed, he suggests that "we seem everywhere to be asked to read Judges as a parody of Genesis and Exodus" (p. 121), a suggestion that invites a full examination.

[16] I first suggested the possibility of reading this intermezzo scene as a parodied replay of the Abraham, Sarah, Isaac story in a 1984 essay co-authored with J. Cheryl Exum; see Exum, ed., *Tragedy and Comedy in the Bible*, p. 11. I am happy to note that S. E. Medcalf draws the same conclusion in his short article on "Comedy," p. 128: "the double story presents man comic before God, ending happily in the conception of Isaac, blackly in the sin and punishment of Sodom." What he misses is that the births of Ammon and Moab represent a perverse parody of Isaac's birth story.   [17] *Ibid.*, p. 94.

His wish is granted, and he flees to Zoar which means "Little" in Hebrew, thus punning on his double use of the word, "little one." The image of Lot as a symbol of delay remains fixed in our memory, and his wife's fatal last peek at the destroyed cities becomes a stock example of the folly of looking back.

More germane to the theme of births of ancestors is the etiological tale concerning Moabite and Ammonite origins: the narrator recognizes the kinship between Israel and its closest geographical neighbors – they are cousins in the Abrahamic family; yet the narrator undercuts the quality of the kinship because Moab and Ammon are the product of an incestuous union, engendered in the paternal bed as the consequence of Lot's daughters' desperate desire to perpetuate life, and permanently embedded in the puns of their names (Moab="from father"; Ben-ammi="son of my people") (19:37–38). Such a use of an invented story about the perverse origins of sometimes hostile neighbors is a stock-in-trade strategy of rather vicious ethnic humor. According to Frye, "the possibilities of incestuous combinations form one of the minor themes of comedy."[18]

The second complication comes in the guise of a repeated story – Abraham's decision once again that his wife's loyal love (*ḥesed*) to him would be best demonstrated by lying about her status and saying that she was his sister, a stratagem designed ostensibly as a self-protective measure whenever Abraham feels threatened on foreign soil (Gen. 20; cf. Gen. 12). Ironically, of course, Abraham's timorous action jeopardizes the future of his family since he gives up his wife (who is now pregnant!) to another man's harem.[19] Here the episode reenacts an earlier cycle of human failing and propitious divine intervention (Gen. 12). Even more significantly, it retards and threatens the long-awaited fulfillment of the promised birth of Isaac. Moreover, it embodies the U-shaped plot-line so endemic to comic tales: the innocuous beginning that locates Abraham and describes his status as resident

[18] N. Frye, *Anatomy of Criticism*, p. 181.
[19] Clines, "The Ancestor in Danger," *What Does Eve Do to Help?*, pp. 75–78.

alien, the decision to have his wife lie about her relationship to Abraham, the induction of Sarah into the royal harem, the timely divine intervention which saves Sarah and averts permanent harm to Abimelech's household, the return of Sarah to her husband along with lavish gifts (once again, as in Egypt, Abraham gets richer!), the rather incongruous prophetic intercession in which the *guilty* Abraham prays on behalf of the *innocent* injured party in order to heal the divinely inflicted childlessness of the royal family – all these elements, whatever their inner complexity, move ineluctably along a traditional comic trajectory, averting potential disaster and ultimately reintegrating all the protagonists into their rightful society.

At last the oft delayed birth of the promised child takes place. Isaac comes as a gift out of season, and his birth is a happy surprise to the aged couple, resolving the long-standing problem of Sarah's childlessness. Hence Yahweh finally fulfills his promise – even if it is not always according to human timetables or expectations. The festive occasion now evokes a laughter from Sarah far different from what we heard before: "God has made laughter for me; everyone who hears will laugh over me. And she said, 'Who would have said to Abraham that Sarah would suckle children? Yet I have borne him a son in his old age'" (Gen. 21:6–7). Once again is heard a play on the name Isaac, sounding the notes of laughter in response to such an amazing turnabout in the fortunes of the formerly childless couple. As we recall, the divine announcement of the promised birth had initially been greeted by skeptical laughter in the face of absurdity; but now promise finally joins hands with fulfillment to create joyous laughter. Sarah's laughter is full-throated, vibrant, and infectious because it is born in one of life's most beautiful moments – the birth of a child. In contrast to Abraham's earlier laughter that was marked by understandable skepticism – or Sarah's initial laughter that was choked back in denial – Sarah's new laughter is wonderfully contagious: she extends it beyond the charmed circle of Yahweh, Abraham, Sarah, and Isaac, announcing that "everyone who hears will laugh over me." But ultimately it is Isaac who becomes the chief bearer of this richly ambiguous tradition of laughter – for his very name ("he laughs") tells the tale. In the end Isaac emerges from this complex of stories as a being who is a sexual joke of sorts, but a joke as profound as it is whimsical, as serious as it is playful, for it contains the mysterious rhythms of laughter and life both human and divine.[20] His birth does fulfill the divine promise, but the sounds of comedy – rich, vibrant, and punningly alive – surround the event, capturing the drive to new life which has been implanted in the cosmos from the first moments of creation.

We would normally expect such a story to end here and finish with a fairy tale flourish, "and they lived happily ever after." But this is not the way of the Genesis narrators, who are telling a series of connected family stories which are open-ended by the necessity of the case. So the story continues, and the narrator strikes a note of discord: Sarah remains hostile about the disturbing presence of Hagar and Ishmael in Abraham's clan (Gen. 21:8ff). During the festive event of Isaac's weaning, Sarah spies Ishmael while he is "playing" (*mesaheq*) (Gen. 21:9). Though we have here apparently still another word-play on Isaac's name, the exact meaning is opaque. Is Ishmael playing with Isaac? (*mesaheq 'im yishaq* – following the Greek). Or is Ishmael simply playing? (So the Hebrew which lacks the name of Isaac.) Or is Ishmael playing Isaac – that is, pretending to be Isaac and thus usurping his role as legitimate heir?[21] We just do not know the precise intent; only the presence of the root *shq* echoes Isaac's name, suggesting some type of word-play. In any event, Sarah is angry

---

[20] See the suggestive exploration of this story of miraculous birth and its varied forms of laughter in Sanders' book, *Sudden Glory*, pp. 43–47. As observed earlier, Sanders overplays his hand and draws unwarranted conclusions about the role of laughter in Judaism; for example, note his sweeping generalization that flies in the face of what we know of religion and Judaism: "Religion – Judaism in particular – has little tolerance for the unsettling effects of laughter" (p. 49). Unfortunately, this claim is based on a very limited sampling of the relevant evidence.

[21] George W. Coats, "Strife Without Reconciliation: A Narrative Theme in the Jacob Traditions," in *Werden und Wirken des Alten Testaments*, R. Albertz, *et al.*, eds. (Goettingen: Vandenhoeck & Ruprecht, 1979), p. 97.

over Ishmael's behavior and demands the permanent expulsion of a rival wife and a potential rival to her own son: "Cast
out this slave woman with her son; for the son of this slave
woman shall not be heir with my son Isaac" (Gen. 21:10).
Though Abraham is displeased – after all Ishmael is his first-
born son – he complies with Sarah's demand, but not until he
receives further clarification from Yahweh about the exact
status of his two sons: "through Isaac shall your descendants be
named; yet I will make a nation of the son of the slave woman
also, because he is your offspring" (Gen. 21:12–13).

Again, as in Genesis 16, we have a bitter-sweet conclusion:
Hagar and her son are banished to the desert where the
forlorn mother laments the imminent death of her son; but
God hears (*shm'*) Ishmael's voice (note the twofold play on
Ishmael's name in Gen. 21:17) and rescues boy and mother,
reiterating one last time the promise of a great future for this
other son of Abraham. This little narrative offers in miniature
a U-shaped plot-line. Beginning with an integrated society
(the larger family unit of Abraham, Sarah, Hagar, and the two
sons), the story has a downturn in the expulsion of Hagar and
Ishmael; but in contrast to a tragic ending, the story has a dramatic upturn when Yahweh intervenes, saving both mother
and son and reaffirming the promise of a new society – "a
great nation" to which Ishmael and his descendants will rightfully belong.

If Hagar's story has moments of pathos and veers toward
tragedy, the portrayal of Abraham's greatest trial represents
the sharpest descent of Isaac's whole story into what is potentially a terrifying tragedy. The imperious voice seems to come
from nowhere, startling us with its horror: "Take your son,
your only son Isaac, whom you love, and go to the land of
Moriah, and offer him there as a burnt offering upon one of
the mountains of which I shall tell you" (Gen. 22:2). If
Yahweh's action has sometimes been puzzling before, now it
becomes utterly incomprehensible, perhaps even contradictory: Abraham is to take the son of promise, whose name
evokes and echoes "laughter," and sacrifice him to the God
who originally gave him. Talk about the Joban God who gives

and takes away! Here the story indeed comes dangerously close to tragedy, and Edwin Good uses the language of "tragic irony" to characterize the inexplicable command to kill Isaac.[22]

Yet we must once again be alert to the U-shaped plot. Even this sharp, stabbing twist in the story need not catch us completely off guard. As Frye reminds us, "An extraordinary number of comic stories, both in drama and in fiction, seem to approach a potentially tragic crisis near the end, a feature that I would call the 'point of ritual death'."[23] Frye's observation provides, in my judgment, a legitimate and illuminating context for interpreting this famous story. We, the readers, know at the outset that the commanded sacrifice is a test for Abraham: like Job and Jesus, Abraham must pass a trial by ordeal. We also know that despite Abraham's occasional moments of weakness, we can generally count on him to trust Yahweh (cf. especially Gen. 12:1–4 and 15:1–6). Thus we are somewhat prepared for Abraham's instantaneous response in faith: as Kierkegaard's "prince of faith" he is ready to sacrifice Isaac to God. We know further that such heroes of faith, after enduring their trials, receive their due reward. Finally, in such a world, we know about dramatic interventions by a divine figure – the fabled *deus ex machina*. Therefore we are predisposed for Yahweh's last-minute intervention to save Isaac by staying Abraham's hand and substituting a ram. Like the preceding story about the divinely sanctioned expulsion of Hagar and Ishmael, the story of Abraham's most demanding trial ends happily: Isaac is spared, Abraham receives a reaffirmation of the promise of abundant blessing, and father and son return to their rightful society.[24]

Yet it is incontestable that this tale of a father's willingness

---

[22] Good, *Irony in the Old Testament*, p. 195.

[23] N. Frye, *Anatomy of Criticism*, p. 179.

[24] For the most convincing and comprehensive analysis of this incredibly richly textured text, see Levenson, *The Death and Resurrection of the Beloved Son*, pp. 111–142. He highlights well the role of paradox in the story, a paradoxical turn that fits especially well the comic vision: "One paradox of the aqedah is that it is Abraham's willingness to give up Isaac that insures the fulfillment of the promise that depends on Isaac" (p. 142).

to offer up his son to a demanding deity contains special power and depth. Commentators have traditionally stressed its climactic role for Abraham in his relationship with Yahweh, but we must not lose sight of how well it epitomizes Isaac's whole career both in its U-shaped structure and in its characterization of Isaac as a type.

I have already noted how Genesis 22 is *almost* a tragedy.[25] What is crucial, however, in the biblical form is the absence of the actual sacrifice of the son and the lack of any heart-rending cries of either father or son – in sharpest contrast to David's haunting lament over Absalom (II Sam. 18:33; 19:4). Moreover, as I have emphasized, Genesis 22 breaks off from the tragic arc at the strategic moment – as opposed to the genuinely tragic tale of Jephthah's daughter where we hear no voice from heaven to stay the executioner's hand (Jud. 11).[26] But for Abraham and Isaac there is an upswing which puts this story back into a comic light, a bitter-sweet comedy in the darkening shadows of threatened death, but nonetheless a comedy with its celebration of new life. Along with Job's ordeal, Abraham's greatest trial emerges as an apt biblical example of what a recent drama critic has compellingly called, "Comic Agony."[27]

Death, however, does come in the next chapter (Gen. 23), the death of mother Sarah whose total absence from the story of the abortive sacrifice of her only son has often evoked comment both from rabbis at an earlier time and from feminist interpreters in the present era. To the rabbis, the report of the strange proceedings of the unconsummated sacrifice

---

[25] See W. Lee Humphreys' sensitive observations on Gen. 22 under the rubric, "Flirtations with the Tragic Vision," in his illuminating book, *The Tragic Vision and the Hebrew Tradition* (Philadelphia: Fortress Press, 1985), pp. 81–83. "Once more the potential for tragedy is quickly blunted; for again it is the situation that contains the elements of tragedy, while the action of the hero denies them realization" (p. 82).

[26] See Exum's exemplary analysis, in *Tragedy and Biblical Narrative*, pp. 45–60.

[27] See the stimulating exploration of this theme by Albert Bermel, *Comic Agony: Mixed Impressions in the Modern Theatre* (Evanston: Northwestern University Press, 1993), p. 7: "Comic agony . . . brings an experience of sacrifice or suffering into harmony – or, more likely, collision – with an experience of triumph and uplift."

caused Sarah's death, illustrating vividly that "there is . . . a tragic residue . . . in the family of Abraham."[28]

Suddenly Sarah resurfaces in the story line, reappearing in the form of a brief genealogical note and a detailed death and burial report. In particular, it is the burial scene that is most prominent in the chapter, as Abraham enters into rather protracted negotiations for the purchase of an appropriate burial plot for his dead wife. For our purposes it is striking that comic and humorous elements appear, an aspect that has already drawn comment from such scholars as von Rad who remarks on the account's "humorous freshness"[29] and Westermann who finds "subtle humor" in the narration of buying and selling.[30] Good also follows the lead of von Rad, arguing that "the story possesses not only irony but also humor, in what might be taken as a mild satire on commercial bargaining customs . . ."[31]

What these commentators find humorous and ironic is the jarring discrepancy between the intrinsic solemnity of Sarah's funeral and the style and tone of the commercial transaction of a land purchase. Amidst all the proper language we hear studied understatement, euphemism, and polite formality, a combination that pushes the narrative into the comic mode. For example, though the Hittites address Abraham as a "mighty prince among us" (23:6), Abraham identifies himself as "a stranger and alien residing among you" (23:4) – a dramatic contrast that highlights the different perceptions of Abraham's social status. Moreover, the very repetition of the key verbs "give" and "bury" creates a comic effect, especially since all the negotiations apparently take place in the presence of Sarah's corpse. The dialogue says it all:

---

[28] Zornberg, *Genesis*, p. 140. See her richly nuanced discussion of the significance of the life and death of Sarah, a most compelling rendition of the tragic potential of the story, which confirms again the intimate interplay between the tragic and comic visions. In my judgment, however, what is perhaps still most striking about the biblical version is the sounding of comic notes particularly in the humorous depiction of the burial scene.   [29] Von Rad, *Genesis*, p. 241.

[30] Westermann, *Genesis: A Practical Commentary*, p. 166.

[31] Good, *Irony in the Old Testament*, p. 166.

[Abraham] "give me property among you for a burying place, so that I may bury my dead out of my sight" (23:4); [the Hittites] "Bury your dead in the choicest of our burial places; none of us will withold from you any burial ground for burying your dead" (23:6); [Abraham] "If you are willing that I should bury my dead out of my sight, . . . entreat for me Ephron . . . so that he may give me the cave of Machpelah, which he owns; it is at the end of his field. For the full price let him give it to me in your presence as a possession for a burying place" (23:8–9); [Ephron] "No, my lord, hear me; I give you the field, and I give you the cave that is in it; in the presence of my people I give it to you; bury your dead" (23:11); [Abraham] "If you only will listen to me! I will give you the price of the field; accept it from me, so that I may bury my dead there" (23:13); [Ephron] "My lord, listen to me; a piece of land worth four hundred shekels of silver – what is that between you and me? Bury your dead" (23:15).

The exchange graphically expresses the comic mode: the elaborate formalism and excessive politeness, the exaggerated generosity, the euphemistic "give" for "buy" – all capped off by the climax in which an exorbitant price is exacted! Beneath the pedantry we hear parody, beneath commercialism we detect comedy. Yet the detailed report is finally designed to secure for Abraham and his family the first possession of the land that he has been divinely promised, a wonderful albeit incongruous gesture of legal ownership of the land in a time of transition where the "dead" mother passes from the scene, but her burial plot ironically assures her and her people a permanent place in the promised land. It is a small but symbolic sign of continuity and even permanency in a time of death and discontinuity. If comedy be present, then it sounds a muted laughter of the hope of ongoing familial life even in the midst of death. A "tragic residue" may be left behind, but it stands as a dark shadow within a prevailing comic light.

The famous "matchmaking" account in the immediately following story is an appropriate sequel to the obituary of Isaac's mother, forming an explicit connection between the events of a mother's death and a son's marriage (Gen. 24). The closing verse of this romantic tale brings the death of a mother into the charmed circle of marriage and love: "And Isaac brought her into his mother Sarah's tent. He took Rebekah, and she became his wife; and he loved her. So Isaac was comforted after his mother's death" (24:67). The story itself is a marvellous example of Hebrew narrative art, a delicate and detailed rendering of the theme of divine guidance in the search for a proper wife for Isaac. It stresses the future fulfillment of the promise of multiplication and mastery, announced poetically in the blessing of Rebekah: "May you, our sister, become thousands of myriads; may your offspring gain possession of the gates of their foes" (24:60). It is noteworthy that only here and in the promise of reward after Abraham's successful passing of his test (Gen. 22:15–17) do we find the promise of numerous progeny coupled with the explicit promise of the possession of the enemies' gates. The story contains magical tests, wonderful improbabilities, striking coincidences of time and chance, and the happy outcome of marriage which even contains love. Such a charming romantic tale easily cohabits with the comic mode, even while retaining its own generic identity.

The close of Abraham's story comes in Genesis 25, a chapter composed of a patchwork of wildly discrepant materials featuring all three patriarchs – Abraham, Isaac, and Jacob – coupled with references to varied other characters such as Sarah, Hagar, Keturah, and Rebekah as well as Ishmael and Esau. Its rich variety and dry genealogical notes concerning Abraham's marriage to Keturah and his siring of still more sons simply continue the focus on the complicated fulfillment of Abraham's promised role as "the father of a multitude." Moreover, its obituary notice shows the perfect ending of a completed life: "Abraham breathed his last and died in a good old age, an old man and full of years, and was gathered to his people. His sons Isaac and Ishmael buried him in the cave of Machpelah . . . with his wife Sarah" (25:8–10). What a wonderful expression of closure with its emphasis on fulfillment, contentment, and communal solidarity! The beautiful image of being "gathered to his people" is a harbinger of Abraham's hallowed place in the company of his people.

Finally, in keeping with the dominant comic mode of the Abraham cycle of stories, it is fitting that the note of "peaceful harmony" be struck: it shows two erstwhile alienated brothers in a gesture of reconciliation when they bury their father. In sum, all the varied members of the Abraham clan are reintegrated in the society to which they rightfully belong.

ISAAC AS COMIC VICTIM AND SURVIVOR

The shadow of death that looms over tragedy lifts when it is comedy's turn, leaving in place the mad buoyancy of life, an urgency that jostles but does not kill.

(GUTWIRTH)[32]

Although the genealogical headline in Genesis 25:19 would lead one to characterize the stretch of texts from 25:19 to 35:29 (the death notice of Isaac) as Isaac's story, Jacob so dominates the action that he is typically made the hero of this whole section. Similarly, Isaac is so overshadowed by father Abraham in the first part of his story that he is all but eclipsed. Indeed, Isaac has only one chapter in which he holds center spot on the stage, but even here he plays a scene that forms a "parodic double" of what father Abraham did twice – namely, a little charade in which the Hebrew husband commands his wife to lie about her status, pretending that she is his sister (cf. Gen. 12 and 20 with 26). Hence on the whole Isaac gets caught in a squeeze play between father and son, dependent on personalities and forces stronger than he, a fact that will serve to help establish his type as a comic figure.

Indeed, Isaac's shadowy, suppressed place in the biblical narrative makes him a more apt candidate for a comic role than one might initially think. His very name Isaac – "he laughs" – is perhaps the best key to his comic portrayal. In fact, as I have argued above, the evocation of various forms of laughter in his name precisely finds its most congenial home in comedy. Moreover, though often cast in the role of the

---

[32] Gutwirth, *Laughing Matter*, pp. 188–189.

tragic victim, a close look at his whole story shows that while he is indeed a passive victim who gets manipulated in all sorts of ways, he is also a survivor who gets out of one crisis after another often in humorous fashion.

A rapid review of his story from the vantage point of his usual characterization illustrates his passive, submissive nature: he is born to overaged parents (Gen. 21); he is protected from the assumed threat of his older half-brother whose potential as a rival is taken care of by his mother Sarah (Gen. 21); he is preeminently the victim in his near sacrifice at the hands of his father, emerging as a survivor only because of divine intervention in response to his father's unflinching obedience (Gen. 22); he is nowhere in evidence in the seriocomic scene of his mother's burial (Gen. 23); he is a compliant son in the idyllic, romantic tale of Abraham's match-making on his behalf, the consummation of which brings him comfort for the death of his mother (Gen. 24); he is the one to yield ground to avoid conflict with the Philistines in a series of disputes over water-wells (Gen. 26); he is duped by his shrewd, strong-willed wife and his wily younger son and tricked into giving his deathbed blessing to the "wrong" son (Gen. 27); he somehow survives for apparently twenty more years after the deathbed debacle and is finally buried by his two sons (Gen. 35).

As I have observed, the only time Isaac acts independently he imitates his father's pattern of perpetrating a lie about his wife's marital status in order to protect himself while in foreign territory – a case of like father, like son (Gen. 26). R. C. Culley has perceptively contrasted this episode with the two earlier parallels in the Abraham cycle (Gen. 12 and 20), singling out for special comment Isaac's dull-witted, awkward handling of the situation.[33] First, argues Culley, Isaac misperceives the danger of the situation, since no one wants Rebekah – in contrast to Sarah who both times is taken into a royal harem.[34] Second, misperception is coupled with an

---

[33] Robert C. Culley, *Studies in the Structure of Hebrew Narrative, Semeia Supplements* 3 (Philadelphia: Fortress Press, 1976), pp. 33–41.   [34] *Ibid.*, p. 39.

unnecessary act of deception to create an awkward, abnormal situation: Isaac continues to live with his wife who is purportedly his sister.[35] Not surprisingly, Isaac cannot control his sexual urges and gets caught in a bit of sexual play with Rebekah. It is comically ironic that he is found out in his lie when King Abimelech spies Isaac as he is fondling or "playing around" (*mesaheq*) with his alleged sister. Once again we hear a word-play on Isaac's name – echoing that intimate connection of eroticism, play, and earthy humor which are staple ingredients of the comic mix from time immemorial. Abimelech's discovery leads to a sharp rebuke of Isaac from a justifiably angry king because of the danger of guilt and divine punishment: "What is this you have done to us? One of the people might easily have lain with your wife, and you would have brought guilt upon us" (Gen. 26:10). Here again, however, the U-shaped pattern asserts itself: despite his reprehensible conduct Isaac gets off scot-free, and Yahweh bountifully rewards him: "Isaac sowed seed in that land, and in the same year reaped a hundredfold. Yahweh blessed him, and the man became rich; he prospered more and more until he became very wealthy. He had possessions of flocks and herds, and a great household, so that the Philistines envied him" (Gen. 26:12–14). So once more a liar is divinely protected and even rewarded, and the innocent become envious! Sometimes crime does pay! So Isaac merits special divine favors simply because he is Abraham's heir (cf. Gen. 26:2–5). "All ends well," as Culley laconically puts it. In fact, "the shape of the story suggests . . . the hero as a bumbler who in spite of his inept handling of the situation comes out on top."[36] Thus on the one occasion when Isaac acts on his own he hardly appears as a strong, resourceful individual and emerges successfully only because of who he is – passive recipient of divine favor – not because of his ability to act wisely and independently.

In sum, apart from the *partial* exception of the episode in Genesis 26 involving his wife, Isaac through and through is a

---

[35] *Ibid.*   [36] *Ibid.*

victim, characteristically acquiescent to personages stronger and more clever than he. Paradoxically, the brightest, happiest moment in Isaac's whole life perhaps occurred when he was most passive – the occasion of his birth. A child of his parents' old age, he bore a name that evoked laughter; yet, as we have seen, laughter can have many faces, often mirroring skepticism as well as joy, embarrassment as well as amusement, cruelty as well as relief. As passive victim Isaac is one who is laughed at or over, not one who laughs himself or laughs with others (though he does enjoy a little sexual play with his wife! – Gen. 26:8). Although sometimes a victim is a candidate for tragedy (Jephthah's daughter is the chilling biblical example), such is not the case with Isaac: he is survivor as well as victim, emerging from difficult and even dangerous circumstances as one who is successful and blessed. His story has always a comic upturn, aborting the possibility of tragedy. He is typically an innocent, passive man who is set up again and again – a classic half-pathetic, half-humorous dupe whose story is filled with ludicrous moments. His role is widely attested in comedy through the ages.

To illustrate most vividly Isaac's role as dupe and victim who is manipulated but who nonetheless comes forth as a survivor, we can turn briefly to Genesis 27. If Genesis 26 is the center of Isaac's story,[37] then surely the climax – or perhaps better the anti-climax – comes in Genesis 27: the account of the famous deathbed scene when he is deprived of what should have been his last noble gesture – the passing on of his inheritance in the form of the paternal blessing to his first-born son who is also his favorite. Here we have a classic conspiracy of a mother and her favorite son who become "co-tricksters"[38] in a plot to deceive the old, blind father and thereby rob the rightful heir of the paternal blessing. Both father and brother are egregiously victimized, yet the

---

[37] I owe this observation to Francis Landy whose penetrating comments on an earlier form of this representation provided insightful and corrective stimulus. See Francis Landy, "Are We in the Place of Averroes? Response to the Articles of Exum and Whedbee, Buss, Gottwald, and Good," in *Tragedy and Comedy in the Bible*, ed. Exum, p. 138.   [38] Niditch, *Underdogs and Tricksters*, p. 100.

victimizers get away with their deception and theft, even though Isaac and Esau realize they have been cheated. Despite the potential for violence and murder (Esau does threaten to kill his brother – Gen. 27:41), the story ends favorably for all parties. The brothers will both be blessed with material wealth and big families, coming together in a kind of reconciliation (cf. Gen. 33). As I will try to show in my analysis of Jacob as a comic figure, the episode does contain many comedic elements (see below); but for now it is sufficient to highlight Isaac's role as innocent victim who is duped by his wife and younger son.

This bitter-sweet encounter between Isaac and his twin sons at their father's deathbed, a scene so decisive in determining the dynamic of the subsequent story of Jacob and his family, meshes with the recurrent pattern of comical moments in Isaac's story which begins with the dramatic announcements of his birth. His name, "he laughs," indeed bespeaks his character and destiny, but in a different sense from what such a happy appellation might initially suggest. Apart from the one occasion of his birth, he is not usually the source of joyous laughter, nor is he a clever wit himself. Again and again he is laughed over, often manipulated, victimized, even duped; but his life at bottom is not tragic, for he survives and survives and survives. In fact, Isaac lives longer than either his father, Abraham, or his son, Jacob. According to biblical chronology, he lives twenty years after the deathbed scene. In the conventional style that describes a complete and successful life, the narrator tells us that "Isaac breathed his last; and he died and was gathered to his people, old and full of days" (Gen. 35:29). As in the Abraham story, the burial scene epitomizes the typical ending of comedy, stressing that the different protagonists are reintegrated into the society to which they properly belong: the dead father "gathered to his people," and his two sons united together at his burial.

In conclusion, the Isaac story contains several vital ingredients of the comic vision. Hence, its plot-line both in the parts and the whole follows the U-shaped pattern intrinsic to comedy. Though it indeed has its moments of near tragedy and pathos, each time we find the decisive upturn to a happy ending. Moreover, style and theme display typical comic traits: word-plays are plentiful, especially the pivotal pun on Isaac's name; ludicrous and farcical moments abound (recall only the one scene from Isaac's marriage where he has his wife lie for him and where he is found out when he is seen fondling her); and comic irony and incongruity are pervasive (cheaters sometimes prosper in this topsy-turvy world). Lastly, the characterization of Isaac as passive victim is best construed as comic. A hallmark of his role is his ordinariness; things typically happen to him, he is never the powerful protagonist actively shaping events. But in his very ordinariness, in his tendency to drift along on currents that sometimes threaten to submerge him, in his ability to survive and somehow to muddle through – in all these ways he is a comic hero familiar to us all, one who evokes from us a secret smile of recognition, a half-comic, half-pathetic figure who incarnates and mirrors the human, the all too human, and is therefore a laughing survivor who is also laughable.

THE ADVENTURES OF A WANDERING ROGUE: THE
COMEDY OF JACOB (GENESIS 25–35)

Unless we become as rogues, we cannot enter the kingdom of heaven.
(EMILY DICKINSON)

*[T]rickster myths . . . have a hero who is always
wandering . . ., who is not guided by normal conceptions of
good and evil, who is either playing tricks on people or
having them played on him and who is highly sexed. Almost everywhere he has divine traits.*
(PAUL RADIN)[39]

Jacob may be the most problematic character in the gallery of the Genesis heroes, but he emerges as the most colorful and complex of all the patriarchs – and possibly "the most

[39] Paul Radin, *The Trickster: A Study in American Indian Mythology* (New York: Schocken, 1972), p. 155.

fully comical of all" – to echo one recent interpreter.[40] In particular, I wish to argue that Jacob is a trickster or rogue who by dint of wit and guile makes his way successfully in the world, a rogue who emerges ultimately as the spiritual namesake and ancestor of the nation Israel. As a rogue, his ability to survive and even flourish inheres in his cleverness, in his ability to deceive, and in his skill in manipulating people and animals and even God to do his bidding. Jacob therefore fits within the model of the trickster, a widespread and ancient type in myth and folklore which had a vital afterlife in literature as the English rogue and the Spanish *picaro* – to name two later European incarnations. To cite only one typical definition of the *picaro* or rogue: he is "an outsider" or "half-outsider" who "adapts himself to diverse situations by serving different masters, inventing clever ruses, or wearing a variety of masks during a peripatetic life alternating good and evil fortune."[41] His adventures and wanderings usually appear in episodic, open-ended narratives which often have an intrinsic comic and humorous character.[42]

Recently Susan Niditch has given a fine analysis of Jacob as a trickster, utilizing anthropological insights into the folkloristic ambience of what she aptly calls in the title of her stimulating book, *Underdogs and Tricksters*.[43] In my view, the major shortcoming of Niditch's helpful treatment lies in her failure to set her delineation of the trickster more fully within its appropriate home of comedy. Apart from one brief, inciden-

[40] Russ, *The Terrain of Comedy*, p. 50.
[41] Richard Bjornson, *The Picaresque Hero in European Fiction* (Madison: The University of Wisconsin Press, 1977), p. 6.
[42] See the helpful collection of essays on tricksters and trickery edited by J. Cheryl Exum and Johanna W. H. Bos in *Semeia* 42 (1988): *Reasoning with the Foxes: Female Wit in a World of Male Power* (Atlanta: Scholars Press, 1988). Especially germane for my analysis are the essays by Naomi Sternberg and Esther Fuchs and the responses by Kathleen M. Ashley, Edwin M. Good, and Mieke Bal. Sternberg, for example, avers that the trickster tales are always comical, but does not argue the point (pp. 2,7). I find, too, that they are often comical, as I attempt to bring out in my analysis, but by no means are they always so (e.g., the trickery involved in the treacherous actions of the sons of Jacob in revenge for Shechem's rape of Dinah in Gen. 34 is hardly comical – see below).
[43] Niditch, *Underdogs and Tricksters*, pp. 70–125.

tal remark, she fails even to mention the possibility of a dominant comic backdrop for Jacob's adventures as rogue and trickster.[44]

We need now to move to the Jacob story where we may begin at the beginning, the account of his birth. Like other typical trickster tales, Jacob's entrance into the world fits what Niditch calls an "unusual birth."[45] Not only is Jacob born to a formerly childless couple where as usual the problem is attributed to the woman's barrenness, he is also a twin, still another frequent element of such stories. Moreover, the divine announcement about the struggling twins ominously foreshadows the destiny of the two brothers:

> Two nations are in your womb,
> Two separate peoples shall issue from your body;
> One people shall be mightier than the other,
> And the older shall serve the younger. (Gen. 25:23)

As in birth, so in life will be their fate: separation and strife will define their relationship, and familial positions will be reversed. Finally, the naming of the twins, with the usual love of word-play and folk etymology, inscribes the character of the two boys, again with a foreshadowing of their future struggle for power and position: "The first one emerged red (*'adomoni*), like a hairy (*se'ar*) mantle all over; so they named him Esau [playing on his reddish color – *'adomoni* – and hence his identification with *Edom*; and his hairiness – *se'ar* – playing on his future habitation in *Se'ir*]. Then his brother emerged, holding onto the heel of Esau; so they named him Jacob [*Ya'aqob*, playing on *'aqeb* "heel" – hence "heel-grabber"]." Esau is humorously characterized, or better, caricatured: his reddish skin color was apparently a cause for laughter, and his hairy body marked him as an animal-like creature, slow of wit and savage in appearance. In contrast, Jacob's name as heel-grabber reflects his role as supplanter

---

[44] *Ibid.*, pp. 105–106. One should note, however, that Niditch points to comical and humorous features in subsequent publications; see her treatment of Genesis in *The Women's Bible Commentary*, pp. 16, 20.

[45] Niditch, *Underdogs and Tricksters*, p. 94.

and usurper. Though Jacob may be second born and thus legally in second place, he is from birth a grasping, greedy individual whose strength is his tenacity, his ability to hold on for dear life whether in his mother's womb or later in his wrestling match with a divine adversary. In sum, the twins' beginnings in the womb and in the world reflect comic touches which mirror their character and destiny.

With those rapid shifts of perspective we associate with the episodic movement of Genesis, we come to the first portrayal of the twins after they are grown up. The brief, bold strokes of the narrator give striking representation of the brothers' occupations, characteristic modes of living, and primary parental attachments – all of which set the stage for subsequent events. "When the boys grew up, Esau became a skillful hunter, a man of the outdoors; but Jacob was a mild (*tam*) man who stayed in camp. Isaac loved Esau because he had a taste for game; but Rebekah loved Jacob" (Gen. 25:27,28). Though they are twins, they are hardly identical: neither in looks, nor in living and working habits, nor in parental affection. This split between twins is a favorite motif of folklore, a split that uses twinness and its seeming similarity to highlight difference and intensify hostility. Twinness, with its fundamental image of doubleness, will play itself out in a drama of double-dealing and duplicity. Moreover, the principle of twoness will animate the movement of the whole story. So much of our tale of twins proceeds by twos: twin brothers who represent two nations; two sisters who become Jacob's two wives; two slave women who become Jacob's secondary wives; two names for Jacob; two camps of divine beings (*mahana'im*); two sons by his favorite wife, the second of whom is given two names; two visits to Bethel, and so on.

For now, however, the twins' character and destiny, prefigured earlier within the birth narrative, receives further amplification and extension in this first description of their adult roles. The seeds of future conflict between the twins are sown, and the narrator will now begin to show how these seeds will grow and eventually bear bitter fruit.

The next episode recounts the famous incident in which

Jacob buys Esau's birthright for a pot of stew (Gen. 25:29–34). The narrator presents for the first time the twins in their most characteristic comic roles: Jacob emerges as a trickster, here in the guise of a shrewd bargainer, whereas Esau plays the role of the classic simpleton, a dull-witted dupe victimized by his wily brother. Though we have just been told that Esau was a "skillful hunter," he must not have been too skillful, for he has apparently returned home emptyhanded. The narrator also uses the occasion to play once again on the redness of the stew (*ha'adom*) which suggests to him the name of *Edom* (Gen. 25:30). Most decisively, Esau emerges as an appetite-driven creature who cannot think beyond his needs of the moment and who exaggerates his hunger to the point of ludicrousness: "I am about to die, so what use is my birthright to me?" (Gen. 25:32). In contrast, Jacob is shrewd and perceptive, able to size up a mark and seize the moment to win an advantage. As the price for a meal, he makes Esau trade his most valuable asset: his birthright, the ostensible key to paternal inheritance and hence blessing and wealth.

To illustrate most blatantly Jacob's role as trickster who can resort to the strategies of disguise and deception when the occasion demands it, we must invoke again Genesis 27, the well-known account of Jacob's theft of his father's blessing. Disguise and deception are common characteristics of comedy; indeed, as Frye puts it, "craft or fraud is the animating spirit of the comic form."[46] Moreover, a classic comic triad of trickster, dupe, and innocent victim appears, with the two sons and their senile father playing these roles and the shrewd, scheming mother performing backstage as a "co-trickster" in collusion with her favorite son.[47] Though the story indeed has a bitter-sweet character, it is dominantly in the comic mode, as I argued earlier in conjunction with the delineation of Isaac's role.

Let us look more closely at the story in terms of the comic vision. The opening lines of the deathbed scene, where we

---

[46] N. Frye, *The Secular Scriptures*, p. 74.
[47] Niditch, *Underdogs and Tricksters*, p. 100.

read how Isaac thinks first of his stomach, strike a humorous note: "prepare for me delectable food such as I love and bring it to me that I may eat; that I may bless you before I die" (Gen. 27:4). (The earthiness of the Genesis narratives comes out often in the eating scenes: as we may recall, Isaac's favorite son, Esau, already has manifested a similar propensity for thinking of food first, the future second – a case of like father, like son.) The clever rogue Jacob pulls off the deception, though he expresses doubts and misgivings when his enterprising, resourceful mother first conceives the plan and urges him simply to follow her instructions. The story is marked by turns with both ludicrousness and pathos. Picture the scene: the old man is on his deathbed, hungrily awaiting his beloved elder son's arrival with choice cuisine; but meanwhile the younger son, the favorite of his mother, enters and identifies himself as Esau. The dissembling Jacob has been ludicrously outfitted with animal skins on his arms, aping the appearance of his hairy brother, lest his blind father feel his smooth, hairless skin and discover the hoax. To complete the disguise Jacob wears his brother's garb in order to emit the right body odor. In brief, Jacob attempts to become his twin brother. He proceeds to tell a series of bold-faced lies when his blind, befuddled father becomes suspicious. To appreciate fully the scene one must read the inimitable dialogue between lying son and dying father, a dialogue immediately followed by the moving account of Esau's late arrival and his anguished plea for a blessing (Gen. 27:19–40). Pathos is indeed here – but more dominant are incongruity and comic irony: Isaac blesses the *wrong* son who is paradoxically the *right* son according to the prenatal oracle (Gen. 25:23). Esau's bitter words explicitly highlight the duplicitous character of Jacob in his dealings with his brother, echoing the pun on Jacob's name and the pun on birthright and blessing (27:36). What a ludicrous way of working out the divine will! Though God is somehow involved, he is curiously absent. Moral categories are not invoked; they are just not appropriate in this kind of folklore which revels in the ability of the trickster to transgress conventional boundaries and in blurring the lines between good and evil.[48] Yet nobody gets seriously hurt – at least not in any ultimate sense.

So far as I know, Gunkel was the first modern critic to discern the comic, humorous aspects of Genesis 27: ". . . the substance of the story," argued Gunkel, "is and remains that a deception ultimately has a happy ending: Jacob the rogue really wins for himself the blessing; Esau draws the shorter one, without being morally guilty, and the hearers are the happy heirs of the deceiver."[49] This tale of duplicity therefore has the happy outcome characteristic of comedy, though this ending must await the later adventures of Jacob the rogue during his sojourn in a strange land where he will use his marvellous ability as a trickster to come out on top. Thus Isaac's wrong blessing for his two sons will ultimately be right for both of them: Jacob as deceiver will emerge as Israel, a prince of God who can prevail against both God and man, whereas Esau appears as a simpleton who is usually outwitted and manipulated by personages more clever than he, but who nonetheless emerges as a magnanimous, generous survivor. Apropos of the plot-line of comedy, the two brothers will become at least temporarily reconciled by the end of the story, but all this is to anticipate the rest of this comic tale of twins and tricksters.

The narrative about the stolen blessing, where Jacob shows his true colors as deceiver, establishes a dominant pattern for the rest of the Genesis narrative. Deception and counter-deception will animate human relationships, as one trickster is pitted against another. Blessing remains the prize, but blessing can be manipulated and even gained deceitfully; yet perhaps the strangest paradox is that divine sanction and support is almost always granted to the deceiver, thus setting aside traditional moral criteria. Indeed, the divine interventions in the story generally will confirm the prenatal birth oracle which decreed the favored destiny of the younger brother, though there will be some ironic turn-abouts in

[48] Hermann Gunkel, *Genesis* (Goettingen: Vandenhoeck und Ruprecht, 1964), p. 308.   [49] *Ibid.*, p. 307.

Jacob's career where he is victimized by deceivers (see below). But for now the deception evokes hatred and the murderous desire for revenge on the part of the aggrieved Esau, a danger to which Rebekah is alerted and which she handles with her usual shrewdness. She sends her favorite son to her brother Laban in order to avoid fratricide.

The most dramatic event in the midst of Jacob's journey is his awesome encounter with God at Bethel, a dream of divinity that confirms God's choice of Jacob and reiterates the promise of land and numerous progeny given earlier to Abraham and Isaac (Gen. 28:10–22). The narrative contains a cultic aetiology for Bethel, but for our purposes the most important dimension of the text is how Jacob, even at this moment of rare and exalted religious experience, remains true to form: he bargains with God, using an ancient form of vow, thus shrewdly binding God to the promises of blessings and protection. Jacob, the heel-grabber, once more grasps the opportunity, revealing his wisdom in things both human and divine, and so manifesting his multiple skills as a master negotiator who will use any strategy to gain a favorable position.

Jacob's sojourn at Laban's house, set within the larger circle of the Jacob-Esau cycle, forms the center of the story of Jacob. As always Jacob will continue to be a trickster, though here he will almost meet his match in his uncle Laban, still another trickster in a family of tricksters (remember Rebekah is Laban's sister).

Within these colorful tales, the narrative exploits age-old themes of broad *comedy*, where bed-switches, mistaken identities, domestic strife, and sexual competition dominate the action. Edwin Good even more specifically adduces the pattern of classical Greek comedy to describe our roguish patriarch, arguing that "the conflict between Jacob and Laban . . . is presented with an almost Aristophanic gusto, the comic confrontation of *eiron* with *alazon* . . ., of the ironical man with the impostor."[50] Moreover, though interpreters

---

[50] Good, *Irony in the Old Testament*, p. 101.

have often pointed out the chiastic and concentric structure of the story, no one to my knowledge has observed that the Jacob-Laban cycle also follows the U-shaped plot we customarily associate with comedy. The story begins on a note of family harmony and happiness, plunges downward into deception, conflict, and alienation, and then moves up at the end into reconciliation when Jacob and Laban form a covenant. Taken all together we indeed have all the ingredients of what we can aptly name "domestic comedy within the household of faith."

When Jacob arrives in the land of his northeastern relatives, he repeats an age-old pattern: he goes to a well in order to meet the local inhabitants, a pattern so conventional that Robert Alter has called it a "type-scene."[51] In any case, a charming scene unfolds, marked not simply by conventional hospitality but by idyllic family harmony as Jacob is welcomed with open arms into his mother's family in the old country. The narrator describes the scene best (see Gen. 29:10–14).

What a wonderful beginning for Jacob! Here for once generosity seems to be dominant. Jacob even displays a delightful impulsiveness. He is a bit of a show-off, for he single-handedly moves a huge stone that blocked the water-hole, apparently a Herculean feat, since it was a task usually requiring a whole group of shepherds. Even more impulsively, he kisses cousin Rachel before he takes the time to introduce himself. When Laban hears of his nephew's arrival, he embraces him with warmth and apparent enthusiasm, inviting Jacob into his house. He then affirms the bond of kinship, "You are surely my bone and flesh" (Gen. 29:14), echoing Adam's words to the woman in the garden (Gen. 2:23).

The auspicious beginning of Jacob's time with Laban is further enhanced when Laban generously offers to pay Jacob for his work: "Just because you are a kinsman, should you serve me for nothing? Tell me, what shall your wages be?" (Gen. 29:15). Meanwhile, we learn that Jacob has fallen in

---

[51] Alter, *The Art of Biblical Narrative*, pp. 47–62.

love with Rachel, the younger, beautiful daughter of Laban;
his love for his cousin makes his answer easy: he wants Rachel
as a wife; she would be his wages. He then names seven years
as his term of service, a time that "seemed to him but a few
days because of his love for her" (Gen. 29:20). Romantic love
appears rarely in Genesis, but in Jacob's case it is not that surprising. At last, the wedding day arrives, and Laban hosts a
festive banquet. But when the wedding night comes, Laban
substitutes Leah, his older daughter for Rachel, the love of
Jacob's life. The bed-switch works, and the amorous Jacob is
tricked, only discovering in dawn's early light that he has slept
with the wrong woman. The narrator tersely remarks, "When
morning came – there was Leah!" (Gen. 29:25). Jacob is
understandably upset and complains to his deceitful father-
in-law: "What is this you have done to me? I was in your service
for Rachel! Why did you deceive me?" (Gen. 29:25). Laban
simply retorts, "It is not the practice in our place to marry off
the younger before the elder" (Gen. 29:26) – a painfully
ironic rebuttal to Jacob who had once cheated his elder
brother. But turn-about is fair play, and there is a kind of
poetic justice in Jacob's world, as the trickster is tricked.

Jacob, however, finally does win his beloved Rachel as his
bride, although Laban exacts the pledge of seven more years
of work from his new son-in-law. So after Jacob completes the
bridal week for Leah, he takes Rachel as his second wife. Thus
Jacob gets two wives, but not for the price of one!

God has not been totally absent from this topsy-turvy
match-making, for he intervenes now on behalf of another
underdog, this time favoring the unloved Leah with fertility,
while allowing Rachel to be barren. What ensues is an intense
and humorous domestic drama involving heated sexual
competition. Whereas earlier we witnessed a battle for birthright, blessing, and brides, now we behold a battle for babies.
For the divinely favored Leah, "babies pop out with clock-
work regularity"[52] as she bears four sons in rapid succession

---

[52] Anne Bingham, "Ruse, Romance, and Resolution: The Comedy of Jacob," unpublished essay (Pomona College, 1981), p. 3.

before she temporarily ceases. Meanwhile, Rachel looks on with increasing frustration and jealousy, consumed by pent-up rage which finally bursts forth in an exaggerated demand to her husband: "Give me sons, or I die" (Gen. 30:1). Jacob angrily retorts, "Can I take the place of God who has withheld sons from you" (Gen. 30:2). In an act of desperate compensation, Rachel gives Jacob her slave woman, Bilhah, as a surrogate wife and mother, who bears two more sons for Jacob. Not to be outdone, Leah also gives Jacob her slave woman, Zilpah, who likewise bears two sons. In this bedroom competition between rival wives, Jacob appears as a kind of "super-stud" who bounces from bed to bed as he is passed from woman to woman. Pregnancy and childbirth are all, and woe upon the woman who remains childless.

In this domestic drama, each son bears in his name the marks of the battle and the colorful word-plays echo the individual triumphs in the baby-making contest. The notes of earthy eroticism, sexual competitiveness, and divine involvement in human fertility reverberate through the narrative and become permanently embedded in the names of Jacob's sons. Two examples suffice to highlight this bedroom drama. Leah's first-born son is named Reuben (*re'u ben*="Look, a son"); for she said, "Because the Lord has looked upon (*ra'ah*) my affliction; surely now my husband will love me" (Gen. 29:32). When Rachel's servant woman, Bilhah, bears a second son, Rachel exclaims, "with mighty wrestlings (*naphtulim*) I have wrestled (*Niphtalti*) with my sister, and have prevailed; so she called his name *Naphtali*" (Gen. 30:8).

Probably the most farcical moment comes when Rachel hires out Jacob to Leah for the night in exchange for mandrakes, a kind of ancient aphrodisiac. What a ludicrous situation when one wife must play the pimp for her husband and sells him to her rival wife and sister! Once again, however, Leah is put back on track and bears for the sexually prodigious patriarch two more sons and one daughter for good measure before she ceases.

At long last Rachel is also favored with a pregnancy, and she gives birth to Joseph, whose name contains a double pun:

"God has taken away (*'asaph*) my reproach"; and she called his name Joseph (*yoseph*), saying "May the Lord add (*yoseph*) to me another son" (Gen. 30:23–24). For the moment the battle for babies comes to an end, though one remembers Rachel's petition embedded in Joseph's name, "May the Lord add to me another son" – a petition that foreshadows the birth of Benjamin, the second son of Rachel and the twelfth and last son of Jacob.

The birth of Joseph apparently rekindles in Jacob the desire to return home, and he requests Laban's permission to go (Gen. 30:25). Once more Laban raises the issue of wages, and the two wily figures enter into negotiations. Jacob asks only for the spotted and speckled sheep; Laban agrees, but before Jacob has a chance to take these sheep, Laban has already segregated them and sent them off to be in the charge of his sons. Once again deception clouds the transaction. This time, however, Jacob proves to be more than a match for his tricky father-in-law, and he resorts to a magical trick of having the stronger sheep and goats breed in front of peeled tree branches in order to have the flocks bring forth spotted and striped animals; the weaker of the flock he lets alone and leaves them for Laban. Thus Jacob increases his flock at the expense of his father-in-law. So the man with many sons now acquires many flocks, hence fulfilling the divine promise of blessing and wealth.

After Jacob perceives that Laban and his sons have become increasingly hostile against him, God commands him to return to the land of Canaan. Jacob confers with his two wives, who agree with his decision to return. For one last time Jacob deceives Laban, keeping his departure a secret. When Laban learns that Jacob and his retinue have fled, he takes up pursuit and catches up, though not before God warns him in a dream not to harm Jacob. The dialogue between the two tricksters reveals vividly the character of the two men in their history of deception and subterfuge (see Gen. 31:26ff). In particular, Laban accuses Jacob of stealing his household gods. Not knowing that Rachel has stolen her father's gods, Jacob pronounces a death sentence on anyone with whom the gods are found (Gen. 31:32). When Laban searches through the tents he fails to find the gods. A comically ironic moment comes when Rachel stays seated on the camel's saddle where she has hidden the gods, claiming not to be able to get up because the "way of women was upon her" (Gen. 31:35). Rachel shows herself to be Laban's daughter, for she, too, emerges as one adept at deception. We have here also a fine parody of the idolatrous household gods which would be profaned because of Rachel's alleged menstrual state. Finally, Jacob and Laban effect a partial reconciliation in the form of a covenantal agreement designed for mutual self-protection. Thus the drama of deception in the Jacob-Laban relationship comes to a good end, and the two men part peaceably.

Jacob, however, must still return home to Canaan and face his angry brother. The journey of return, like the journey of flight, is marked by an encounter with a divine being (Gen. 32:22–32). The fateful encounter on the bank of the Jabbok river is the most significant event in Jacob's whole career. A lone Jacob meets a mysterious assailant at the fording-place of the Jabbok, an adversary initially identified only as a "man," but finally recognized as God. In the struggle Jacob must again hold on for dear life, but it is Jacob's nature to be tough and tenacious. What is decisive for our purposes is that Jacob once again is simply being true to form, refusing to let go of his assailant until he exacts a blessing from him. Jacob gets even more than he bargained for, since he receives both a new name, the honorific name Israel, and a crippling blow which leaves him permanently marked by his ordeal. Jacob fails to learn his opponent's name, but he does name the place *Peniel* ("face of God"), saying simply, "For I have seen God face to face, and yet my life is preserved" (Gen. 32:30). Jacob's departure from this momentous encounter is one of the most compelling in Scripture: "The sun rose upon him as he passed Peniel, limping because of his thigh" (Gen. 32:31).

From now on Jacob bears a double name: thus he retains his old identity as Jacob, as "heel-grabber," as supplanter and usurper; but he takes on also a new image and identity as

Israel, as one who has "striven (*sarita*) with God and men and [has] prevailed" (Gen. 32:28). Although Jacob is permanently changed after this event, he is not totally transformed: he continues to remain a trickster and deceiver. The name Israel simply confirms him as one who has struggled with divine and human adversaries and has won, but the wonder is that he is a trickster who is triumphant even with God.

Jacob still must meet his brother. Although he has seemingly been fearless in facing a divine adversary (whom some interpreters consider to be the divine ally of Esau), he still fears to face his brother. He makes elaborate preparations to provide maximal self-protection; but ironically all his worry is in vain, for he in fact has nothing to fear. Jacob reverts to his usual role of trickster, displaying exaggerated servility to the brother he once cheated. Indeed, in a delightfully ironic twist, Jacob's action of self-prostration to Esau subverts one key part of the original birth oracle which forecast that Esau would bow down before Jacob (Gen. 25:23). In any case, Esau proves to be magnanimous, generous, and forgiving, welcoming home a long absent brother with open arms and apparently open heart (note the disparaging note the rabbis added which describes Esau biting Jacob's neck). The biblical narrator affirms the spirit of reconciliation, emphasizing how Jacob is reintegrated into the charmed circle of the land and society to which he properly belongs. Even in this time of surprising and joyous reconciliation the sly Jacob once more deceives his overly trusting brother, lying about his intentions of meeting Esau for a later rendezvous (Gen. 33:12–17). Yet the two brothers are united one last time at the burial of their father Isaac (Gen. 35:29).

The story of Jacob in his relationships with both Esau and Laban always has the comic upswing no matter how dark and threatening particular episodes might appear. Not so with the story of the rape of Dinah by young Shechem (Gen. 34). Here a rape which incongruously turns into a romance – Prince Shechem falls in love with Dinah and wants to marry her – takes a severe down-turn into murderous revenge when Jacob's sons deceive the men of Shechem about the marriage agreement, using the condition of circumcision as a means to render all the men of Shechem weak and vulnerable. Like their father, the sons of Jacob prove adept in the art of deception; but in contrast to his more benign deceptions, theirs is a cloak for a savage murder of all the males in Shechem plus wholesale pillage of Shechemite flocks and seizure of all the women and children. Jacob and his sons still emerge as God's favored and protected ones, yet at the price of mass murder. Nonetheless this remains but one gory episode in the more dominant comic movement, showing that a comedy can sometimes contain darkly ambiguous and even tragic moments.

This bitter-sweet side of the comic vision is perhaps most poignantly revealed in the birth story of Jacob's twelfth son, the second son of Rachel. Rachel dies while bearing this son which ironically fulfills her wish at the time Joseph was born and fulfills Jacob's curse on the one who had stolen the household gods (Gen. 31:32). As she lies dying she names this child of her last breath, *Ben-oni* ("son of sorrow"); but Jacob calls the child by another name, *Benjamin* ("son of the right hand"), an honorific name designed to negate the significance of the sorrow-laden name of Ben-oni (Gen. 35:18). But the sensitive reader will remember this heart-rending scene, which leaves Jacob bereft of his beloved Rachel who dies while giving birth to a child. The comedy of Jacob continues in the story of his family, but it is a comedy which also knows suffering and death even in the midst of the coming of new life.

COMIC NARRATIVES OF JACOB AND HIS SONS: JOSEPH, JUDAH, AND THEIR BROTHERS (GENESIS 37–50)

As the story of Jacob moves into its next major stage, the focus shifts from the wily patriarch to the fortunes of his twelve sons, a shift represented in the genealogical formula that begins Genesis 37 (vs. 2a). Usually interpreters have simply taken the major character of this last section of Genesis and named it the "Joseph Story," arguing that it represents an originally independent novella, and segregating out as a later interpolation the story about Judah and Tamar in Genesis 38. More recent interpretation, especially the insightful literary analysis of Robert Alter, has demonstrated convincingly the integral place of Genesis 38 in the ongoing story of Jacob's family.[53]

I wish to concentrate only on the possible play of comedic forms in this last major segment of Genesis. In my judgment, this complex story that focuses on Joseph and Judah simply continues and confirms dominant comic trajectories both in the earlier Jacob story as well as in the entire book of Genesis. Thus the themes of deception and disguise, amazing reversals of fortune, restoration and reconciliation, and the celebration of survival and new life continue to wend their often circuitous and comical way through Genesis.

"A Comedy of Errors": Tamar's seduction of Judah (Genesis 38)

The story of Judah and Tamar (Gen. 38) stands out as a masterpiece of ironic comedy, revealing one of the most brilliantly conceived female characters in Genesis. It forms an inspired digression within the surrounding Joseph story (Gen. 37, 39–50), yet it is an imaginative interpolation which reflects an artful set of structural and thematic interconnections with the more dominant narrative about Joseph.[54]

Paralleling somewhat Joseph's descent into Egypt (using the same root form – *yrd*, "going down" – that will reappear in Gen. 39:1, "Joseph was taken down" – *hurad*),[55] Judah has gone down away from his brothers and has taken a Canaanite woman as wife, a daughter of Shua (Gen. 38:1–2). In quick succession they have three sons, the first-born of whom also takes a Canaanite wife named Tamar. For mysterious reasons Er, Judah's first-born, is struck dead by Yahweh; Onan is then commanded to perform the duty of a brother-in-law, but he spills his semen on the ground lest he impregnate his

---

[53] Robert Alter, *The Art of Biblical Narrative* (New York: Basic Books, 1981), pp. 3–12.
[54] *Ibid.*, pp. 5–6, 10.   [55] *Ibid.*, p. 6.

widowed sister-in-law, an action that costs him his life. Only an under-age third son remains alive, and Judah falsely promises him to Tamar after he grows up. Meanwhile Judah orders Tamar to reside in her father's house until Shelah can marry her. Judah, however, has deceived Tamar out of fear for his one surviving son, a fact that Tamar perceives. When Judah's wife dies and his period of mourning is over, Tamar, who up to this point has been utterly passive, shows her mettle as a true daughter of Eve and enacts a bold plan to get herself pregnant. Life must continue, her husband's line must be perpetuated.

Learning that her father-in-law is going to a sheep-shearing festival, Tamar dons the veil characteristic of a prostitute and strategically stations herself on the road where she can meet Judah. It is clear that she knows well her father-in-law who sees her and wants her: the brisk business-like negotiations are dispatched quickly: he makes his proposition, and she names her price – and it is a high price indeed! She wants his staff and his signet and cord, the ancient equivalent of a credit-card.[56] He accepts her terms and sleeps with her, leaving behind his signet and cord and staff with her.

After Judah arrives back home, he entrusts his payment of the promised goat with a friend who goes in search of the prostitute in order to get back his collateral, but he could not find her. Moreover, when he inquires about her whereabouts, the local citizens say there is no prostitute. Showing a delightful and revealing ironic touch, he uses a special Hebrew word – *qedeshah* (sacred functionary or votary) – rather than the usual word for prostitute (*zonah*), thus trying to put the best possible face on Judah's sexual transaction. In any case, he returns to Judah empty-handed. Judah thinks the affair is over, shrugging off the whole matter: "Let her keep the things as her own, otherwise we will be laughed at; you see, I sent this kid, and you could not find her" (Gen. 38:23). Little does Judah know that the joke is on him and the laugh will finally be on him.

---

[56] The apt analogy is Alter's, *ibid.*, p. 9.

A few months pass, and Tamar's pregnancy is discovered and duly reported to Judah: "Your daughter-in-law Tamar has played the whore (*zantah*), and she is pregnant as a result of her whoredom (*zenunim*)" (Gen. 38:24a) – once again adroitly playing on the root *znh* which appears above. Judah's judicial sentence is brief and brutal: "Bring her out, and let her be burned" (Gen. 38:24b). But just as she was being brought, she coolly informed her father-in-law: "It was the owner of these who made me pregnant . . . Take note, please, whose these are, the signet and the cord and the staff. Then Judah acknowledged them and said, 'She is more in the right than I, since I did not give her to my son Shelah'" (Gen. 38:25,26).

So the joke was on Judah, but it was a joke in the service of life. Judah had attempted to block the drive to new life by holding back his third-born son. Tamar did what she had to do to perpetuate the line of Judah, showing the savvy, boldness, and coolness under fire characteristic of the heroines of Genesis. Thus she bore twin boys whose manner of birth and resulting names reveal the narrator's love of apt and compelling puns: "While she was in labor, one put out a hand; and the midwife took and bound on his hand a crimson thread, saying, 'This one came out first.' But just then he drew back his hand, and out came his brother; and she said, 'What a breach [*peretz*] you have made for yourself!' Therefore he was named Peretz. Afterward his brother came out with the crimson thread on his hand; and he was named Zerah ["brightness"]" (Gen. 38:28–30).

In sum, the narrative is one of the comic masterpieces of the Bible, highlighting the resourcefulness and determination of a heroine who refused to be stopped in her pursuit of life. Being unjustifiably deceived, she resorts to "justifiable deception."[57] She thus takes her place with the other tricksters of Genesis who move out from their marginalized, subordinate position and plot a viable future even when it

---

[57] *Ibid.*, p. 11. Alter also calls attention to the ironic linking of Tamar's deception with Judah's deception of his father.

requires that they must force themselves onto the center stage of action. Adroitly using disguise and deception, Tamar steps boldly into the light of history and claims her status as mother of Judah's heirs of the blessing.

A comedy of deception and deliverance: Joseph and his brothers (Genesis 37, 39–50)

The Joseph story has long been considered one of the superlative achievements of Hebrew narrative art. Typically it is deemed a parade example of an early form of a short story or novelette with a tightly woven plot-line, superb character portrayals, and deft delineation of theme. Usually interpreted in a more serious key, it has only recently been analyzed from a comic perspective, though Thomas Mann perceived its resonance with a high view of ironic comedy. Following in Mann's train, Bloom sees vital segments of the story (which he calls a "romance" or "wonder tale") as further evidence of the Yahwist's comic genius.[58] Alter has also described it in passing as "rich comedy," though without offering a detailed argument.[59] Once one begins to entertain the possibility of a comic reading, some fascinating insights emerge which show just how attuned the so-called Joseph story is with the dominant comic strains of Genesis.

For my purpose it is not necessary to rehearse the incredibly vast array of interpretations of the Joseph story. I wish to concentrate only on those key structural and thematic dimensions that suggest the category of comedy. First, the story begins with that same note of parental favoritism as was displayed earlier by Jacob's parents: here it is a case of like parents, like son as Jacob repeats the character trait of both his father and mother: "Now Israel loved Joseph more than any other of his children, because he was the son of his old age . . ."(Gen. 37:3). The theme of brotherly disharmony has already emerged in the narrator's earlier observation about

---

[58] Bloom, *The Book of J*, p. 224.
[59] Robert Alter, *The World of Biblical Literature* (New York: Basic Books, 1992), p. 168.

Joseph's "bad report of [his brothers] to their father" (37:2). Hence Joseph is initially portrayed as a "tattle-tale and spoiled brat"[60] whose symbol of paternal favoritism is blatantly advertised in his fabled "coat of many colors" (or long robe with sleeves). Such favoritism can often lead to tragedy, for which it sometimes has the potential in Genesis; here it serves to pinpoint at the beginning the domestic tensions at work in Jacob's family and the primary factors involved.

Joseph compounds his problematic standing within his family by reciting his two famous dreams of his future glory, dreams which offer in partially duplicate form the plot announcement for his whole story. For now the recital serves to inflame further his brothers' animosity toward young Joseph: "So they hated him even more because of his dreams and his words" (37:8). After Joseph's recital of his second dream, even father Jacob has had enough and "rebukes" him (37:10), while his brothers become even more jealous (37:11). No one at the outset responds favorably to Joseph's "I have a dream" speeches. What the brothers will do with their pampered, pretentious younger brother motivates the decisive action in the opening scenes of this family drama, setting the stage for the whole movement of the story. Moreover the brothers' hostility toward Joseph will trigger the initial descent of the story down the U-shaped pattern that we have connected with comedy, whose first major phase plunges the story into danger and threatened death.

Sent on a mission to check on the welfare of his brothers, Joseph promptly gets lost and is found wandering in a field. Finally learning the location of his brothers, he walks into a murder plot: "They saw him from a distance, and before he came near to them, they conspired to kill him. They said to one another, 'Here comes this dreamer. Come now, let us kill him . . .; then we shall say that a wild animal has devoured him, and we shall see what will become of his dreams'" (37:18–20). The initial plan to do away with Joseph, though altered critically by the decision not to kill their brother, but

---

[60] Bloom, *The Book of J*, p. 229.

sell him into slavery, gives the key terms of the deception of their father: they will say that wild animals have eaten him, using Joseph's bloodied coat as proof. Like the preceding stories of Jacob, so much of the Joseph narrative will involve disguise and deception which will then be coupled with scenes of deliverance. Here Joseph's bloody robe serves to mask the truth of what happened, a garment used to elicit the painful recognition of father Jacob: "They had the long robe with sleeves taken to their father, and they said: 'This we have found; recognize (*haker*) whether it is your son's robe or not.' He recognized it (*wayyakkir*), and said, 'It is my son's robe! A wild animal has devoured him; Joseph is without doubt torn to pieces'" (37:32–33). Jacob's response is to engage in untempered mourning rites, showing his tendency to be a man of extremes who will not be comforted for the death of his favorite son. Father Jacob, once the master of deception, is now deceived for a second time, this time involving not a bed-switch but a faked death.

As we noted above, the story of Judah and Tamar is subtly interrelated with the more dominant movement of the Joseph story. Hence Genesis 39 echoes the descent of Judah away from his brothers (38:1) by using the same root (*hurad*) as we heard in the earlier account. Both brothers are thus separated from their brothers but in very different ways: Judah by choice leaves his brothers to fall into his amorous adventure with the disguised Tamar, whereas Joseph has been sold as a slave and taken against his will down to Egypt where he too is tempted to fall into the sexual embrace of a foreign woman. The tales of the two brothers will follow similar patterns in their basic movement, especially involving deception and counter-deception, pivotal scenes of recognition, and the birth of two sons whose birth-position will be reversed.[61]

The tale of Joseph's resistance to the attempted seduction by Potiphar's wife serves not only as a contrastive parallel to Tamar's successful seduction of Judah, but also "becomes

---

[61] Once again I must acknowledge my debt to Alter's fundamental analysis; see *The Art of Biblical Narrative*, pp. 3–12.

great comic writing in J, comedy for its own sake . . ."[62] While I agree in general with Bloom's assertion, I find here comedy for the sake of the whole story: the comic twist shows not only Joseph's innocence and virtue to good advantage (the emphasis that Fielding gave his hero, Joseph Andrews), but features the persistence of Joseph's amazing luck – no matter how adverse the circumstances, he ultimately emerges unscathed. Thus the fraudulent charge of attempted rape leads not to Joseph's death, but to a prison sentence which sets the scene for his rise to power in Egypt. Once again Joseph's garment becomes key evidence for a false claim (see Gen. 37; cf. Tamar's important use of clothing in still another case of deception as well as the ludicrous attire of Jacob when he steals the blessing). Joseph has now been wrongly stripped of two different garments, but later he will receive a third kind of attire that will symbolize his royal position and prestige (cf. 41:42).

In prison Joseph immediately begins to prosper because "Yahweh was with him" (39:21,23) and rises to a kind of head trustee status. Meanwhile Pharaoh became angry with two of his officials, a chief cupbearer and chief baker, who also were put in prison. After a while, they both had dreams which troubled them. Young Joseph continues to show both sensitivity and sympathy – and no little self-confidence: noting that their faces were downcast he asks them "why?" (40:7), to which they respond: "We have had dreams, and there is no one to interpret them" (40:8). Joseph's reaction is classic: "Do not interpretations belong to God?" – a pious commonplace – but then makes the audacious request: "Please tell them to me," suggesting that he is privy to God's own thoughts, which is indeed the case. Joseph's implicit self-view squares with the narrator's observation about the divine presence with Joseph. Providential power both protects and prospers Joseph.

Joseph's interpretation of the two dreams is both accurate and witty. Superficially similar, each dream in fact discloses a radically different destiny for the two officials. After three

---

[62] Bloom, *The Book of J*, p. 208.

days Pharaoh will "lift up the head" of both cupbearer and baker: for the cupbearer this will mean restoration to his former position of favor, but for the baker it will mean decapitation and public hanging ("within three days Pharaoh will lift up your head – from you! – and hang you on a pole; and the birds will eat the flesh from you" [40:19]). The interpretations prove to be true, but the cupbearer forgets the young Hebrew dream specialist.

Two years later when Pharaoh has his duplicate dreams, the cupbearer remembers Joseph who is brought before Pharaoh and interprets his dreams. In rapid fashion Pharaoh rewards Joseph with an exalted position in Egypt, installing him as vizier, second only to Pharaoh: Joseph receives Pharaoh's signet ring, royal garments, a new name, and an Egyptian wife who bears him two sons, whose names bear the tale of Joseph's "rags to riches" career: Manasseh ("For God has made me forget [*nassani*] all my hardship and all my father's house") and Ephraim ("For God has made me fruitful [*hiprani*] in the land of my misfortunes") (41:51,52). Once more puns on the sons' names carry the history of the father.

With Joseph installed in his new position of authority, the stage is set for the appearance of his brothers who must come to Egypt to buy grain given the extent of the famine. When Jacob learns about the grain in Egypt, he is quick to chide his sons: "Why do you keep looking at one another?" (42:1). His question reveals that marvelous ability of the narrator to disclose in simplest fashion a father's impatience at his sons' befuddlement in a crisis situation, a small but telling indication of the long history of Jacob's tendency to think lightly of the qualities of his surviving sons.

Once the brothers arrive in Egypt and have an audience with Joseph, he is quick to recognize them, but he masks his knowledge by treating them "like strangers" (playing upon the root *nkr*). Viewing his prostrate brothers, Joseph remembers his earlier dreams of exaltation (42:9). Showing himself a true heir of his father, he displays similar gifts of disguise and dissimulation, harshly interrogating his brothers and accusing them of being spies. Ostensibly testing his brothers (42:15,16), he ferrets out information about his father and his youngest brother, even while discerning whether his brothers might have changed in character. Many interpreters have been troubled with Joseph's rather harsh, manipulative manner, but when one thinks of the *leitmotif* of deception at work in the larger story his behavior is not at all out of place. To be sure, since he is the preeminently successful survivor, he is no longer an underdog figure who must resort to tricks; he is now the master puppeteer who can manipulate his brothers to bring about his desired end, thereby orchestrating events to reach the happy ending of reunion and reconciliation.

Joseph's series of tests is in fact a carefully staged "play within a play" which focuses on the mysteriously returned money as a way to highlight the brothers' dilemma. When Joseph's brothers discover a bag of money in their sacks, they are at first utterly dismayed, exclaiming to one another, "What is this that God has done to us?" (42:28). It is comically incongruous that the brothers invoke God to explain their predicament, whereas we the readers know that it is all Joseph's doing. Their victimization at the hands of Joseph is further heightened when they confess to their father how and why they left one of his sons as surety that Benjamin would come down. In the reprise of their speech before Joseph, they emphasize how they are "honest men" (repeating the phrase three times!), an emphasis that is then ironically subverted when they discover their bags of money. Though they are dismayed (how often in the story are the brothers dismayed), their father stresses how the loss of Joseph and Simeon coupled with the threat of Benjamin's loss would bring him to an early grave (42:36–38). He accuses them of bereaving him of his children. Although the poignancy of the scene from Jacob's side is compelling, any thought of tragedy is undercut not only by Jacob's "poor me" routine ("All this has happened to me" [42:36b]), but also by our knowledge of the survival of Joseph. The whole scene continues the elaborate trick Joseph is playing on his brothers and his father, a charade that may appear to be cruel, but one designed to get the brothers to bring down Benjamin and not allow them to perpetrate further deception of their own. That is, if Joseph had simply identified himself to his brothers at the outset and sent them back to bring down their father and youngest brother, they could have gone home and never said a word about Joseph's survival and brilliant success. After all, it is hardly to their advantage to become honest now.

The famine is relentless in its severity and forces Jacob to permit Benjamin to accompany his sons in their return to Egypt. When Joseph sees that Benjamin is with them, he orders that they be brought into his house. Of course the brothers draw the wrong conclusion and remember the returned money: "It is because of the money, replaced in our sacks the first time, that we have been brought in, so that he may have an opportunity to fall upon us, to make slaves of us and take our donkeys" (43:18). As often, the brothers are characterized as rather witless simpletons whose fear makes them lose their sense: Joseph has the power to seize them any time and hardly needs to bring them into his house. Their falsely perceived predicament is further compounded by their explanation about the returned money to Joseph's steward who simply declares that God must have done it: "Rest assured, do not be afraid; your God and the God of your father must have put treasure in your sacks for you; I received your money" (43:23).

When the brothers finally have their audience with Joseph, he inquires about the health of his father and then sees Benjamin, a scene that is so moving to Joseph that he must step out of the room to weep and recompose himself. But he continues to mask his identity, returning only to order the serving of the meal. Maintaining initially the strict separation between Egyptians and Hebrews (43:32), Joseph has his brothers seated before him, "the firstborn according to his birthright and the youngest according to his youth," an action that amazes his brothers. He further confounds his brothers by means of the seating arrangement with clear-cut favoritism for Benjamin, giving him five times more than the other brothers – still another mystifying turn when viewed from the brothers' perspective. Given the strange pattern of events, the concluding note is perhaps belied: "They drank and were merry with him" (43:34b). Just how merry could they be under the circumstances?

But Joseph is still not finished with his charade and stages one more act in setting up his brothers for the climactic recognition scene. Once more Joseph instructs his steward to replace their money in their sacks, this time adding his special silver cup in the sack of his youngest brother Benjamin. After his brothers begin their return trip, Joseph directs his steward to give chase and to accuse them of stealing the cup: "Why have you returned evil for good? Why have you stolen my silver cup? . . . You have done wrong in doing this?" (44:4b, 5b). The steward complies and confronts the brothers with the charge of thievery to which they offer an impassioned defense, climaxing with the offer: "Should it be found with any one of your servants, let him die; moreover the rest of us will become my lord's slaves" (44:9). Mitigating the self-pronounced death sentence, the steward says that the guilty party need only to be enslaved. When the search is made, the cup of course is discovered in Benjamin's sack, which makes the brothers tear their clothes and then return to the city once more to confront Joseph.

Joseph repeats the charges against the brothers which Judah seeks to answer: "What can we say to my lord? What can we speak? How can we clear ourselves? God has found out the guilt of your servants; here we are then, my lord's slaves, both we and also the one in whose possession the cup has been found" (44:16). Joseph counters and says that only the guilty one – namely Benjamin – needs to stay, whereas the others can "return in peace to their father" (44:17).

Once again Judah steps forward, giving an eloquent and moving speech which recapitulates the unhappy events of the family history, and pleading that if Benjamin does not return Jacob will die. Judah then offers himself in Benjamin's place.

Judah's speech has its effect on Joseph who can no longer control himself and at long last reveals his identity to his

brothers: "'I am Joseph. Is my father still alive?' But his brothers could not answer him, so dismayed were they at his presence" (45:3). Joseph commands his brothers to come closer,
and he again identifies himself, this time telling a fuller story
and mitigating their guilt by invoking divine providence as
the fundamental reason for his Egyptian sojourn: "I am your
brother Joseph, whom you sold into Egypt. And now do not
be distressed, or angry with yourselves, because you sold me
here; for God sent me before you to preserve life" (45:4–5).
Joseph continues and tells about his appointment to high
and honored position in Egypt, urging his brothers to bring
his father and the whole family down to Egypt in order to be
near them and take care of them. Joseph kisses his brothers
and weeps over them, an act which loosens their tongues so
that they can finally talk with Joseph.

This climactic recognition scene includes both revelation
and reconciliation, a climax which simultaneously serves as
the turning-point of the whole narrative. Interpreters have
often focused on Joseph's long build-up to his revelation of
his identity, centering on Joseph's seeming "cruelty."[63] One
may note that Coats consistently calls the Joseph story a
"family tragedy" which illustrates again how close comedy
and tragedy can be. Here, however, one must consider
Joseph's role as master trickster, well-versed in the arts of disguise and deception who can out-do both father and brothers in engaging in tricky tactics. Joseph must resort to such
tactics in order to manipulate his brothers to recognize not
only his identity as their brother, but to see also his powerful
status as the one who had in fact fulfilled his dreams of grand
accomplishment. In contrast to his brothers' deceptive conspiracy against him, Joseph's deception is ultimately benign,
done in the service of reconciling love and designed to effect
reunion with his father and all the family. Here the narrative
is marked by irony, "the irony of ultimates and incommensu-

---

[63] See the discussion in George W. Coats, *From Canaan to Egypt: Structural and
Theological Context for the Joseph Story*, The Catholic Biblical Quarterly Monograph Series
4 (Washington, DC: The Catholic Biblical Association of America, 1976), pp.
82–89.

rates."[64] Characterizing Joseph as an "ironic theologian," Bloom strikes to the heart of Joseph's intimate relationship with Yahweh, whose "restless dynamism becomes in Joseph affectionate mischief, or the cunning resourcefulness of his father Jacob, free now to turn itself to play, since everything comes as easily to Joseph as it comes so desperately hard to Jacob."[65] Joseph's ironic play is absorbed in a comic vision of reconciliation and restoration.

In the reunion of the whole family on Egyptian soil I want to single out three moments which highlight the comic spirit. First, in the reunion itself between the aging father and his long-lost son, we hear once again the triumph of life in the midst of the shadows of death. When Jacob meets his beloved Joseph, he simply declares amidst the joyful tears: "I can die now, having seen for myself that you are alive" (46:30). Second, in Jacob's audience with the Pharaoh, he shows that he is ever the typical Jacob, responding to the Pharaoh's question about his age with a direct answer which is immediately coupled with a rather self-serving comment designed to elicit sympathy: "The years of my earthly sojourn are one hundred and thirty; few and hard have been the years of my life. They do not compare with the years of the life of my ancestors during their long sojourn" (47:9). Though interpreters usually have imputed to these lines an unduly sombre tone, perhaps a closer look suggests that Jacob is simply playing an old game: one hundred and thirty is no mean life (ten more years than the one hundred and twenty limit of Genesis 6:3), and after all he does live on another seventeen years; his answer smacks more of a "poor me" quality, and the quality of pathos is possibly a little strained. Third, Joseph sets up Pharaoh by instructing his brothers how to answer the Egyptian sovereign, an answer designed to elicit from the generous but not too bright Pharaoh an assignment to the land of Goshen which was the most favorable from the Israelite perspective. As Gunkel saw long ago, the narrator here delights in exposing the stupid-

---

[64] Bloom, *The Book of J*, p. 233.   [65] *Ibid.*

ity of Pharaoh, demonstrating the superiority of Joseph in shrewd manipulation.[66]

Two other scenes in the context of Jacob's death express a comic sensibility. In the series of death-bed blessings, Jacob wants to bless Joseph's two sons, Manasseh and Ephraim. In executing the blessing, Jacob crosses his hands so as to place his right hand on Ephraim, second-born son, and his left hand on the first-born Manasseh. In Joseph's eyes, Jacob seems to make a mistake due to his failing vision, since the first-born Manasseh ought to receive the primary blessing signaled conventionally by the strategic right hand. Joseph tries to correct his father: "'Not so, my father! Since this one is the first born, put your right hand on his head.' But his father refused, and said, 'I know my son, I know; he also shall become a people, and he also shall be great. Nevertheless his younger brother shall be greater than he, and his offspring shall become a multitude of nations'" (48:18–19). Evoking the memorable scene of Jacob's wresting by deceit the blessing from his old blind father, history here repeats itself, this time by conscious design: so primogeniture is again set aside, and the greater blessing goes to the younger son. The exchange between Jacob and Joseph not only echoes the past reversal, but shows again the comic spirit, subverting the conventional pattern and thus making a seeming mistake to be exactly correct. Bloom rightfully calls our attention to the Yahwist's "comic powers" which are at work, a comic sensibility that indirectly and ironically reenacts the fateful earlier scene of blessing and manifesting thereby "the humor of Jacob's lifelong habits persisting to the end . . ."[67]

The last scene has sometimes been called the climax of the Joseph story, coming immediately in the wake of father Jacob's death and funeral. The brothers remain forever their uncertain, hapless selves, thinking Joseph will at last exact revenge now that their father was gone. So they approach their brother and tell what seems to be a bold-faced lie: "Your father gave this instruction before he died, 'Say to Joseph: I

[66] Gunkel, *Genesis*, p. 465.   [67] Bloom, *The Book of J*, p. 239.

beg you, forgive the crime of your brothers and the wrong they did in harming you.' Now therefore please forgive the crime of the servants of the God of your father. Joseph wept when they spoke to him. Then his brothers also came, fell down before him, and said, 'We are here as your slaves'" (50:16–18). We have no record that Jacob gave any such instructions which in their thrust and tone smack of the same old habitual behavior of the brothers who are constantly unsure of their position in regard to Joseph and who therefore resort to deception. They cannot believe that all is really forgiven. Note, for example, how they repeat twice the imploring words that Joseph should forgive them, substituting "the servants of the God of your father" for "your brothers" (50:17). The language and situation is too staged, reflecting the age-old patterns of behavior that mark the brothers.

The brothers' anxious ploy, however, sets the stage for Joseph to offer a climactic commentary on his whole history with his brothers: "Joseph said to them, 'Do not be afraid! Am I in the place of God? Even though you intended to do evil to me, God intended it for good, in order to preserve a numerous people, as he is doing today'" (50:19–20). Do we not find here a fitting consummation not only to the Joseph story per se, but to the entire book of Genesis? As we recall, the creator affirms and celebrates his creation with the repetition of "good," a good that is threatened by human actions of "evil," but a good that cannot be completely effaced or erased. The opening scenes of creation which also feature the contested possession of "the knowledge of good and evil" reach their appropriate climax by Joseph's reaffirmation of the divine purpose to bring about good in the face of evil, life in the midst of death. So good continues to be wrought, and the divine purpose expressed in the command to be fruitful and multiply continues to be fulfilled: "God intended it for good, in order to preserve numerous people, as he is doing today" (50:20). The affirmation of the divine goodness in preserving life becomes Joseph's pledge that God continues to act on behalf of the whole world. That Joseph concludes his healing, reconciling speech with added reassurance to his brothers is especially touching: "'So have no fear; I myself will provide for you and your little ones.' In this way he reassured them, speaking kindly to them" (50:21). In the end Joseph ironically does stand in the place of God, offering consoling words and gestures for his anxious, doubting brothers. What we find in the Joseph story can perhaps best be called a "comedy of forgiveness,"[68] a comedy which revels in the reconciliation of broken families, in the reaffirmation of life, and in the revelation of a mercy beyond merit or measure.

CONCLUSION

Now I must end my deliberations on Genesis, and in the spirit of most comedies, it is best to close with a happy ending. I have attempted to argue the case for the comedy of Genesis from three interrelated perspectives. (1) The characterization of the major figures in the Genesis story shows a cast dominated by tricksters, dupes, and innocent victims. Jacob of course is the master trickster, but Eve, Abraham, Sarah, Rebekah, Laban, Leah, Rachel, Tamar, and Jacob's sons also are all adept in playing this role. Adam, Esau, and Isaac, in particular, appear as dupes and victims, outwitted, manipulated and deceived by stronger and smarter persons. (2) The usual stylistic and thematic strategies of comedy – word-plays, especially the powerful and pivotal puns on key names such as Adam, Eve, Noah, Abraham, Sarah, Isaac, Jacob/Israel and Esau/Edom, as well as the twelve sons of Jacob; ironic twists and turns; hyperbole; and parody – run through the narrative. (3) The U-shaped plot of comedy recurs throughout the whole story; indeed, the narrative contains what Anne Bingham aptly calls a "series of little u's,"[69] all set within a comprehensive pattern which typically moves from fragile harmony to conflict and estrangement and finally upward to reconciliation and restoration. Thus the book of Genesis pos-

---

[68] I owe this designation to Robert Grams Hunter, *Shakespeare and the Comedy of Forgiveness* (New York: Columbia University Press, 1965).

[69] Bingham, "Ruse, Romance, and Resolution," p. 3.

sesses the fundamental ingredients of the comic vision as I
have characterized it.

Yet one may still legitimately ask the question, "so what?"
One might rightly wonder what larger meaning and intention the comic forms convey. As I observed in the introduction, interpreters have long found comic and humorous
elements in Genesis. Usually these elements have been connected with the folkloristic milieu of these ancient tales,
comical residues that have been left in the narratives perhaps
to add a touch of color, to spark laughter, or to serve as
entertainment. Though this view may have its validity, I do
not think it goes far enough.

In my judgment, the comic vision contributes rich insight
into the dynamic that animates the whole Genesis story. First,
the comedy performs a *critical* function. It does not just entertain. As Brueggeman puts it in reference to the Jacob story,
its humor is "partisan and polemical."[70] As comedy with a
cutting edge it uses the age-old comic strategies of caricature,
parody, and satire, strategies directed against many of the
principal characters. Adam, for example, surely comes off
second best in relationship to mother Eve, who is much more
resourceful and decisive than her husband. Moreover, Lot is
satirized in his relationship with his daughters. Esau of course
emerges as a classic simpleton and is caricatured as a dupe,
one who is slow-witted and stupid, unable to think of the
future; one, in short, who sells his birthright for a pot of stew.
But even Jacob is satirized – a trickster who himself can be
duped, a rogue who sometimes engages in deception even
when it is unnecessary. Yet Jacob can be lovable. After all he
falls in love and is willing to work fourteen years for his
beloved; he is therefore resilient and tenacious in his struggle in life and for life. He is a figure intensely and warmly
human, one who is realistically drawn as a complex, contradictory, and wonderfully colorful man. That Jacob/Israel
especially mirrors Yahweh in all his ways compellingly represents the divine-human bond in Yahwistic faith and literature.

[70] Walter Brueggemann, *Genesis* (Atlanta: John Knox Press, 1982), p. 250.

Second, the comic vision, as unfolded in the Book of Genesis, is usually *conciliatory*. Typically, the antagonists ultimately reconcile, and violence and death are exceptional occurrences which nonetheless show the shadow side of tragic existence that hovers over the story of human beings. But the way of peace and reconciliation prevails. Hence negotiation and the possibility of rapprochement remain open. How much better this comic emphasis on conciliation than the way of violence, war, and death, a way represented, for example, in all its horror in the Deuteronomic ideology of holy war (adumbrated in the macabre story of rape and revenge in Genesis 34). The way of Genesis is much more humane in its winsome comedy of compassion, reconciliation, generosity, and forgiveness.

Finally, the comic vision is *celebrative*: it affirms *life* even in the midst of exile, loneliness, and death. Again and again we have seen how the U-shaped plot presses on toward the reaffirmation and celebration of life – especially focused on the continuation of life, a theme that has been a decisive determinant from the first commandment to be fruitful and multiply in the original creation (Gen. 1:28). Just as marriages and births are the driving force of the Adamic and Abrahamic cycles, so marriages and births coupled with conflict over blessing and inheritance continue to dominate the dramatic action of the Jacob/Israel story. The difficulties and delays in fulfilling the commandment to multiply and master come out repeatedly in the Genesis stories. Isaac – whose name ought to evoke laughter and celebration – is born to over-age parents and is almost sacrificed, though he survives and lives to see the blessing continue is spite of various obstacles. Moreover, in securing the blessing for himself and his family, Jacob may be a trickster, but he is still a maddeningly lovable figure, a delightful, irrepressible rogue who embodies in his double name and identity of Jacob/Israel the fears and hopes, sorrows and joys, failures and triumphs of the people he mirrors. Thus the story of Genesis focuses on families that are often unhappy, but it unfolds ultimately within a comic vision, a vision aware of the threatening, terrifying shadows of loneliness and death, yet a vision at the same time vibrant with the drive to blessing and new life within a human community. The story may be filled especially with trickster tales, but the tales finally revel in the comic rhythms of a universe alive with the divinely charged power of rebirth and regeneration.

PART II

Generating comedy: biblical texts and the drive to comic regeneration

CHAPTER 3

Liberation and laughter: Exodus and Esther as two comedies of deliverance

The central myth of the Bible, from whatever point of view one reads it, is also a myth of deliverance.

(Northrop Frye)[1]

The essential drive of comedy is toward liberation, whether of the central characters, a pair of lovers, or its whole society, and so comedy has the same narrative shape as many of the programmes in religion that lead toward the goals of salvation or enlightenment or beatitude.

(Northrop Frye)[2]

True ambivalent and universal laughter does not deny seriousness but purifies and completes it . . . Laughter does not permit seriousness to atrophy and to be torn away from the one being, forever incomplete. It restores this ambivalent wholeness.

(Bakhtin)[3]

INTRODUCTION

Exodus and Esther do not come readily to mind as related stories, yet one can make a case for the mutually illuminating potential of the combination. In fact, Gerleman has argued the thesis of explicit inter-linkage most vigorously, though his proposal has not commanded wide assent.[4] In his judgment,

---

[1] N. Frye, *The Great Code*, p. 50.
[2] Northrop Frye, *The Myth of Deliverance: Reflections on Shakespeare's Problem Comedies* (Brighton: The Harvester Press, 1983), p. 14.
[3] Bakhtin, *Rabelais and His World*, p. 123.
[4] Gillis Gerleman, *Esther* (Neukirchen-Vluyn: Neukirchener Verlag, 1973), p. 11.

Esther was consciously and explicitly written as an antithetical response to Exodus involving a desacralizing thrust. While not agreeing with all the various parallels he cites or the over-arching model that he delineates, I nonetheless think that heuristic use can be made of his proposal to look at the two books in tandem. In particular I think that the two books may be fruitfully viewed as two comedies of deliverance, comedies that not only share certain similarities in plot-line, but also similar characterizations of major figures as well as common rhetorical strategies that feature incongruity, irony, hyper-bole, repetition, and satire.

Rather than Gerleman's model of Esther as a conscious antithesis to Exodus, I share the insight of other interpreters that it is more compelling to set the two books in a larger circle of affiliated texts, a complex nexus of "intertexts" which create a rich and suggestive pattern of inter-linkages. Hence both Exodus and Esther have vital resonances with Genesis, especially the Joseph and Jacob stories, connections long recognized.[5] Moreover, the Joseph story, Esther, Daniel, Judith, and other narratives form an even wider circle of affiliation, comprising various sorts of stories of deliverance within an exilic setting, tales which create and foster "a life-style for the diaspora."[6] Where I hope to go beyond the usual patterns of interconnection is to show how Exodus and Esther also draw upon the comic vision to express their differ-ent narrative versions of deliverance.

EXODUS AS COMEDY

Exodus has not usually been considered as an embodiment of the comic vision. To be sure, David Robertson has offered an ingenious, provocative interpretation of Exodus 1–15 as a comedy. Using Frye's model of comedy in which the hero is

---

[5] See the handy summary in the useful dissertation by Sandra Beth Berg, *The Book of Esther: Motif, Themes and Structure*, Society of Biblical Literature Dissertation Series 44 (Missoula: Scholars Press, 1979), note 45, p. 24.

[6] See the illuminating study by W. Lee Humphreys, "A Life-style for the Diaspora: a Study of the Tales of Esther and Daniel," *Journal of Biblical Literature* 92 (1973), pp. 211–223.

reintegrated in the society to which he or she rightfully belongs after a long struggle to establish the power of the deity, Robertson argues that Exodus 1–15 is a comedy whose conventional structures become more sharply profiled when contrasted with Euripides' tragedy, *The Bacchae.*[7] With the notable exception of the indefatigable Gottwald, most biblical scholars have paid little heed to Robertson's suggestive interpretation, which is unfortunate.[8] I think Robertson has presented an illuminating possibility, but I contend, on the one hand, that he unduly narrows the parameters of his comic theory to become oversimply a factor of plot and, on the other hand, that he has a limited view of comedy in relationship to its potential to express ambiguity and irony which he rather arbitrarily excludes.

In my view Exodus contains a complex, many-faceted vision of comedy that not only possesses the plot-line identified by Robertson, but also represents key characters in typical comic guise and reveals a powerful manipulation of such stock and trade comic strategies as parody, satire, repetition, exaggeration, ironic reversal, and word-play. Moreover, it is important not only to delineate the literary dimensions of the alleged comedy of Exodus, but it is vitally important to highlight its social and theological functions within the life-settings of ancient Israelite and Jewish communities of faith.

Whatever the complexity of various sources that lie behind our present story, its structure is highly stylized and reveals skillful artistry. Its major elements are fairly clear, manifesting a purposeful structure: Exodus 1 serves as *bridge and background*, recapitulating Israel's story of migration to Egypt in the time of Jacob and Joseph and refocusing the Genesis story's benign conclusion in light of the subsequent oppression which comes with a new Pharaoh "who no longer knew

---

[7] Robertson, "Comedy and Tragedy: Exodus and the Bacchae," in *The Old Testament and the Literary Critic*, pp. 16–32.

[8] Norman K. Gottwald, *The Hebrew Bible: A Socio-Literary Introduction* (Philadelphia: Fortress Press, 1985), pp. 220–221. Gottwald finds Robertson's study "useful in posing questions about the larger design and intent of Exodus 1–15" in comparison with the Greek tragedy, but faults it for failing to "take sufficient account of their differences in literary genre and sociohistoric setting" (pp. 220–221).

Joseph" and who issues the genocidal decree to kill all the Hebrew baby boys. Against this dark, forbidding backdrop, Exodus 2 leads off with the story of Moses' *birth* (2:1–10) which is matched at the end of the Pentateuch by the story of Moses' *death* (Deut. 34), the two stories functioning as frames for the rest of the Pentateuchal narrative which becomes an ancient "biography of Moses."[9] Hence our narrative of deliverance (Ex. 1–15) is the first major part of a comprehensive biography of Moses whose story becomes the context for a foundational telling of Israel's story. After the *birth of a hero* (2:1–10) we find a series of episodes which depict *the unmaking and remaking of a hero* (2:11–4:31), a section which begins with Moses' failure and flight (2:11–21), centers in his call and commission (3:1–4:17), and concludes with his return and reintegration into his true community (4:18–31). All of these episodes are preliminary to and preparatory for the major confrontation between Moses and Pharaoh, an encounter appropriately termed *the contest between Moses and Pharaoh* (5:1–15:21) which takes the form of an elaborately constructed series of plagues (7–11) and which ends with a climactic double triumph: the slaying of the first-born on Passover Night (12–13) and the victory over Pharaoh and his army at the Red Sea (14–15).[10]

But is this famous story of deliverance a comedy? On one level, it qualifies as such by Frye's definition as suggested in the chapter's epigraphs and presented in Robertson's comic reading; hence, like comedy, the story drives toward the liberation of Moses' people from slavery (3–15) and its constitution as a new covenantal society (19–24), a deliverance severely threatened by the people's worship of the Golden Calf and only restored by an act of divine compassion

---

[9] Rolf P. Knierim, "The Composition of the Pentateuch," in *Society of Biblical Literature Seminar Papers* 24, Kent Harold Richards, ed. (Atlanta: Scholars Press, 1985), pp. 393–416; see also John Van Seters' volume, *The Life of Moses: The Yahwist as Historian in Exodus-Numbers* (Louisville: Westminster/John Knox Press, 1994), pp. 2–3.

[10] Robertson offers several compelling observations in his delineation of the contest between Yahweh and Pharaoh which he aptly calls an *agon*; see *The Old Testament and the Literary Critic*, pp. 20–27.

and forgiveness (32–34).[11] Moreover, within this grand journey toward freedom Moses and Yahweh as the two major heroes are reintegrated into the society to which they rightfully belong;[12] thus Moses becomes the divinely legitimated leader of his people, and Yahweh reunites himself with his people in fulfillment of his covenantal pledge to bring them back to the promised land. If Frye and Robertson are correct, then Exodus may be fittingly called a comedy. However, one can go further. As I earlier intimated, Robertson hurts his case when he limits himself too much to the basic plot-line of comedy and arbitrarily excludes irony from his version of the comic vision. Moreover, though he includes characterization as a part of his analysis, I feel that one must look even more closely at how the major (and even minor) characters are depicted in light of comic types and especially at how the rhetorical strategies and pivotal themes operate from a comic perspective.[13]

---

[11] Recently the exodus narrative has been especially coupled with the claims of liberation theology, claims that have been vigorously contested. I do not wish to enter into this area of debate; suffice it to say that greater concentration on delineating the dramatic qualities of the genre would contribute to sorting out the issues at stake in the debate. It is my view that appreciation of the comic character of the Exodus narrative would help to avoid false polarities often at work in "idealist" and "materialist" interpretations of the Exodus event. For a finely nuanced and balanced assessment of this ongoing discussion, see Walter Brueggemann, "Pharaoh as Vassal: A Study of a Political Metaphor," *The Catholic Biblical Quarterly* 57 (1995), pp. 27–51. Though Brueggemann never explicitly mentions the possibility of comedy as an appropriate interpretation of the Exodus narrative, his comments sometimes reveal a congeniality between his assessment of the dramatic properties of the narrative and my comprehensive comic focus; for example, compare his observation about the "playfulness" of the plague narrative: "Throughout the drama of the plagues, Yahweh is single-minded and relentless. The narrative playfulness of the drama turns much more on Pharaoh's devious, parrying, vacillating responses to the relentlessness of Yahweh than it does to Yahweh's behavior. This vacillation on the part of Pharaoh greatly enriches the dramatic, liturgical power of the narrative. That is, the witnessing Israelites, generation after generation, schooled in *ressentiment*, were invited to delight in the pitiful performance of Pharaoh" (p. 37). See below my discussion of the characterization of Pharaoh in the contest with Yahweh.

[12] Robertson, *The Old Testament and the Literary Critic*, pp. 25–26.

[13] Here Robertson has made some helpful identifications of Pharaoh and Pentheus in terms of the *alazon* or boaster who claims to know more than he does and Moses and Dionysus as examples of "the *eiron* or the one who, to expose the pretentious *alazon*, pretends to be less than he is and to know less than he knows" (*Ibid.*, p. 21).

A careful consideration of the characters shows various figures that will play roles befitting their analogues in comic narratives. Thus we have Moses as the somewhat bumbling, hesitant leader who can appear as an "anti-hero"; Aaron as the hero's helper who sometimes momentously confuses the issues and functions as a "parodic double" of Moses (cf. his role in the Golden Calf incident in Exodus 32 and his comically lame rationalization of his actions); Pharaoh as a classic villain or blocking agent (*alazon*) who appears as the oppressive, foolish tyrant; the winsome daughter of Pharaoh who surprisingly disobeys her father's decree to save the infant Moses; the court magicians who initially can match the feats of Moses and Aaron but who finally lose; the clever, resourceful Hebrew women (the midwives, Moses' mother and sister) who along with Pharaoh's daughter serve as saviors; a foreign priest and his daughters who provide home and family for the fugitive Moses; and finally the fickle Israelite masses who are easily swayed by changing fortunes and who ironically and incongruously give Moses more difficulty than the Egyptians. Fox has offered an apt description of the Israelites as "a collective anti-hero, an example of precisely how *not* to behave."[14] All these characters of course do not exclusively belong to comedies, but their particular depictions in the Exodus narrative often take on comic attributes (see below).

It is especially when one notes how the plot-line, characters, and themes work in concert within the specific rhetorical strategies of the ancient story-tellers that the comedy comes alive. Thus we need briefly to re-tell the story, highlighting for special effect its distinctly comic features. In my view, the foundational story of Israel's deliverance contains the energy of life and laughter we associate with comedy that revels in liberation and relishes the drive for the creation of a new community.

The first two chapters of Exodus are crucial in both recapitulating themes already at work in Genesis as well as antici-

---

[14] Everett Fox, *These Are The Names: A New English Rendition of the Book of Exodus* (New York: Schocken Books, 1986), p. 7.

pating the action of the major drama of deliverance in the remaining story (Ex. 3–15). From the first line of the book Jewish tradition, following ancient Near Eastern custom, derives the title of the book: "These are the names . . ." (1:1a), thus characterizing it as a "Book of Names" and furnishing it thereby with the major thematic trajectory that courses through the whole narrative of Exodus. Starting with this seemingly innocuous beginning, "These are the names . . .," Exodus may be read as a retrospective summation of the key names of the patriarchal story (the names of Jacob's sons) and a progressive revelation of the significant new names intrinsic to the drama of deliverance and disclosure, names both human and divine. At two pivotal junctures, for instance, the name of Yahweh is revealed (Ex. 3 and 6) and then powerfully proclaimed (Ex. 33:19 and 34:5–7), with echoes and reverberations throughout the entire narrative. Moreover, the book is also an intensely human tale of naming, moving from the names of Israel's sons (1:1–6) to the names of the lowly midwives (1:15) to the various names of Moses and his sons (2:10;2:22;18:3–4). (The lack of name for Pharaoh is conspicuous by its absence!) For our purposes these names are especially important because they will often contain striking word-plays that reveal not only comic wit but express in condensed versions pivotal themes of this story of deliverance.

A noteworthy feature of the two initial chapters is the relative absence of God, thus allowing the story to unfold on a human stage of events with any divine presence hidden behind the scenes.[15] This feature not only resonates with a major aspect of the preceding Joseph story, but also will reappear most forcefully later in Esther. Although the divine presence will appear spectacularly in the bulk of the story

---

[15] See the helpful analysis of the theme of God's absence in Exodus 1–2 in Donald E. Gowan's book, *Theology in Exodus: Biblical Theology in the Form of Commentary* (Louisville: Westminster/John Knox Press, 1994), pp. 1–24. Note also the penetrating observations by R. P. Carroll, "Strange Fire: Abstract of Presence Absent in the Text-Meditations on Exodus 3," in *Journal for the Study of the Old Testament* 61 (1994), pp. 39–58. As we will see later, Carroll is sensitive to the place of wit and irony in the presentation of the theme of absence in the Exodus narrative.

beginning with Exodus 3, here in the opening scenes the human actors play out their crucial roles without overt intervention by God. This rhetorical strategy both shows the human possibility for meaningful action apart from explicit divine involvement, but also heightens by way of contrast the subsequent moments of decisive divine participation.

BRIDGE AND BACKGROUND: BONDAGE AND OPPRESSION (EXODUS 1)

Exodus opens with a recapitulation of the Genesis account of the migration of Jacob's family to join Joseph (cf. Gen. 46) and then concentrates on the partial fulfillment of the commandment to "multiply and fill the earth" (Gen. 1:28). After recalling some of the initial problems of having children experienced by the patriarchs and their wives, we note how the Israelites have finally proved to be very fertile: "the descendants of Israel were fruitful and increased greatly; they multiplied and grew exceedingly strong; so that the land was filled with them" (Ex. 1:7; cf. Gen. 1:28; 9:1, 7; 17:2, 6). At long last God is beginning to fulfill his promise to the patriarchs about the multiplication of progeny. However, a cruel irony now enters the picture: the fulfillment is perversely partial – the Israelites have indeed multiplied and filled the land, but they have not mastered it; indeed, they have been mastered. Instead of numbers guaranteeing mastery, their numbers have become threatening to their Egyptian hosts who have enslaved the Israelite migrants. The Israelites have therefore numerous progeny which "fill the land," but the problem is that they are in the wrong land; they cannot become masters until they reach the promised land. The situation grows even worse: despite hard labor, their numbers continue to increase in fulfillment of the divine promise so that the Egyptians come to fear them and consequently Pharaoh enacts a genocidal decree to kill all the Hebrew baby boys.

The first description of the Pharaoh sets a satirical tone for the overall depiction of the Egyptian king: he is satirized as a cruel tyrant who is at the same time a boaster and arrogant fool. Like Haman in the book of Esther, he prides himself with his great wisdom, but he too triggers a chain reaction which ultimately will destroy himself and many of his people. Intending to "deal shrewdly" with the growing Hebrew numbers, he makes them slaves, but the "more they were oppressed, the more they multiplied and the more they spread abroad" (1:12). His policy creates the opposite effect from what he had intended: his wisdom proves to be folly. He then enacts a death decree against all the male babies, a policy which again proves to be stupid and ineffective. The midwives "fear God" and let the male children live, thus thwarting Pharaoh. In their encounter with the king the ensuing dialogue foreshadows a whole series of exchanges between the Israelite leaders and the Pharaoh, confrontations which consistently will show the king to be a short-sighted, stubborn ruler. To his question, "Why have you done this, and let the male children live?", the midwives slyly respond: "Because the Hebrew women are not like the Egyptian women; for they are vigorous and are delivered before the midwife comes to them" (1:19). The clever way the midwives justify their disobedience shows a classic trickster motif in which the quick-witted women counter the king with a deceptive rationalization that in fact is a put-down, thus satirizing both the Egyptian women (who are weak in comparison with the Hebrews) and the Egyptian king (who is not very bright). In contrast, by their "fear of God" and adroit action in the service of life, the midwives emerge as wise women who receive their due reward by having families of their own. Indeed, they are true daughters of mother Eve (note the multiple echoes of Eve's name [*havah*] in the verbal forms of bringing life or embodying life – see 1:18,19) as they live out their roles as midwives and mothers who help to produce and protect life.

The death decree, however, is not set aside, but made even more stringent as Pharaoh commands all his people, "every son that is born to the Hebrews you shall cast into the Nile, but you shall let every daughter live" (1:22). The stage is at last set for the birth of Moses, whose story forms one of the most lovely vignettes in biblical literature. A poignant story filled with human sympathy and sensitivity, it also contains multiple ironies, striking incongruities, and flashes of humor.

THE UNMAKING AND REMAKING OF A HERO (EXODUS 2:1–4:31)

The hero's birth (Exodus 2:1–10)

The story begins with an announcement of marriage between two unnamed members of the tribe of Levi whose namelessness is unusual in a "Book of Names." Conception, pregnancy, and the birth of a son soon follow – normally a joyous cycle of events – but initially missing the customary naming of the new-born child. Echoing God's action of "seeing and approving" his works of creation in Genesis 1, his mother "saw that he was good"; she then "hid him three months" (2:2). Making an ark (the same Hebrew word as in the story of Noah's ark), she casts him adrift on the waters of the Nile. His unnamed older sister then takes up her station to see what would happen to the child. Pharaoh's daughter, likewise unnamed, appears at river's edge, and spying the little ark, she commands an attendant to retrieve it. "When she opened it she saw the child; and lo, the babe was crying. She took pity on him and said, 'This is one of the Hebrews' children'" (2:6). Here is one of the tenderest moments in the story, expressing human sympathy for a condemned child told in the simplest language possible. Moses' sister promptly appears at her side, asking whether the princess wants a Hebrew nurse; she commands her to get one and when his mother comes, Pharaoh's daughter ironically hires her as the baby's nurse. Later the child's mother returns him to Pharaoh's daughter who adopts him as her son and who finally gives him his name, adding a momentous word-play that is richly suggestive of his future role as deliverer.

The story not only reveals tenderness born in basic human

sympathy, but is filled with incongruity and irony. First, it is a tale preeminently about the actions of women, who follow the lead of the midwives in defying the Pharaoh's decree.[16] In contrast to most Near Eastern narratives, the men are utterly passive, and the helpless infant's fate depends on a variety of women who enter into a kind of silent conspiracy in the service of life. The women show compassion coupled with courage and wisdom to defy the king, thus beginning the process of liberation. Second, the supreme irony is that it is Pharaoh's daughter who explicitly disobeys her father's decree by rescuing and raising as her own son the man who will ultimately defeat Pharaoh and rescue his own people. Third, a humorously ironic twist is added when Moses' sister offers to find the infant a wet nurse who of course is his own mother and who even gets paid for her services![17] Fourth, the narrator climaxes the birth story with Pharaoh's daughter's unusual naming of the child with its portentous word-play: "She named him Moses (*mosheh*)," for she said, "because I drew him (*mashiti*) out of the water" (2:10). The earlier image of the tiny ark, recalling Noah's ark, finds its fitting consummation in the rescue of a child out of the waters of death, thus anticipating the later rescue of Israel from the waters of the Red Sea.

Thus we have a wonderful foundling's tale which is ultimately a tale of three women who risk death in their commitment to life – and to the future. It parodies the genre of foundling stories by its ironic reversals and its focus on women as the true heroes. This beautiful birth story serves as a miniature version of Exodus as a comedy of deliverance, following the typical U-shaped plot-line of comedy: beginning with a normally joyous situation – the birth of a baby boy – the story plunges into potential deadliness as the child is cast

---

[16] See the variety of essays on the women in Exodus conveniently collected in Athalya Brenner's edited volume, *A Feminist Companion to Exodus and Deuteronomy* (Sheffield: Sheffield Academic Press, 1994).

[17] Note that James Ackerman also finds here "the humorous irony common to slave literature." See his essay, "The Literary Context of the Moses Birth Story," in *Literary Interpretations of Biblical Narratives*, K. R. Gros Louis, J. Ackerman, and T. S. Warshaw, eds. (Nashville: Abingdon Press, 1974), p. 94.

adrift on dangerous waters, but the traditional comic upturn to a happy ending occurs when the child is saved by Pharaoh's daughter. Moreover, even as Pharaoh's daughter sees and hears the crying of a condemned child and saves him, so Israel's God against all odds will see and hear and save his own first-born son (cf. 2:23–25; 3:7–8).[18] Finally, the stunning irony that it is a foreign princess who saves baby Moses injects a profound sense of ambiguity and comic·irony in the story which blurs absolute distinctions between "evil" Egyptians and "good" Israelites: though her father may be a cruel tyrant capable of genocide, she shows the compassion for the helpless that demonstrates the capacity of humans to be humane and sympathetic toward other humans.[19] In sum, it is a comedy of deliverance whose driving force is compassion, courage, and commitment to life amidst the threatening shadows of death.

Failure and flight of a fearful hero (Exodus 2:11–25)

Who made you a prince and judge over us?

(EX. 2:14)

With the rapid changes of pace we associate with episodic narrative, we are transported suddenly to scenes from Moses' adulthood. A series of three episodes gives striking insight into the initial steps in the making of a hero who ironically appears at first as a failed or unmade hero. Moses reflects a dual identity, marked as an Egyptian, yet still able to identify with the plight of his Israelite kindred. Moreover, he shows a sensitivity toward the oppressed, which echoes the concern for justice registered in the earlier narratives. He also manifests an impetuousness in his desire to intervene and make

[18] I owe this insight to Terence E. Fretheim in his *Exodus: Interpretation: A Commentary for Teaching and Preaching* (Louisville: John Knox Press, 1991), p. 38.

[19] Ackerman along with other interpreters has made a similar point; to be sure, he attempts – unsuccessfully in my opinion – to give a negative reading to the princess' actions. See his "The Literary Context of the Moses Birth Story," p. 93.

things right, an impetuousness which leads to his killing an Egyptian for beating an Israelite (2:11–12). His attempt to intervene in the strife between two Israelites elicits a sharp rebuke for his unwanted meddling and the revelation that the truth about the homicide was known: "Who made you a prince and a judge over us? Do you mean to kill me as you killed the Egyptian?" (2:14). His response is fear – not fear of God but fear of Pharaoh – a fear for his life that causes him to flee to Midian (2:14b–16). To be sure, at another level he is reenacting "a common motif of the hero's withdrawal into the desert before his return to Egypt in 4:18ff."[20]

Following an old convention we recall from the patriarchal narratives (see Gen. 24 and 29), Moses sits down by a well where shepherds gather to water their sheep, and he meets seven daughters of the priest Midian. One remembers the similar "type-scene"[21] where Jacob meets his future wife (Gen. 29), and thus it is not difficult to predict the outcome. Like Jacob, Moses acts the part of a hero,[22] intervening on behalf of helpless women whom rival shepherds were preventing from watering their flock. At least this time he is successful in his intervention, not only rescuing the women – playing a traditional male role – but even watering the flock himself, thus fulfilling what was usually a woman's role. The scene contains a humorous moment when the daughters return early and encounter their father. The ensuing dialogue is delightful (2:18–20): [father] – "How is it that you have come so soon today?" [daughters] – "An Egyptian delivered us out of the hand of the shepherds, and even drew water for us and watered the flock." [father] – "And where is he? Why have you left the man? Call him, that he may eat bread." As hero of the day, Moses has been left standing behind, with no immediate invitation from the rescued women. Nonetheless Moses finds

---

[20] Brevard S. Childs, *The Book of Exodus: A Critical, Theological Commentary* (Philadelphia: The Westminster Press, 1974), p. 29. See also the fine discussion in Van Seters who challenges the usual view (in *The Life of Moses*, pp. 31–33).

[21] Alter, *The Art of Biblical Narrative*, pp. 47–62.

[22] Van Seters, *The Life of Moses*, p. 31.

not only a place to stay, but also a wife when the priest gives him his daughter. Marriage is followed by the birth of a son, and we hear another significant name: "He called his name Gershom; for he said, 'I have been an alien residing in a foreign land'" (2:22).

From the perspective of comedy, the scene is noteworthy for a number of reasons. It has a finely tuned resonance with the earlier birth story in that both feature daughters in their varied relationships with Moses, but this time there is a reversal of roles in that they are daughters whom he helps, thus reciprocating the earlier compassion shown him. Moreover, it shows how the tarnished hero – despite his initial failure, fear, and flight – still attempts to be the hero, intervening on behalf of the defenseless women, and finding a new home where "he was content to dwell" (2:21) and even take a wife and have a child, though he always would remain a stranger. In contrast to Jacob's story, there is "no attempt to develop the love theme"[23] in the fashion of a traditional romance; indeed the humorous dialogue reveals that the excited daughters left their rescuer behind at the well. Van Seters has questioned the heroic nature of Moses' depiction, and perhaps he has a point in describing this episode as "very much truncated and quite unheroic in character."[24] In my view, what seems to be at work can best be explicated from a comic view: as I have indicated, Moses is at best a hero who persistently fails; hence parody of heroic conventions seems to be in play, which is epitomized in the "amusing report"[25] that the daughters in their excitement forgot their manners and embarrassingly left their heroic defender standing out in the heat, and it was only their father's intervention that rescued the rescuer.[26] Parody of his heroic stature is also revealed in his striking pun on his son's name (*gershom*) which

[23] Ackerman, "The Literary Context of the Moses Birth Story," p. 105.
[24] Van Seters, *The Life of Moses*, p. 31.
[25] John I. Durham, *Exodus: Word Biblical Commentary* 3 (Waco: Word Books, 1987), p. 22.
[26] See Childs' elegant rendering of this scene in his landmark commentary, *The Book of Exodus*, p. 30.

bears the identity and destiny of the father: "I have been an alien (*ger*) . . ." (2:22).[27]

The characterization of Moses contains profound ambiguity: identified as an Egyptian by the daughters of the priest and marrying into Midianite society, Moses continues to remain confused about his identity and his sense of place; in naming his son he in fact names himself and defines his status, a man curiously and self-consciously out of place, "an alien in a foreign land," thus experiencing the fate of his ancestors who would be "aliens in a land not theirs" (Gen. 15:13). He is incongruously a hero who has failed both as Egyptian prince and Israelite kinsman, a fugitive who must live in exile, and thus remain a perennial stranger who cannot feel fully at home in his new place with his new people. The ambiguity of his new station highlights his place on the margins of three different cultures: Egyptian court life, Israelite slave community, and Midianite pastoral society. He will always be the outsider. The unspoken question remains – what will become of this man of such mixed cultural identity and confused sense of self? What kind of hero will he make given his "unheroic" lapses? His later question in response to Yahweh's call, "Who am I?" (3:11), says it all![28]

Using a kind of flashback technique, the narrator gives us an updated report about developments back in Egypt (2:23–25), a report that serves as a kind of bracket corresponding to the opening section (1:1–7).[29] However, like the earlier text, it also functions as another bridge between past, present, and future. "The king of Egypt died and the people

---

[27] Note Isbell's perceptive observation on the significance of Moses' naming of his son: "any hint of 'heroism' in Moses is ironically circumscribed. He can be a hero (of sorts) in Midian, but not in Egypt where it really would have counted." Charles Isbell, "Exodus 1–2 in the Context of Exodus 1–14: Story Lines and Key Words," in *Art and Meaning: Rhetoric in Biblical Literature*, David J. A. Clines, David Gunn, and Alan Hauser, eds. (Sheffield: JSOT Press, 1982), p. 43.

[28] Zora Neale Hurston has exploited most effectively Moses' ambiguous sense of cultural identity in her comic adaptation of the biblical story in her novel, *Moses, Man of the Mountain* (New York: Harper & Row, 1991). See also the compelling analysis of Hurston's achievement in Lowe, *Jump at the Sun*, pp. 205–255.

[29] Durham, *Exodus*, p. 26.

of Israel groaned under their bondage, and cried out for help, and their cry came up to God. And God heard their groaning, and God remembered his covenant with Abraham, with Isaac, and with Jacob. And God saw the people of Israel and God knew . . ."(2:23–25). What is especially compelling in this bridge text is the usage of verbs in depicting God's perspective on his people's situation, since God has been notably inactive and unresponsive up to this point in the story. But now in response to the cry of the Israelites, God "heard" . . . "remembered" . . . "saw" . . . and "knew" (2:24–25). That the verse ends with the verb "know" without an object (usually supplied in various translations, e.g., RSV "God knew their condition") is suggestive in its vagueness and open-endedness, connoting possibly both God's empathetic awareness of his people's sufferings and his consideration of what to do. With its view of the past and glimpse into the future, the text is both retrospective and prospective. Also – and especially germane to the potential comedy of the story – the U-shaped plot-line bottoms out here and with the concentration on God's knowing his people's plight an ineluctable upward turn begins: God's remembrance of his covenant with the fathers implies his readiness to act on behalf of his suffering people. How will this promised future unfold? What will be the relationship between the failed, alienated hero Moses and the sympathetically knowing God in the drama of Israel's deliverance?

Call and commission of Moses as a messenger of deliverance
(Exodus 3–4)

Who am I that I should go to Pharaoh, and bring the Israelites out of Egypt?

(EX. 3:11)

Who gives speech to mortals? Who makes them mute or deaf, seeing or blind? Is it not I, Yahweh?

(EX. 4:11)

No text in the Mosaic biography has elicited more commentary than Exodus 3 and 4. It represents a famous call nar-

rative, the fullest and most varied account of prophetic vocation that we encounter in the Hebrew Bible. It is not my
purpose to rehearse the bewildering variety of commentary.
I wish instead to explore the comic potential of the text particularly in its final form. In my view, the text can be fruitfully
interpreted as a parody of Moses as prophetic messenger, a
parody in the service of comic faith which revels in the
incomparability of God's power and presence in relationship
to his reluctant prophet, a parody ironically that serves to
praise God. The use of exaggeration, repetition, and self-
conscious elaboration – in short, a fine excess of rhetoric –
leads me to describe Exodus 3 and 4 as a powerful parody. It's
all so wonderfully overdone and overdramatic.

For a long time scholars have recognized the multiple influences especially from classical prophecy and the Deuteronomic conception of the prophetic office. Indeed, an
increasingly strong case can be made that the prior and principal influences in shaping Exodus 3 and 4 come from the
prophetic and Deuteronomic circles.[30] In my view, the narrators draw upon these sources to represent Moses' call as a
parody of prophetic vocation narratives. Parody helps to
explain the supreme riddle at the heart of this account of
Moses' call to prophetic service: according especially to the
Deuteronomic school, Moses is the incomparable prophet –
such is the consistent claim (see Deut. 18, 34) – yet he shows
the most reticence and resistance of any of the prophets.
Hence the question – how and why is the greatest prophet in
Israelite history the one who most stubbornly resists Yahweh's
patient, but persistent efforts to induct him into divine
service? Why does our hero emerge as a stumbling and stam-
mering resister who resorts to virtually every reason and
excuse imaginable in offering his objections to the divine call?

Childs' incisive and compelling description of the artistic
skill of the narrator's presentation of Moses' extensive objections gives a first clue that parody might possibly be at work
in the dialogue:

---

[30] See especially the recent treatment by Van Seters, in *The Life of Moses*, pp. 35–63.

The Writer shows remarkable skill in sketching his portrayal of resistance. Moses raises five sets of objections to his commission. These are not logically connected, although they do begin with a personal focus. The progression of the dialogue is more visceral than rational. Each time in which the objection is fully met, a new one springs up, unconnected with the latter. No visible gain is ever made. The picture emerges of one person trying to reason with another who is throwing up arguments, but basically whose will, not mind, is resisting the call. Moses' initial objection points to his own inability. Soon, however, his objection can flatly contradict God and attribute the worst to the people. In the end he is trapped and his real doubt emerges.[31]

An egocentric orientation does give an inner cohesiveness to Moses' objections: first, he pleads sheer inadequacy – "Who am I to go to Pharaoh . . . ?"; second, he moves to the people's possible difficulties with the identity of the God whom Moses represents; third, he focuses on their potential disbelief in Moses himself; fourth, he returns to the theme of his inability; finally, he resorts to a plea to send someone else. Childs is right in identifying Moses' "scatter-gun" approach. But is this not a form of parody, in which the greatest prophet is shown to be exaggeratedly and randomly resistant – he simply does not want the job? In his resistance, Moses foreshadows Gideon, Jeremiah, and Jonah, but he outdoes them all in the comprehensiveness of his attempts to evade and escape his prophetic destiny. In particular, the comparison with Gideon, on the one side, and Jeremiah, on the other, helps to illumine the particular kind of call narrative we have in Exodus 3 and 4. Like Gideon, Moses is given "a vastly disproportionate space . . . to the eliciting of the dutiful response."[32] Both characters become caricatures of prophetic figures in their excessively elaborate reluctance and uncertainty. In contrast, though Jeremiah is also reluctant, he pleads his youthfulness as grounds of his inability to speak, and continues in his poignant complaints to voice his resis-

[31] Childs, *The Book of Exodus*, p. 71.
[32] Robert B. Boling, *Judges: Introduction, Translation, and Commentary* in *The Anchor Bible* (New York: Doubleday and Company, 1975), p. 132.

tance to his calling and is more sympathetically portrayed, even tragically so. Moses and Gideon both go on and on to the point of self-parody (think, for example, of the signs Gideon demands [Jud. 6]). But now we must look to the details of the case that Moses makes against his being inducted into Yahweh's service.

Moses' initial "Who am I?" sets the tone for the entire series of objections because it lays bare the basis of his extreme reluctance – namely, a pervasive sense of inadequacy as evidenced by his series of failures, beginning of course with his well-intended but disastrous attempts to intervene in Egypt and then continuing in his sense of estrangement in his adopted land. He is failed hero and fugitive, living out his life as shepherd and sojourner in a strange land: a man without a country, a man without status and significance, a man seemingly without a future. "Who am I?" represents his fundamental problem with the divine summons. The divine assurance, "I will be with you," coupled with the ambiguous sign (3:12) is not sufficient to answer his sense of inadequacy and disqualification.

Moses' second objection focuses on the potential question that the Israelites might pose as to God's identity: "What is his name?" (3:13), a question that various scholars translate as the equivalent to "Who are you?" which serves as a kind of counterpart to Moses' opening question.[33] The question also anticipates Pharaoh's question ("Who is Yahweh?") in the initial meeting between Moses and Pharaoh (5:2). God's answer to Moses' query constitutes one of the most celebrated and disputed texts in the entire Bible: *'ehyeh 'asher 'ehyeh* ("I am who I am"/"I will be who or what I will be") (3:14). For our purpose it is sufficient to underscore the multiple meanings of the cryptic response which on one level repeats the earlier assurance, "I am (*'ehyeh*) with you," but then makes the crucial identification between this "new" God YHWH and

[33] Cf. Martin Buber's enlightening discussion of the semantic range of these sorts of questions in his *Moses: The Revelation and the Covenant* (New York: Harper & Row, 1958), pp. 47–55.

"the God of the Fathers" (3:15,16). Perhaps scholars have sometimes attempted to be too precise in determining the meanings both historical and theological, thus reducing the range and richness of possible symbolism. The response first and foremost embodies a powerful pun, playing on the special name of YHWH, an inspired and ingenious instance of a wonderful word-play that both reveals and conceals, explains and evades – thus heightening the sense of mystery and irony and ultimate comedy of divine communication to humans.[34] It is a joke in language which expresses in its punch-line a profound truth: the mysterious *'EHYEH* ("I am," "I will be") is *YHWH* ("He is/He will be"), a sublimely simple equation which explodes into diverse and ultimately indecipherable symbolic possibilities. Perhaps the best paradox in this comedy of revelation is that the divine name finally translates itself as "The Unnameable." To a certain extent the whole book of Exodus – titled traditionally in Hebrew as a "Book of Names" – becomes "The Book of the NAME."[35] However, it is better to keep the original title in its plural form, because the pivotal names both divine and human continue to proliferate and to repeat themselves always with new and ever-deepening nuances (see most notably, the reiteration of the revelation of YHWH in the so-called Priestly version in Ex. 6:2ff), thus retaining depths of mystery. It is in this dialectic of singular and plural, of revealed meaning and concealed mystery that the comic drama of exodus revels.

After this puzzling, punning revelation of a new name of an old God, the narrator has God both repeat his earlier promise of deliverance in his appearance to Moses (3:16–18) and make additional announcements about what was to

[34] I concur with R. P. Carroll's pithy observations in his essay, "Strange Fire": "I read the simple punning tautology of 3.14 as a dismissive rejection of Moses' kvetching questions . . . I take the response to be somewhat short-tempered and dismissive. It says nothing and then twits Moses by inviting him to speak nonsense to the people of Israel" (p. 47). "If Matthew in the New Testament can have his Christ found the church on a pun . . ., why should the writers of the Exodus narratives not use pun, irony, tautology to evade (even misdirect?) any serious engagement with trying to understand the meaning of name now well beyond their comprehension?" (p. 48).

[35] J. P. Fokkelman, "Exodus" in *The Literary Guide to the Bible*, p. 64.

happen (3:18–22). Thus further themes are anticipated: the positive response of the Israelites to Moses' leadership (3:18); the demand of the Israelites to Pharaoh for a three-day religious holiday to offer sacrifice in the wilderness (3:18); the predicted rejection from Pharaoh that necessitates the performance of "all the wonders" in Egypt, so that he is compelled to let the Israelites go (3:19,20); finally, the "favor" Yahweh will grant in the eyes of the Egyptians that will lead to the "plundering" of Egyptian treasures (3:21,22). This last theme has elicited an incredible variety of explanations, many of which are apologetic. If our reading of the story as some kind of comedy of deliverance is correct, then such a theme of plundering is not at all strange or out of place. The narrators consistently emphasize how the Israelites from Moses on down will win out in the contest for superiority over their Egyptian overlords. This act of plunder will simply fulfill the old adage, "To the victors belong the spoils." Here too we note again how the women will be the agents of this act of despoiling, whereas typically the reference is to male warriors who collect war prizes (cf. Num. 31; Jud. 5:30, etc.). Once more it is women who play the active role of outwitting Egyptian neighbors and even resident aliens living in Israelite houses; the Egyptians are aptly described by Durham as "a marvelously gullible . . . populace"[36] whom the Israelite women only have to ask in order to receive. Of course it is Yahweh who ultimately sets up the Egyptians for their massive give-away of precious goods; he makes the Egyptians either generous or gullible depending on one's perspective concerning the meaning of divine favor in this setting. The recipients of all the jewelry will be the sons and daughters of the Israelites who will be decked out in resplendent attire for the Exodus parade.

One might suppose that the prospects of this grand spectacle of the exodus might be enough to overcome Moses' hesitance, but not so. Moses continues his objections, this time disputing the divine promise that the Israelites will believe

---

[36] Durham, *Exodus*, p. 41.

that "the God of the fathers . . . has appeared" to him (3:16). "But behold, they will not believe me or listen to my voice, for they will say that Yahweh did not appear to you" (4:1). Again Yahweh has a ready answer for Moses' objection: Yahweh moves now from words to magical deeds, enabling Moses to witness the power in his rod that can turn into a snake or his hand that can become leprous and then be restored. Both acts will serve as "signs," proving that Yahweh has in fact appeared to him; if neither of them works, then a third sign – turning Nile water into blood – will be wrought.

Thus the narrator attempts to show how God is as good as his word and will duly equip his prophetic deliverer with sufficient power to work wonders. The folkloristic motifs of the narrative illustrated in Yahweh's giving Moses a magical rod, power in the healing arts, and the ability to transform one substance into another are fairly typical. Touches of humor are even present: when Moses threw down his staff and it becomes a snake, he understandably "fled from it" (4:3). The narrator also adroitly varies the verbs to suggest the extreme caution Moses displayed in his encounter with the staff/serpent. Yahweh commands him to "put forth his hand and grab" ('ḥz) the serpent, but when he obeys he "puts forth his hand and grasps it firmly" (ḥzq, a stronger verb). Moses appears to be both convinced and no doubt relieved when the serpent turns back into a rod.

Returning to the opening theme of his inability, Moses comes up with still another argument in support of his lack of qualifications: he is not eloquent – indeed, he seems to be burdened with a speech impediment ("heavy of mouth, heavy of tongue" – 4:10). As Durham rightly remarks, Moses' "claim is wittily, perhaps even disrespectfully comprehensive,"[37] since he asserts that his condition has long been present and has not improved even during Yahweh's conversation with him (4:10). Yahweh has displayed amazing patience up to this point – now he begins to show signs of strain, though still attempting to answer Moses' objection. Appealing to his cre-

[37] *Ibid.*, p. 49.

dentials as creator, Yahweh invokes basically a wisdom argument: "Who gives speech to mortals? Who makes them mute or deaf, seeing or blind? Is it not I, Yahweh? Now therefore go, and I will be (*'ehyeh* once again) with your mouth, and teach you what you shall speak" (4:11,12). Moses, however, is relentless in his resistance, showing remarkable gifts of language for one who ostensibly lacks powers of speech – surely a striking irony! He now strips away any veneer of giving an argument and bluntly expresses his desire not to be enlisted: "Oh, my Lord, send whom you will send" – that is, send someone else! His plea harbors the real reason for his resistance: he simply does not want to go.

Finally, Yahweh's patience runs out and he becomes angry at his reluctant servant. Yahweh begrudgingly concedes Moses' sense of his rhetorical ineptitude and takes care of the fourth objection by giving him Aaron as his "mouthpiece," as his eloquent spokesman. The divine concession and compromise seem to work – at least for now (see the repetition of this objection in Ex. 6:12,30). At long last Moses dutifully complies with Yahweh's commission to return to Egypt in order to deliver the Israelites.

Return and reintegration of Moses into his true community (Exodus 4:18–31)

Truly you are a bridegroom of blood to me!

(EX. 4:25)

In terms of Frye's basic plot-line of comedy, this next phase signals the completion of a U-shaped pattern: the return of the hero and his reintegration into the community to which he rightfully belongs; to be sure, the community itself is still out of place and must be reunited with its proper homeland, the promised land, but to effect that reunion is precisely Moses' mission. Moreover, right in the middle of the return journey, Moses experiences a harrowing escape from a divine assailant.

After requesting permission from his father-in-law to go

back to Egypt, and after receiving information from Yahweh
that "all the men who were seeking [his] life [were] dead"
(4:19), Moses takes his wife and two sons and returns to Egypt
(or does he? According to Ex. 18:2–3, he had sent her away
and Jethro had taken care of her and the boys). The narrator
is careful to add that "Moses took in his hand the rod of God"
(4:20b). Yahweh then announces in advance the basic scenario in Moses' coming confrontation with Pharaoh: Moses
is to peform all the miracles, but Yahweh will harden
Pharaoh's heart so that he will not let Israel go. Moses is
directed to make a crucial announcement in Yahweh's name:
"Thus says Yahweh, 'Israel is my first-born son, and I say to
you, "Let my son go that he may serve me; if you refuse to let
him go, behold, I will slay your first-born son"'" (4:22,23). As
one looks back over Exodus 4, one notices how the text functions both programmatically and proleptically; thus the narrator offers the outline of the script in advance, supplying the
basic plot-line of what is to come: 4:9 – turning water into
blood – and 4:23 – the slaying of the first-born sons – will
serve as the first and last of the plagues that Yahweh will visit
upon the Egyptians in order to liberate his people.

Moses apparently has all that he needs to confront Pharaoh
and begins his journey back to Egypt. We then encounter an
episode that has all the marks of some primordial stranger
that disrupts and disturbs the narrative and casts a dark
shadow across the page:

At a lodging place on the way Yahweh met him [apparently Moses]
and sought to kill him. Then Zipporah took a flint and cut off her
son's foreskin, and touched Moses' feet with it, and said, 'Surely you
are a bridegroom of blood to me.' So he [Yahweh] let him alone.
Then it was that she said, 'You are a bridegroom of blood,' because
of circumcision (Ex. 4:24–26).

On the surface the text is short and straightforward, but it
has evoked enormously varied comment. For my purpose it is
not necessary to rehearse all the different opinions;[38] it suf-
fices simply to suggest how this text might fit into Exodus as

---

[38] Childs, *The Book of Exodus*, pp. 95–101, 103–104.

a "comedy of deliverance." First, I want to underscore that I do not find the characterization of Yahweh or Moses or even Zipporah strange in light of the dominant modes of representations we have encountered so far. Yahweh has consistently appeared as a complex, puzzling deity whose behavior is often seemingly capricious, fickle, even whimsical; he displays what Bloom, following Freud, calls the "uncanny."[39] We seek too quickly to domesticate or normalize Yahweh as a character in the biblical drama who often is forced to fit a scaled-down model of what allegedly a proper God should be (the apologetic intent of such safer versions is most apparent). Recall only the God who wrestles with Jacob in another night-time encounter (Gen. 32) or the God who commands Abraham to sacrifice Isaac (Gen. 22) or the God who later wants to kill all the Israelites save Moses and start over with him (Ex. 32). Yahweh's behavior is not really strange, nor is this night-time attack particularly out of place. After all, Yahweh is a God who "kills and brings to life" (I Sam. 2:6a; see also Deut. 32:39 and Isa. 45:7).

So this episode does have its own rationale and precedent: it fits into a kind of trial by ordeal that the Genesis examples illustrate (see discussion above). But it is precisely over against these oft-cited models that Exodus 4:24–26 does show some curious twists and turns. Whereas the hero is usually active and passes the test by his strength or wisdom (think of Abraham and Jacob), Moses in his deadly test is once again utterly passive. God attacks him; Zipporah saves him by her timely intervention. At this point, however, the episode fits the prevailing model of our hero who typically is "unheroic": once more a woman's action saves the day – and the hero. And it is a foreign woman who ironically knows exactly what to do and say by executing the age-old rite of circumcision on her son and transferring its benefits to Moses; thus she incorporates both males into the covenantal community, thereby making them eligible for participation in the Passover rite (see Ex. 12:48). Zipporah takes her place in that line of notable women who have rescued Moses.[40] Earlier the would-be killer was Pharaoh, who twice sought to kill Moses; but this time Yahweh is the night-time assassin who tries to kill Moses apparently because of a ritualistic lapse. Though we are prepared for this type of divine behavior (which, in fact, is "in character"), its timing seems strange – or does it? Is it not another example of the narrator's delight in changing pace, of injecting the element of surprise, of intensifying suspense? The seeming strangeness of the scene highlights God's unpredictability, his uncanniness which shows the vulnerability of any and all – hence evoking awe and fearful trembling. It is a God who apparently takes pleasure in "making sport" or "amusing himself" at the expense of all those who offend or oppose him (cf. Ex. 10:2) even when death and destruction come as a consequence.

If comedy is at work, it is a dark, sardonic comedy which is keenly aware of death and violence and yet which revels in quick-witted intervention by a woman who seeks to protect and preserve life. Thus Zipporah heroically rescues the unheroic male who is a passive victim of the divine assailant's attack which can be unleashed even against his own servant when he fails to obey (see the later divine punishment of Moses to die outside of the promised land – Num. 20; Deut. 34). The episode dramatically illustrates the type of narrative we are dealing with – a sometimes darkly comic representation of deliverance which revels in ironic reversals and "aweful" events – all in the service of life that comes in the midst of death, life and death together entwined in a dance of opposites, each one intensifying and illuminating the other. Immediately prior to this night-time attack, Yahweh had announced in advance that the climactic plague in Egypt would be the slaying of Pharaoh's first-born son as the context and condition for the liberation of Yahweh's first-born son. Yahweh will engage Pharaoh via Moses' mediation in a spectacular contest where it is foreordained that Yahweh will

---

[40] See the illuminating analysis in Pardes, *Countertraditions in the Bible*, pp. 79–97; Pardes also underscores the continuity in the roles of the female saviors as well as the subversion of Moses' role as hero (note particularly pp. 81–83 and 84–85).

demonstrate his power to free his people, but the freedom will ultimately be purchased with the blood of the first-born.

Here the story takes on the potential of tragedy, but as Robertson reminds us, our response to the story depends fundamentally on how the narrator manipulates the conventions and thus helps to determine whether or not we read it as tragedy or comedy.[41] I share with Robertson the conviction that the story dominantly falls into the domain of comedy, though tragic dimensions still play a decisive role within the story; but the comedy finally allows the tragic component to be transcended without being fully eliminated. The issue now will turn on our reading of plot, character-portrayal, and rhetorical strategies in the dramatic conflict between Yahweh and Pharaoh (Ex. 5–15).

THE CONTEST BETWEEN YAHWEH AND PHARAOH (EXODUS 5–15)

Who is Yahweh, that I should heed him and let Israel go?

(EX. 5:2)

Who is like thee, O Yahweh, among the gods? Who is like thee, majestic in holiness, terrible in glorious deeds, doing wonders?

(EX. 15:11)

All the preliminaries are now over, and we come to the main event of the exodus story which is brilliantly conceived and rendered as a series of confrontations between Moses and Pharaoh – and ultimately between Yahweh, god of the Israelites, and the gods of Egypt. Whatever the complex sources and traditions out of which the story has been spun, the story as we now have it is a highly stylized and staged event; it is a spectacle of grand proportions. I will argue that it is a complex, colorful comedy which moves between the two "Who" questions I am using as my epigraphs. Pharaoh poses the first question in his initial meeting with Moses and

---

[41] Robertson, *The Old Testament and the Literary Critic*, p. 28.

Aaron. Setting the pace for the subsequent encounters, the two Israelite emissaries open with a prophetic demand: "Thus says Yahweh, the God of Israel, 'Let my people go, so that they may celebrate a festival to me in the wilderness'" (5:1). Pharaoh then responds with his question: "Who is Yahweh, that I should heed him and let Israel go? I do not know Yahweh, and I will not let Israel go" (5:2). Whatever the digressions and disruptions in the subsequent narrative, it will function as a massive answer to this question. As we will see, the answer ultimately will move from Pharaoh's arrogant, sarcastic "Who is Yahweh?" to the climactic "Who" question sung out in the triumphal Song of Moses/Miriam: "Who is like you, Yahweh, among the gods?" (15:11). Revelation of the divine name and power is central and crucial to the narrative, but revelation must be completed by recognition. As we will see, knowledge is indeed power in the Exodus narrative, but power becomes knowledge which will be gained at great cost.

The first round of negotiations between Moses and Pharaoh proves to be disastrous as a trial run. After a forceful opening speech replete with the prophetic messenger formula to authorize the demand for release, Pharaoh responds with sarcasm and dismisses Yahweh and refuses the demand to let Israel go. Moses and Aaron attempt to counter Pharaoh, but the shift in their mode of argumentation is noteworthy. Their reply is chastened and toned-down; they no longer speak of Yahweh and refer simply to "the God of the Hebrews" who had met them unexpectedly; they ask more politely for permission to go on their three-day religious holiday in order to sacrifice to their God – "or he will fall upon us with pestilence or sword" (5:3). What is striking is not only the change of style and approach, but their addition of a divine threat if they fail to go. Nowhere in the previous instructions God gave to Moses and Aaron do we find such a threat. They seem to be making up part of their argument, saying that Yahweh has threatened to destroy the Israelites for failure to obey, whereas consistently God threatens to destroy the Egyptians if they fail to let the Israelites go. Moses' and Aaron's appeal, however, fails to persuade

Pharaoh. What follows is a classic delineation of a tyrannical regime and its ruthless efficiency in crushing the spirit of a potential revolt. The Pharaoh rebukes Moses and Aaron for · distracting the Israelites from their tasks and demands that they be responsible for the same quota of bricks, but they must now collect the straw themselves. Counterposed to the prophetic messenger formula – "Thus says Yahweh" (5:1) – is the royal word – "Thus says Pharaoh" (5:10) which authorizes the new work order. A delegation of Israelite supervisors complain to Pharaoh about the new policy, but they get no farther than Moses and Aaron (5:15–19). When these Israelites meet Moses and Aaron who were waiting for them, their words of rebuke are sharp, bitter, and incontestable: "Yahweh look upon you and judge! You have brought us into bad odor with Pharaoh and his officials, and have put a sword in their hand to kill us" (5:21). Moses has no counter-argument, taking his own complaint to God: "O Yahweh, why have you mistreated this people? Why did you ever send me? Since I first came to Pharaoh to speak in your name, he has mistreated this people, and you have done nothing at all to deliver your people" (5:22–23). Yahweh's answer is also classic: "Now you will see what I will do to Pharaoh: Indeed, by a mighty hand he will let them go; by a mighty hand he will drive them out of his land" (6:1).

I have paraphrased and quoted key parts of this long dialogue to highlight its function within what I am calling a comedy of deliverance. At first glance the scene is hardly funny, imaging realistically the harshness of an oppressive regime.[42] But then comedy is not necessarily about being funny. A closer look shows a sardonic, even cruel humor at work. God has indeed promised deliverance because of his mercy and his memory of covenantal pledges (see again 2:23–25; 3:7–8, 16–17); he has called and commissioned Moses and Aaron to be his emissaries to engage Pharaoh and demand freedom for the Israelites; he has even given them forewarning about how he would "harden Pharaoh's heart"

[42] Childs, *The Book of Exodus*, p. 106.

and only after powerful signs would the deliverance occur. Yet in the first round Moses and Aaron fail abysmally to get anywhere; in fact, the would-be deliverers are simply dismissed as nobodies. The whole scene is rife with parody of traditional prophetic-royal encounters (cf. II Sam. 12 or Isa. 7 as vivid examples of the normative pattern of such dramatic meetings). The parody signals the intent to prolong the sense of failure that has marked Moses' career as a would-be hero and deliverer from the outset. Why does this intent to dramatize failure of the commissioned prophet continue to dominate the picture? Why is Moses depicted in such a poor light, crumpling here before the pressure of Pharaoh's rebuff, even to the point of adding to the divine script he is to follow by inserting a threat that God never made? (A true prophet is not supposed to make up the divine message!) The answer to these questions seems to lie in the characterization of Yahweh as the major figure, whose relentless will is dictating the script, but whose resulting behavior contains some unflattering components. The normative tradition has focused on Yahweh's mercy and compassion as the determinative forces behind Israel's redemption from Egyptian slavery, and that theme is clearly present. But there is another side, an unpredictable side, a "demonic," destructive side that portrays a God who involves both his advocates and his opponents as pawns in a power-game, a game designed ultimately to gain greater glory for God at the expense of all the other players. If a "comedy of deliverance" is an apt description, then it is a bitter-sweet comedy that gains its power from the tense interplay between the "bitter" and the "sweet," a comedy in which horror and hope, tenderness and terror bounce off one another, culminating in Yahweh's triumph. Thus Moses as incomparable prophet must be shown up first as a failure who didn't even want the job; Pharaoh is exposed as a proud, stubborn ruler whom God will make sport of in bringing him down (see 10:2); and even God himself is also parodied as a capricious, whimsical deity who delights in his own power and glory, gloating over the defeat of any and all rivals, even when it means destruction and death.

In the documentary hypothesis, God's extended answer to Moses' complaint continues in the distinct voice of the Priestly Writer, reiterating both a revelation of the "new" name Yahweh to Moses as well as repeating Moses' objection about his lack of oratorical skill (Ex. 6:2–7:7). Though it is recapitulative and thus partially parallels the earlier Yahwistic version (see Ex. 3–4), it functions now in its present context as a "sequel, not a parallel to the call in Midian."[43] What I want to underscore is precisely the character of the text as sequel, arguing that the parallelism with the earlier texts (Ex. 3–4) is only superficial and that the more decisive parallelism comes in the complementary role of Ex. 6:2–13, 28–30 and Ex. 7:1–7. Thus the Israelite reaction to Moses is ironically paralleled by the Egyptian reaction: both will refuse to listen to Moses' prophetic words (6:9 and 7:4), yet both nonetheless "shall know that I am Yahweh" (6:7 and 7:5) – the Israelites because of their deliverance from bondage in fulfillment of the promises to the patriarchs and the Egyptians because of the same act of deliverance which meant disaster for the Egyptians. The parallelism creates a striking effect: both Egyptians and Israelites will come to recognize Yahweh by the same set of acts, one to know liberation and new life in a blessed land, the other to know death in the wake of the Israelites' liberation from an oppressive land. The revelation of the divine name Yahweh in all its power and glory is the keynote, thus confirming the Jewish title of Exodus as a "Book of Names." That the Priestly Writer has spliced in a genealogical list giving fuller identification and hence legitimation of Moses and Aaron should not cause surprise since naming in this book is the name of the game.

Yet Moses is caught in the middle of these opposing groups of Egyptians and Israelites; rebuffed by the one, rebuked by the other, he reiterates his climactic objection from his earlier encounter with God at Sinai. Two times he adverts to his weakness in being a persuasive speaker (6:12, 30), but it is repetition with a difference since his question this time

---

[43] *Ibid.*, p. 114.

about his ability is grounded in the concrete experience of rejection: "The Israelites have not listened to me; how then shall Pharaoh listen to me, poor speaker that I am?" (6:12). Neither the revelation of the new name Yahweh (6:2–3) nor the genealogical legitimation of Moses and Aaron (6:14–26) seems to make a difference: Moses remains "a man of uncircumcised lips" (6:12 and 30), whose divinely mandated speaking is simply ineffective. The contrast between the exalted, eloquent language of revelation and Moses' complaint about his inability in speech sharply illustrates both his horizontal failure in his initial encounters with Israelites and Egyptians and his vertical failure in dutifully fulfilling his divinely imposed role of prophetic messenger.

The parallel roles of Egypt and Israel with Moses thrust into the middle of this drama of revelation enhance the comedy of deliverance, since the goal of recognition of Yahweh's power and presence contains such sharply contrasting destinies for Egyptians and Israelites. If comedy revels in opposites, spotlighting unexpected turns in the major story line, then Exodus surely deserves such a characterization. Rather than excluding irony as Robertson argues, the Exodus storytellers exploit to the full various forms of comic irony as they present curiously complementary and contradictory depictions of the Israelites and the Egyptians.[44] Both nations will come to know Yahweh, but the consequences of their knowing him are dramatically different.

Round two of the contest between Moses and Aaron and Pharaoh and his magicians now takes place after the reassurances to Moses. The ante is raised to include a wondrous deed as well as prophetic word. So Moses directs Aaron to do the trick of turning the staff into a snake. Not to be outdone the Egyptian magicians duplicate the feat – but the narrator then adds the "punchline" in this battle of wonders: "Aaron's staff swallowed up theirs" (7:12b). This humorous twist symbolizes the ultimate victory of Moses over Pharaoh; yet as predicted, the whole display has no real effect on Pharaoh, whose "heart

---

[44] Robertson, *The Old Testament and the Literary Critic*, pp. 28–29.

was still hardened, and he would not listen to them, as Yahweh had said" (7:13).

At last the contest between Pharaoh and Moses has been joined, focusing at the beginning on the "face-off" between Aaron as Moses' representative and Pharaoh's magicians. The first two plagues – water into blood and frogs – end in a draw. Here one cannot overlook the ironic and humorous elements in the contest with the magicians: normally one would expect the magicians to show their power by taking care of the problem, i.e., reversing the effects of the plague – but strangely they get caught up in matching the wonders, thus incredibly worsening an already bad situation. They consequently emerge as fools instead of wise magicians who get locked into a pattern of self-defeating competition that can only lead to their utter defeat and humiliation. The comical picture of frogs hopping everywhere is rendered in humorously fulsome detail: "The river shall swarm with frogs; they shall come up into your palace, into your bedchamber and your bed, . . . and into your ovens and your kneading troughs. The frogs shall come up on you and on your people and on all your officials" (8:3–4). After the land is overrun with frogs (whose numbers have been further multiplied by the Egyptian magicians), Pharaoh appeals to Moses and Aaron to "pray to Yahweh to take away the frogs from me and my people, and [he] would let the people go to sacrifice to Yahweh" (8:8). Prayer works, the frogs die off; but Pharaoh's promise was a ruse, and he continues in his obduracy (8:15).

The third plague – gnats – continues this contest, but with a difference; now for the first time the magicians cannot duplicate the wonder (why would they want to?): "the magicians tried to produce gnats by their secret arts, but they could not" (8:18). We then read their begrudging admission: "This is the finger of God," but their recognition has no impact on Pharaoh whose "heart was hardened, and he would not listen to them, just as Yahweh had said" (8:19).

The fourth, fifth, and sixth plagues unroll with everincreasing deadliness: the plague of flies ruins the land of Egypt, but the land of Goshen where the Israelites dwell is spared, "so that you might know that I Yahweh am in this land" (8:22). The next plague is a "deadly pestilence" that strikes the livestock of the Egyptians, while sparing the livestock of the Israelites. Both these plagues unite in showing how Yahweh distinguishes between the Egyptians and the Israelites; both show with thudding monotony how Pharaoh continues to harden his heart and refuse to let the Israelites go. The sixth plague – "festering boils" (9:9–11) – strikes both humans and animals, thus rendering the magicians unable to "stand before Moses" (9:11). The magicians present a painful but ludicrous pose, forfeiting any further role in the contest. Moreover, along with the disappearance of the magicians, we note that Aaron ceases to play any active role. The place of the various assistants is over, and now the confrontation is directly between the divinely guided Moses and the increasingly stubborn Pharaoh. Finally, this time it is Yahweh who "hardens the heart of Pharaoh, and he would not listen to them, just as Yahweh had spoken to Moses" (9:12).

Decidedly different notes are struck in the next two plagues: they are more elaborate; they are said to be unprecedented (9:18,24; 10:6,14); they have the effect of making Pharaoh more accommodating and even contrite in the negotiations; and most important for determining the general intention of the plague narratives, they both contain programmatic descriptions of the overarching divine purpose in the series of disasters. These announcements convey vividly the stakes of the game and the character of the dramatic action. The first comes in connection with the seventh plague, serving as a prologue for the next display of divine judgment, but also offering a comprehensive explanation for the whole series of plagues.

For this time I will send all my plagues upon you yourself, and upon your officials, and upon your people, so that you may know that there is no one like me in all earth. For by now I could have stretched out my hand and struck you and your people with pestilence, and you would have been cut off from the earth. But this is why I have let you live: to show you my power, and to make my name resound through all the earth. (9:14–16)

Yahweh's intention here is crystal-clear: he could have totally destroyed Egypt, but he held his hand in order that Pharaoh would recognize and acknowledge Yahweh's incomparability in the demonstration of divine power and that Yahweh's name would be proclaimed throughout the world. Here we have a rather blatant representation of the plagues as a power game designed for Yahweh to win the contest at the expense of Pharaoh. Pharaoh is only kept alive to witness the power of God; he becomes thereby a puppet in Yahweh's drama of self-promotion: Pharaoh would "know that there is no one like me in all the earth." That the apostle Paul chooses this text to support his argument about the absolute sovereignty of God reflects an accurate reading and appropriation of the Exodus text (cf. Rom. 9:17).

The nature of the confrontation as a grand contest becomes even more sharply profiled in the second programmatic text which is the prologue to the locust plague; once again it is a speech of Yahweh to Moses:

Go to Pharaoh; for I have hardened his heart and the heart of his officials, in order that I may show these signs of mine among them, and that you may tell your children and grandchildren how I have made fools of the Egyptians and what signs I have done among them – so that you may know that I am Yahweh. (10:1–2)

Once more we hear a reiteration of Yahweh's overweening power and need to be recognized not just in the present, but long into the future. Yahweh commands Moses to be the master narrator of a tale that is to be told and retold for future generations of Israelite children. One is especially struck by the specific content of this narration for the future: "How I have made fools of the Egyptians and what signs I have done among them." The notice about "signs" is a general category for the divine acts in Egypt, but the lead-off statement about Yahweh's "making fools" of the Egyptians is unique, though it catches precisely and comprehensively Yahweh's (and the Israelites') showing up of the Egyptians and especially the Pharaoh from the beginning of the Exodus story until the climactic end of the Egyptians at the Red Sea. The word itself is interesting and has received a variety of translations. S. R. Driver still catches succinctly the semantic range: "The Heb. word is applied in a bad sense, to 'divert oneself at another's expense,' to *make a toy of*, or by a slight paraphrase, to *mock.*"[45] Other typical translations are "make sport of" or "amuse oneself" or "make a fool of." The word appears, for example, in the context of battle where the victor revels in triumph over the fallen hero; after Saul is mortally wounded he commands his armorbearer to kill him lest the Philistines "come and thrust me through, and make sport of me" (I Sam. 31:4). Or in the humorous encounter between Balaam and his donkey, the prophet is so angry at his donkey that he beats it and when challenged justifies his action by saying: "Because you have made a fool of me! I wish I had a sword in my hand! I would kill you right now!" (Num. 22:29). Yahweh intends to keep Pharaoh alive only so that he can "make a fool of" his opponent, toying with him and making sport of him so that Yahweh gains the "glory." The result will be a compelling story to narrate to children in the future who will take delight in Yahweh's glorious victory over the foolish Pharaoh. (The Passover Haggadah is the best illustration of the success of this ancient intention.) It is not surprising therefore that the Deuteronomistic historian chose to put this memorable episode on the lips of Philistine priests and diviners as an instance of Yahweh's power when they were consulted about what to do with the Ark of Yahweh: "Why should you harden your hearts as the Egyptians and Pharaoh hardened their hearts? After he [i.e. Yahweh] had made fools of them, did they not let the people go?" (I Sam. 6:6). Not only Israelite children know the tale, but foreigners as well. Yahweh delights in toying with – and then destroying – those who challenge his absolute sovereignty.

Yahweh's desire to engage in a contest where he will "amuse himself with" Pharaoh creates a comedy of horrors for the Egyptian king and his people. The whole movement

---

[45] S. R. Driver, *The Book of Exodus* (Cambridge: Cambridge University Press, 1953), p. 78.

of the contest from the initial confrontation to the climactic victory at the Red Sea dramatically illustrates this divine intent to play with his opponent even as a cat plays with a mouse. As I indicated earlier, Pharaoh's arrogant response to the divine demand to let Israel go throws down the gauntlet in the contest: "Who is Yahweh, that I should heed him and let Israel go?" (5:2). The plague narratives offer a convincing answer to Pharaoh's question. The relentless progress of the narratives through the first nine plagues shows a monotony of predictable reactions on the part of Pharaoh: his heart remains hardened both by Yahweh's action and his own stubborn will; but Yahweh's purpose to be known and recognized and feared also stays the same.

However different the origins and development of the tradition of the tenth plague and its combination of the slaying of the first-born and Passover Night, it clearly functions as the first of the two climaxes in the confrontation between Yahweh and Pharaoh. Along with the story of the Red Sea victory, the Passover supplies the festive consummation of the Exodus. Though Passover celebrates the sparing of the Israelites in the midst of the mass slaughter of Egyptian first-born, it features more prominently and decisively the celebration of life and liberation and thus moves appropriately in the field of the comic vision. To be sure, such a vision shows the sometimes blurred line between comedy and tragedy, between tears and laughter. Thus it is not surprising that some interpreters have called the Passover's bitter-sweet intermingling of death and life, "A Tragic Night, A Joyful Day."[46] Similarly, Robertson is correct when he says that the narrators have manipulated us to have our sympathies dominantly, if not exclusively, with the Israelites, because if we listen too intently to that "loud cry in Egypt [where] there was not a house without someone dead" (12:30), then we could feel the irony and ambiguity of the story, dwelling too much on the deaths of so many Egyptians.[47] But in this ancient tale

---

[46] Fretheim, *Exodus*, p. 140.
[47] Robertson, *The Old Testament and the Literary Critic*, pp. 28–29.

of a contest between gods the stakes are typically deadly: "I will pass through the land of Egypt that night, and I will strike down every first-born in the land of Egypt, both human beings and animals; on all the gods of Egypt I will execute judgments: I am Yahweh" (12:12). The narrators do not really raise this kind of implicit moral issue, since with their theological and moral criteria Yahweh was eminently just and right in his dealings with the Egyptians.[48] In any case, Passover remains a dominantly joyous event, an apt and compelling celebration of the comedy of deliverance, even though it also contains a tragic potential that is unfulfilled.[49]

As we have already noted, the story moves on to a second climax, Yahweh's final victory over the Egyptians at the Red Sea. The story performs a double-duty function: not only does it climax the story of Israel's deliverance from the Egyptians, but it initiates the time of Israel's wanderings in the wilderness.[50] In the final form of the narrative, it is wiser not to place a faulty "either-or" as to where the story primarily belongs – to the Exodus traditions or to the wilderness account. We have seen that the Exodus story-tellers again and again use a recapitulative and anticipatory strategy. Thus the Red Sea event ends the first major phase of the journey from bondage to liberty, but begins the second major part: the wilderness wanderings.

After their hasty but successful departure from Egypt, "God led the people by the roundabout way of the wilderness toward the Red Sea . . ." (13:18a), avoiding the more direct route by way of the land of the Philistines. Providing a touching link with the conclusion of Genesis, the narrator also informs us that "Moses took with him the bones of Joseph

---

[48] Later interpreters do raise such questions – see Childs' discussion in his excursus on the theme of "hardening" in *The Book of Exodus*, pp. 70–74.

[49] One should note, however, that Ezekiel the Tragedian, a Hellenistic Jewish dramatist of the third century BCE, composed a tragedy based on the Exodus story modeling it after classical conventions especially drawn from Euripides. See the summary in John J. Collins, *Between Athens and Jerusalem: Jewish Identity in the Hellenistic Diaspora* (New York: Crossroads, 1983), pp. 207–211. Here, again, one notes the fine line of separation between comedy and tragedy (see my chapter on Job below as well as the conclusion).

[50] See Childs' incisive review of the possibilities in *The Book of Exodus*, pp. 222–224.

who had required a solemn oath of the Israelites, saying, 'God will surely take notice of you, and then you must carry my bones with you from here'" (13:19). The Israelites then camp "on the edge of the wilderness" (13:20). Yahweh supplies his own signal-corps to guide the Israelites: "Yahweh went in front of them in a pillar of cloud by day . . . and a pillar of fire by night . . ." (13:21). We read then about another change in the itinerary, when Yahweh directs Moses to "tell the Israelites to turn back and camp in front of Pi-hahiroth, between Migdol and the sea, in front of Baal-zephon; you shall camp opposite it, by the Sea" (14:2). All this rather arcane geographical information – which has led historians on a merry-chase to find the "real" route of the Exodus – is offered as a piece of deliberate manipulation on Yahweh's part. Again Israel's God delights in being a trickster. Thus the narrator finally gives us insight into the purpose for Israel's divinely ordered meanderings: it is all an elaborate ruse, a twisting trail designed to create a false perception on the part of Pharaoh who will think the Israelites are lost and entrapped: "Pharaoh will say of the Israelites, 'They are wandering aimlessly in the land; the wilderness has closed in on them'" (14:3). Why does Yahweh want to cause such confusion for Pharaoh? The answer lies in Yahweh's purpose for Pharaoh from the very beginning: "I will harden Pharaoh's heart, and he will pursue them, so that I will gain glory for myself over Pharaoh and all his army; and the Egyptians shall know that I am Yahweh" (14:4; also 14:17–18 with even more emphasis on God's desire for self-glorification). Yahweh has not finished with Pharaoh and the Egyptians, nor has Pharaoh finished with Yahweh and the Israelites. The contest for supremacy must continue to its relentless climax: Yahweh will be superior – indeed incomparable – at all costs. So Pharaoh and his advisers do as predicted, changing their minds about letting the Israelites go and giving chase with the elite chariot-corps. Pharaoh also will not give up the game so easily.

What of the Israelites in this drama of deliverance? Old habits of being and behaving also die hard for them. Despite all the diverse signs of Yahweh's superior "fire-power," they revert to a persistent pattern of complaining (which will be repeated over and over again in the wilderness wanderings). When confronted with the spectacle of the rapid advance of the Egyptian army, the Israelites panic and give vent to old gripes, now repeated with sarcasm and a bitter "we told you so" attitude:

Was it because there were no graves in Egypt that you have taken us away to die in the wilderness? What have you done to us, bringing us out of Egypt? Is this not the very thing we told you in Egypt, 'Let us alone and let us serve the Egyptians'? For it would have been better for us to serve the Egyptians than to die in the wilderness. (14:11–12)

The Israelites' complaint is both "poignant and humorous,"[51] for we hear the sounds of genuine fear coupled with an amazing inability to remember the previous displays of divine power and protection. Moreover, the Israelites fall prey to a form of self-parody when unknowingly they engage in a form of protest that curiously mimics the Egyptian reaction to the Israelites' escape: "What is this we have done that we have let Israel go from serving us?" // "What is this you have done to us . . . in bringing us out of Egypt?"[52] Childs explains that the "two reactions are parallel because neither reckoned with God's plan."[53] This explanation is accurate so far as it goes, but it is the irony that is especially striking. The Israelites should have known better because they had received ample instruction; the Egyptians also should have known better (recall the litany of plagues and the "recognition" scenes), but a double-dosage of "hardening" at least makes the Egyptian obduracy more understandable.

Moses answers their terrified protest by calling them to stillness and stability, to a form of trust that casts out fear; all they must do is "see the deliverance that Yahweh will accomplish . . . today; for the Egyptians whom [they] see today, [they] will never see again" (14:13). Seeing indeed will be believing, but the biblical narrator reverses the order – believing will be

---

[51] Durham, *Exodus*, p. 191.   [52] Childs, *The Book of Exodus*, pp. 225–226.
[53] *Ibid.*, p. 225.

seeing. The play on the word "seeing" recalls the story of Moses' deliverance from the waters of death; now Israel will see its own deliverance when Moses draws them through the parted waters, thus fulfilling the symbolism of his Egyptian given name as one "drawn out of water" (2:10). Here too the passivity of the earlier birth story is present, since the Israelites are to remain "still" as they see with their own eyes Yahweh's victory over Pharaoh and his army. In this case the passivity comes out of the strength of faith that "stands firm." All they must do is walk and watch, going forward in trust on the path between the parted waters. Yahweh thereby has set up both the Egyptians and the Israelites ironically to join together in finally and fully knowing Yahweh's power to destroy – and to save; to deal out death and destruction – and to bestow life and restoration: "Thus Yahweh saved Israel that day from the Egyptians; and Israel saw the Egyptians dead on the seashore" (14:30). Lastly, the total triumph over the Egyptians effects the full reintegration of Yahweh, Moses, and the Israelites in the community of faith: "Israel saw the great work that Yahweh did against the Egyptians. So the people feared Yahweh and believed in Yahweh and in his servant Moses" (14:31).

If the Exodus story is a comedy of deliverance, then Yahweh's victory at the Red Sea fittingly evokes a hymn of praise as the festive consummation we expect in such stories. The Song of Moses and Miriam thereby reiterates and reinforces the note of triumph registered in prose in Exodus 14, effecting a powerful poetic closure of the first major movement of the Book of Exodus.[54]

The Song itself has evoked endless commentary which I need not repeat; I want only to underscore a few dimensions of this brilliant poem which contribute to our general theme of Exodus as festive comedy. First, the ambiguous attribution of the hymn to Moses and Miriam has usually been analyzed from the perspective of historical priority; for my purpose the

---

[54] "The caesura marking the end of the first section of Exodus is signaled by dense and powerful poetic language" (Fokkelman, "Exodus," p. 56).

dual attribution dramatically rounds off the fascinating presence of female and male voices in the narrative. Rather than
being overly concerned with historical priority, it is more illuminating to note how the two voices represent a wonderful
set of antiphonal responses: first of all, pride of place goes to
Moses, the primary human hero of the Exodus event; but
surprisingly, yet appropriately, Miriam and her women step
boldly forward at the end to celebrate with singing and
dancing the triumph of Yahweh over the Egyptian forces,
thus corresponding with the active presence of the diverse
women at the very beginning of the story. Once again therefore the story of Moses' role as leader of the Exodus is
enframed between the account of notable women who are
the first saviors in the story and then become at the last
singers and dancers in a choreography of the comedy of
deliverance. That Moses steps forward as the inspired "I" of
the community ("I will sing to Yahweh, for he has triumphed
gloriously") is appropriately matched by the commanding
prophetic voice of sister Miriam ("sing to Yahweh, for he has
triumphed gloriously"). Brother and sister, male and female,
join harmoniously together as two prophets with one voice
leading the Israelite community in their song of praise.

The Song gives dramatic poetic form to the whole sweep of
the dramatic Exodus event and reaches ultimately to the conquest of the Land and the establishment of Yahweh's sanctuary on Mt. Zion. It has an expansively imaginative horizon,
invoking, on the one hand, the mythological imagery of the
divine warrior's victory over the mighty waters of primordial
chaos, now personified as Pharaoh and his army (15:1–10);
and anticipating, on the other hand, the conquest of the
promised land and the installation of Yahweh as King in his
holy sanctuary on Mt. Zion (15:13–18). Right in the center
of the poem, serving as decisive pivot in the poetic movement
and powerful reprise of the thematic focus on Yahweh as the
ultimate and unique hero, is the two-fold "Who" question
that underscores Yahweh's incomparability: "Who is like you,
O Yahweh, among the gods? Who is like you, majestic in holiness, awesome in splendor, doing wonders?" (15:11). The

rhetorical questions with the accompanying narrative of victory effectively answers Pharaoh's sarcastic question: "Who is Yahweh?" It also expresses vividly the theme of Yahweh's glory, now pinpointed in the impressive claim of Yahweh's incomparability which has been demonstrated in his victory in the war of gods: "Yahweh is a warrior; Yahweh is his name" (15:3). The contest between rival divine powers reaches its dramatic conclusion in this song of Yahweh's triumph.

ESTHER AS COMEDY

Esther of late has received considerable attention as a comic work of first rank. Several scholars have made the case for a comic interpretation, offering valuable insight into the variety of dynamics that combine to render Esther as a magnificent illustration of the comic vision in ancient Israel. Indeed, in a most stimulating study of Esther, Michael Fox makes the striking claim: "The book of Esther begins a tradition of Jewish humor."[55] I would agree that Esther contains a rich vein of "Jewish humor," but I would argue that Esther, in fact, continues a tradition of Jewish comedy that begins in Genesis and Exodus. Indeed, the central thrust of this chapter is that Exodus and Esther may be fruitfully brought together as two exemplary instances of biblical comedy.

In my judgment, Esther emerges as perhaps the clearest embodiment of the comic vision among all the biblical narratives, representing a brilliantly conceived story in which plot-line, characterization of major figures, and rhetorical strategies combine to produce a finely told comedy. Sandmel expresses well the comic achievement of Esther, though his assertion is a bit extravagant: "Esther discloses a tremendous narrative skill, for it is as comic a story as has ever been told."[56] Jack Sasson gives substance to this claim; contrasting the Greek version's suppression of the comic dimensions of

[55] Michael V. Fox, *Character and Ideology in the Book of Esther* (Columbia: University of South Carolina Press, 1991), p. 253.
[56] Samuel Sandmel, *The Enjoyment of Scripture* (Oxford: Oxford University Press, 1972), p. 498.

Esther, Sasson convincingly puts his case for the comedy of
Esther:

In the Hebrew rendering . . . the comic potential of the story is
richly exploited, and laughter at human vanity, gall, and blindness
becomes the vehicle by which the writer gives his tale integrity and
moral vision. Were it not for its modern pejorative connotation,
'travesty' (wherein serious subjects are treated lightly) would suit
Esther as a literary category. Setting aside the questions of intellectual influence or contact, we can say that this is essentially the same
literary mode adopted by Hellenistic romances (for example,
Apuleius' *Golden Ass*), by the medieval fabliaux, and by Voltaire in
his satiric *Contes philosophiques* (such as *Candide, Zadig,* and
Micromegas). In all such stylized, farcical narratives, the laughter is
broad and comes from the incongruity of situations and from the
sharp reversals of fate.[57]

All in all Sasson has expressed well the comedy of Esther,
citing apt analogues from comparative literature. I agree with
Sasson that "travesty" is too open to misunderstanding, and
prefer to subordinate the satirical elements to a more comprehensive vision of comedy. Hence I think that "comedy of
deliverance" is a more compelling designation involving both
form and content. Moreover, as comic tale par excellence,
Esther finds its perfect setting in the festival of Purim which
provides a carnivalesque atmosphere for the annual remembrance and reenactment of this comedy of deliverance.

First, as Sasson and several other scholars have rightly
noted, the theme of reversal is key to the movement of the
book.[58] What no one has observed – at least to my knowledge
– is that this thematic trajectory of reversal follows the U-
shaped plot-line so endemic to comedies. Beginning on the
high note of festivity and seeming harmony involving a
sumptuous banquet scene, the narrative plunges downward
into a series of crises of increasing seriousness which are ultimately resolved by the combined efforts of Mordecai and
Esther; the story then swings upward to consummate in a
traditional "happy ending" as the deliverance of the Jews

[57] Jack M. Sasson, "Esther," in *The Literary Guide to the Bible,* Robert Alter and Frank
Kermode, eds., p. 339.   [58] *Ibid.,* pp. 340–341.

from the genocidal plot of wicked Haman is celebrated and then permanently inscribed in the festival of Purim.

Second, plot combines with characterization of the major figures to reinforce and deepen the comic movement. To be sure, the characters are subordinated to the plot-line, so that the rather flat, stereotypical figures predictably play out their roles in the relatively simple plot.[59] Thus we see such stock characters as a foolish, fickle king, a beautiful, wise heroine, a loyal courtier, and a wicked villain. It is precisely in the adroit combination of plot and characterization in the narrator's employment of various rhetorical strategies that the comic intentionality forcefully and funnily emerges. We must now turn to the concrete details of the story to see the embodiment of the comic vision in Esther.

The story opens up with an opulent description of the greatness of the Persian Empire as illustrated by the wondrous wealth of the royal court in Susa. As Berg and others have cogently argued, banquets bracket the major episodes of the narrative, focusing the theme of festivity at beginning, middle, and end, and creating the setting for the significant actions.[60] Already in the exaggerated representation found in the opening scene one discerns comic hyperbole. The vast extent of the empire stretching "from India to Ethiopia" is highlighted by the sheer number of provinces: one hundred and twenty-seven (in contrast to the twenty satrapies Herodotus mentions). The citadel of Susa becomes a microcosm that mirrors the grandeur of the huge empire: the king "displayed the great wealth of his kingdom and the splendor and pomp of his majesty" (1:4). No less than three banquets are given (two by the king, one by the queen), the first and most sumptuous feast lasting no less than one hundred and eighty days. On the seventh day of the second banquet, the king "was merry with wine" (to echo a quaint, euphemistic translation), thus setting a good (or bad) example at a party

---

[59] Edward L. Greenstein, "A Jewish Reading of Esther," in *Judaic Perspectives on Ancient Israel*, Jacob Neusner, Baruch A. Levine, and Ernest S. Frerichs, eds. (Philadelphia: Fortress Press, 1987), p. 231.

[60] Cf. Berg, *The Book of Esther*, pp. 31–48.

where "drinking was . . . without restraint, for the king had given orders to all the officials to do as each one desired" (1:8). In this drunken atmosphere the king orders his seven eunuchs "to bring Queen Vashti before the king, wearing the royal crown, in order to show the people and the officials her beauty; for she was fair to behold" (1:11). What we have here amidst the glitter of excessive display is a finely honed satire of a royal court that knows no restraint in its pursuit of pomp and circumstance, and a king who embodies and exemplifies the principle of unbridled desire. This satire gives a tone not only to the beginning, but continues throughout the story: it is satire designed to expose the overweening king to ridicule and laughter.[61]

The first explicit sign that King Ahasuerus' extravagant display of power has its limits comes from an unexpected corner: the queen refuses his command to appear in all her beauty before the ogling eyes of his compatriots, a refusal that evokes immediate rage from the king and creates a crisis that takes on monumental proportions. To deal with this breach in royal etiquette, the king feels compelled to consult his sages and his seven leading officials who know the law and inquire what he should do with his disobedient queen. One woman's brave refusal to appear becomes a *cause célèbre*, setting off a crisis not just for the king, but for the whole empire: after all, the queen's disobedience might give ideas to all the women in the realm who might thereby fail to obey and honor their husbands. The counselors advocate the deposition of Queen Vashti and the selection of a more suitable replacement. The effect of such action implemented in a royal decree would cause all women to give honor to their husbands.

The comic spirit is at work in this grand opening scene. Not only does it offer an exaggerated, satirical portrait of a vast, splendid kingdom marked by incredible wealth and a smoothly functioning bureaucracy, it presents a king who

---

[61] See David J. A. Clines, *The Esther Scroll: The Story of the Story* (Sheffield: JSOT Press, 1984), pp. 31–33.

delights in excessive display and who appears as a buffoon in his awkward attempts to rule. Beneath the apparent efficiency and stability of the kingdom, a spirit of excess rules which becomes a case of comic misrule. The banquet becomes a scene of unlimited drinking and drunkenness presided over by the king himself. The king revels in pompous display, in showing off everything including his beauteous queen who alone manifests a sense of dignity and appropriate royal decorum, even though it costs her dearly. The vaunted efficiency of the kingdom is placed in the service of controlling the queen when ironically the king is the one who is in need of some control. He appears as a master only of excess, thus ironically and paradoxically emerging as its slave. He responds mainly to the moment, demonstrating an amazing stupidity in his actions. He is consistently short-sighted, forgetful, and hot-tempered. His rebuff from his queen sets off a major crisis which was only caused by the king's intemperate command to his queen to appear (naked?) before his drunken male guests. The scene is a masterfully executed burlesque in which the king is ridiculed. He fits well the character type of a royal buffoon, thus forming a parallel to the foolish Pharaoh: both kings reflect a self-defeating nature, whose solutions to the problems of ruling their kingdoms usually backfire and make the situation worse.

In the elaborate process of choosing a new queen, a process involving an empire-wide beauty contest, the narrator pauses to introduce the two major Jewish heroes, Mordecai and Esther. Mordecai is a Benjaminite, particularly in the line of Saul, a Jew who had apparently experienced first-hand the Babylonian exile. Bereft of father and mother, Esther is his cousin and adopted daughter (recalling possibly the motif of the adopted Moses). As a beautiful virgin Esther is swept up into the search for a new queen. Esther not only is beautiful, thus fulfilling the first requirement, she also seems to do all things well and evokes the admiration of everyone, including the king. For once in his life the king acts independently and makes a wise choice: he falls in love with the "right" woman, the beautiful, winsome Esther. "The king loved Esther more than all the other women; of all the virgins she won his favor and devotion, so that he set the royal crown on her head and made her queen instead of Vashti" (2:17). To be sure, he does not initially understand fully who and what he has acquired in choosing Esther as his new queen, since her guardian Mordecai had instructed her not to reveal the identity of her people (2:20). Typical for his court, the king gives a "great banquet" for Esther in celebration of her coronation (2:18).

Using the technique of foreshadowing, the narrator relates how Mordecai discovers a plot against the king. Mordecai discloses the identity of the conspirators to Esther who in turn informs the king in Mordecai's name. Investigation reveals the truth of the information, and the two assassins are hanged. Even though the matter is duly "recorded in the book of the annals in the presence of the king" (2:23), it is clear from later in the story that the matter was promptly forgotten with no commensurate reward for the loyal Mordecai.

With chapter 3 we meet the fourth and final major figure in the story, the wicked villain Haman. Coming on the heels of the disclosure of Mordecai's good service of the king, the promotion of Haman to second rank in the kingdom comes as a surprise (why was Mordecai not rewarded with such a promotion?), yet the tale needs a villain and so the spotlight falls on Haman. Like Mordecai, he is briefly identified in terms of familial lineage: he is son of Hammedatha the Agagite, thus linking him fatefully with the Amalekites, the age-old enemy of the Jews (see Ex. 17 and I Sam. 15). The king commands that everybody should bow to his new chief official, a posture that Mordecai stubbornly refuses to take. When Haman sees this rank insubordination, he becomes enraged (not unlike the king's response to Vashti's disobedience), but his rage turns into a genocidal plot against all Jews, not just Mordecai himself (4:7). Here the plot-line descends to its lowest point in the U-shaped plot-line, reaching the moment that Frye names "the point of ritual death."[62] Execution of genocidal

---

[62] N. Frye, *Anatomy of Criticism*, p. 179.

decree would of course break off the comic movement, turning the story into a tragic tale of holocaust; but the comic trajectory descends to the bottom of the "U" in order to show how the wicked plot will be negated by heroic intervention. The "Who knows?" question Mordecai later poses to Esther becomes a symbolic way of injecting suspense and surprise in a narrative marked by striking coincidences, wise, courageous decisions of the human protagonists, and amazing reversals of fortune.

After the decree of death for Jews has been disseminated throughout the empire, Mordecai leads the way for a widespread manifestation of Jewish mourning rites. Donning sack cloth and ashes, Mordecai parades around the city and comes up to the "entrance of the king's gate, for no one might enter the king's gate clothed in sackcloth"(4:2) – thus suggesting that he is most conscious about transgression of limits, even while issuing a kind of distress signal that can reach Esther who is apparently isolated within the harem walls. Indeed, when she hears about the state of Mordecai, she sends some fresh clothes for him, which of course he refuses and returns a message to Esther via the queen's emissary. The message involves both the information about the genocidal decree and the command for Esther to intercede for the Jews. Esther's immediate response is disappointing both to the reader and especially to Mordecai, for all she can do is to express her reluctance given that a death sentence awaits anyone who enters before the king without an express invitation – with only the one escape clause hanging on the king's decision of holding out the golden scepter as sign of his favor. Mordecai, however, is not to be thwarted and sends back a message that forces Esther to confront the existential moment: "Do not think that in the king's palace you will escape any more than all the other Jews. For if you keep silence at such a time as this, relief and deliverance will rise for the Jews from another quarter, but you and your father's family will perish. Who knows? Perhaps you have come to royal dignity for just such a time as this" (4:13–14). Mordecai is ruthless in the logic of his reaction to Esther's reluctance to act: a decree to kill all the Jews will not allow Esther to escape;

whatever she decides to do, he himself is certain of Jewish survival. This is a time to speak, not to keep silence; the fateful "Who knows?" forces her to sense and seize the moment. This time her reply is immediate and decisive, boldly taking the initiative: "Go, gather all the Jews in Susa, and hold a fast on my behalf, and neither eat nor drink for three days, night or day. I and my maids will also fast as you do. After that I will go to the king, though it is against the law; and if I perish, I perish" (4:16). Here she begins to show her mettle as a heroine, reversing positions with her mentor and now for the first time issuing the orders which he completely obeys. If not the fundamental turning-point in the entire book, this key decision of Esther to intervene at the risk of her life is clearly a pivot on which the story turns, giving us a foretaste of the courage and wisdom of the Jewish queen who now becomes the most significant actor in this drama. She takes her stand with other brave, resourceful biblical heroines who take their stand in times of danger to bring "relief and deliverance for the Jews."

On the third day of her fast, Esther makes her uninvited appearance before the king, who shows that he is not always caught up in the rigidities of law and holds forth the golden scepter as soon as he sees his queen (after all he once was described as "loving" her and favoring her over all her other rivals). Indeed, he not only favors her by signaling that her life is spared, but he shows once again his most characteristic attribute – a love of excess – for he asks her simply to name her request, "even to the half of my kingdom" and it would be given to her (5:3). Showing that she is a master of the waiting game, Esther does not immediately name her real request, but simply invites the king to what is one of his favorite pastimes: attending a banquet, this time a rather private affair with only his queen as hostess and Haman as the only other guest. "While they were drinking wine" (apparently the king's favorite activity at a banquet), the king once more asks her to indicate her wish up to half the kingdom; once more she strategically delays and wants the king and Haman to come to another banquet on the morrow and then she would finally name her petition (5:8).

In the intervening time between Esther's two banquets for Ahasuerus and Haman, two striking coincidences occur which are pivotal in the whole movement of the story. First, when Haman leaves the first banquet, "he went out that day happy and in good spirits" (5:9) – that is, until he saw the utter lack of Mordecai's obsequiousness before him, which made him "infuriated," though he "restrained himself and went home" (5:10). He then manifests behavior which reveals insight into his character: he calls for his wife and friends to whom he relates all his "greatness" – as demonstrated by "the splendor of his riches, the number of his sons, all the promotions with which the king had honored him, and how he had advanced him above the officials and the ministers of the king" (5:11). Switching from third-person to first-person language, he climaxes with his latest honor of being the only other guest at the private banquet Esther gave for the king: "Even Queen Esther let no one but myself come with the king to the banquet that she prepared. Tomorrow also I am invited by her, together with the king" (5:12). But all his honors – all denoted by external circumstances – come to nothing in light of Mordecai's unbowed presence. Two things come to mind: first, Haman is all too like his king in his love of outward display, a balloon of illusory happiness which can be quickly punctured by one recalcitrant figure; second, again like the king, he becomes uncertain what he should do until counseled and manipulated by others. Both are characters who show no depth or inner substance, being easily puffed up by external marks of success while becoming quickly angered by resistance or disobedience and consequently becoming almost paralyzed until others dictate a course of action. Zeresh and his friends respond to Haman's discomfiture over Mordecai with a rather extravagant proposal which appeals to Haman's love of excessive display: get rid of the offender by hanging him on a gallows seventy-five feet high (!) and then go to Esther's party "in good spirits" (5:14). The narrator adds the laconic note: "This advice pleased Haman, and he had the gallows made" (5:14b). Little does he know that this exaggerated symbol of execution will become all too visible and ironically become the instrument for his own death.

Meanwhile, on that very same night, King Ahasuerus is restless and calls for a reading of the royal annals as a soporific.
By another surprising coincidence, the king hears about
Mordecai's loyal service of informing against the assassins.
The king also learns that nothing was done to reward
Mordecai. At that very moment, Haman's presence is noted
in the outer court, since Haman had come in order to ask the
king's permission to hang Mordecai. When Haman comes
before the king, the king asks his prized official the key question: "What shall be done for the man the king wishes to
honor?" (6:6). Of course Haman can only think of himself as
the obvious candidate, saying to himself, "Whom would the
king wish to honor more than me?" (6:6b). Haman emerges
as an egocentric fool, whose imagination becomes fixated on
himself to the exclusion of other possibilities. He thus pre-
scribes the fullest array of royal honors imaginable, supposing he would be the recipient: the king's robes to wear, the
king's horse (duly crowned) to ride, and one of the king's
most noble officials to clothe and lead the honoree through
the open square of the city, proclaiming, "Thus shall be done
for the man whom the king wishes to honor" (6:11). Sasson
rightly calls this a "first-rate example of rude comedy and
reversal of expectation."[63] One can well imagine the shattering effect of the king's response to Haman: "Quickly, take the
robes and the horse, as you have said, and do so to the Jew
Mordecai who sits at the king's gate. Leave out nothing that
you have mentioned" (6:10). In a deft stroke the narrator
simply describes Haman's immediate compliance with the
king's orders and only afterwards lays bare Haman's sense of
abject humiliation: "Haman hurried to his house, mourning
and with his head covered" (6:12b). After Haman recounts
his shattering reversal of fortune, his wife Zeresh and his
advisers once again offer their chilling assessment: "If
Mordecai, before whom your downfall has begun, is of the
Jewish people, you will not prevail against him, but will surely
fall before him" (6:13b).

---

[63] Sasson, "Esther," p. 341.

It is easy to understand why many interpreters have named this episode as the major pivot of the whole story, since it effectively encapsulates the ironic reversal in the positions of Haman and Mordecai – and by anticipation in the positions of the Jews and their enemies. The fortuitous timing of the events, the sudden rise of Mordecai to royal favor coupled with the beginning of Haman's decline, and the change from joy to mourning for Haman in anticipation of other dramatic mood-swings – of such stuff are fairy tales made as well as comedies. In terms of the U-shaped plot-line we have begun the upward swing of the tale, but more momentous events are still to come.

Just as Haman and his intimate circle were discussing the bewildering change of events, attendants arrive to whisk Haman away to Esther's second private banquet. Again, amidst drinking that continued into the second day of feasting, Ahasuerus raises again the question about Esther's petition, the answer to which Esther had insisted on delaying to heighten suspense as well as to await the most propitious moment. Now Esther no longer equivocates or dissimulates; her answer is a skillfully wrought piece of rhetoric designed to play upon the king's generosity toward her: "If I have won your favor, O king, and if it pleases the king, let my life be given me – that is my petition – and the lives of my people – that is my request. For we have been sold, I and my people, to be destroyed, to be killed, and to be annihilated. If we had been sold merely as slaves, men and women, I would have held my peace; but no enemy can compensate for this damage to the king" (7:3–4). Displaying an amazing forgetfulness about the earlier death warrant against the Jews he had authorized under Haman's prodding, the king asks sharply: "Who is he, and where is he, who has presumed to do this?" (7:5). Esther answers pointedly: "A foe and enemy, this wicked Haman!" (7:6). Angry beyond words, the king rises in his wrath and goes into the palace garden, while Haman stays behind to "beg for his life from the queen, for he saw that the king had determined to destroy him" (7:7). But Haman's humiliation is not yet complete, as this comedy of errors and miscalculations continues. Having prostrated himself before the queen on the very couch where the queen was reclining, Haman pleads for his life – only to be discovered in this compromised position by the king who thinks that Haman is trying to make sexual advances toward the queen: "Will he even assault the queen in my presence, in my own house?" (7:8). Here the king continues to be rather witless, one who consistently misconstrues appearances. Esther's silence here is ominous, for she does nothing to correct the king's misconception. Haman is now utterly beyond hope or help, and one of the eunuchs indicates to the king that the very gallows that Haman had prepared for Mordecai stand ready; the king's pronouncement of sentence is short and swift: "Hang him on that" (7:9). Thus Haman is hanged on his own gallows, the king's anger is appeased, Esther is given Haman's house, Mordecai is installed in place of Haman, but the Jews must still be saved since the earlier death decree remains in force.

Esther once again pleads her case to the king, asking for the revocation of the genocidal decree against the Jews. King Ahasuerus responds favorably, giving a carte blanche to Esther and Mordecai to avert the disaster: "You may write as you please with regard to the Jews, in the name of the king, and seal it with the king's ring; for an edict written in the name of the king and sealed with the king's ring cannot be revoked" (8:8). The king reveals how malleable he can be, giving Esther what she wants, without being able to escape the irrevocability of Persian law. Once again Persian king and Persian law are satirized: the king shows how he becomes victimized and stymied by the irrevocable character of Persian law, giving to his Jewish supplicants the seemingly impossible task to negate an irrevocable decree. The wise Mordecai, however, is up to the task of undercutting the earlier decree, without having to revoke it; he dictates letters whereby the Jews are allowed to defend themselves against their enemies (8:11, 13). The issuance of the second decree throughout the empire evokes widespread celebration: "For the Jews there was light and gladness, joy and honor. In every province and in every city, wherever the king's command and his edict came, there was gladness and joy among the Jews, a festival and a holiday" (8:16, 17a). To be sure, the edict also evokes fear among the Gentiles, many of whom convert to Judaism (8:17b). For all intents and purposes deliverance of the Jews has been accomplished – with the added boon of Gentile converts who will increase the population and hence power of the Jews. O happy, happy day! – hence the outbreak of jubilation throughout the kingdom.

Although I find Clines' perceptive analysis for the secondary and stylistically inferior quality of 9:1–10:3 generally persuasive, one still can inquire as to the comic function of the book's final part.[64] In its present form it serves as a conclusion which describes the events of the fateful day of conflict between the Jews and their enemies and moves into rather redundant prescriptive language about the institution of Purim.

At last the momentous day arrives, the thirteenth day of Adar, "the very day when the enemies of the Jews hoped to gain power over them, but which had been changed to a day when the Jews would gain power over their foes" (9:1). The fates had in fact been reversed, and the day of potential destruction is turned back on the enemies of the Jews. No one could withstand the power of the Jews, since the fear of them and notably the "fear of Mordecai had fallen upon them" (9:2–4). Five hundred people die in Susa on the thirteenth day including the ten sons of Haman all of whom are named (9:6–10). When the king hears the casualty report, he in turn reports to the queen; apparently perceiving that she is still not fully satisfied (why she might be is not really disclosed), he renews again his request that she make known to him her petition which he pledges to fulfill. Esther obliges by asking for an additional day in Susa for the Jews to take vengeance on their enemies and to hang the corpses of the ten sons of Haman on the gallows (9:13). The king grants her wish, and three hundred more people in Susa fall to the Jewish defend-

[64] Clines, *The Esther Scroll*, pp. 39–49.

ers. Meanwhile on the previous day the Jews have killed seventy-five thousand people in the various provinces, gaining "relief from their enemies" (9:16). So the day of doom is averted, justice is served, and the Jews not only preserve their life but strengthen their standing in the Persian world. The fourteenth day of Adar in the provinces and the fifteenth day in Susa become days for "gladness and feasting, a holiday on which they send gifts of food to one another" (9:19).

Many interpreters have been troubled not only by the stylistic awkwardness that appears in Esther 9, but also by the "moral problem" involved in the Jewish retaliation against their enemies and their exultation in revenge and mass slaughter. Now certainly it is easy to understand this kind of reaction, though often it has been along partisan lines with Christians excoriating the Jews for excessive nationalism and vengeful slaughter. However, some attention to the comic spirit that animates the tale should help to mitigate the problem. As Bruce Jones has suggested, it is possible to discern in the casualty reports a continuation of the kind of hyperbole and macabre humor that run through the whole book.[65]

First, the decree designed to reverse the initial genocidal decree only grants the Jews the right of self-defense, though this seems to be contradicted by the offensive gestures ("gain the mastery," "no one could withstand them"). Moreover, the studied way of reporting King Ahasuerus' actions continues the parody of this relatively benign albeit witless king. Serving as a messenger boy to his queen, he does not have all the information; thus after reporting the deaths of five hundred people plus the deaths of Haman's ten sons, he still must ask about the provinces ("What have they done in the rest of the king's provinces?" [9:12]). Without receiving an answer to his question, he then without any urging or motivation repeats his question to the queen about any additional petition she

---

[65] Bruce W. Jones, "Two Misconceptions about the Book of Esther," *Catholic Biblical Quarterly* 39 (1977), pp. 177–181.

might have. Here he shows his characteristic trait of being overly compliant and even subservient to the will of others, now appearing completely malleable to the directives of his queen. The king means that his queen will be satisfied – whatever her wishes; ironically, a king who at the beginning is completely caught up in fulfilling his own desires can now think only of his queen's desires. In this repetition of his request to know the queen's wishes, he even drops the earlier limitation of her petition up to half of the kingdom. The scene continues its comic face, even if "serious" themes of death and destruction are being treated.

A kind of coda follows the story proper (9:20–32), a coda that permanently inscribes the festival of Purim in the Jewish liturgical calendar. What had been presented as a one-time historical event is now perpetually embedded as an annual commemoration in the future of Jewish festivals (cf. 9:27–28). The rather prosaic recapitulation of the fundamental story serves to institutionalize Purim, memorializing the "days on which the Jews gained relief from their enemies, and the month that had been turned for them from sorrow into gladness and from mourning into holiday" and enjoining that the Jews "should make them days of feasting and gladness, days for sending gifts of food to one another and presents to the poor" (9:22).

Significantly, at the end of the tale both Esther and Mordecai appear as equals, second only to King Ahasuerus in the vast Persian empire: "Queen Esther daughter of Abihail, along with the Jew Mordecai, gave full written authority, confirming this second letter about Purim" (9:29). The book concludes with the exaltation of Mordecai the Jew who "was next in rank to King Ahasuerus, and [who] was powerful among the Jews and popular with his many kindred, for he sought the good of his people and interceded for the welfare of all his descendants" (10:3). The final note recalls the exaltation of Joseph (cf. Gen. 41:40–45). The elevation of Esther and Mordecai as twin heroes of this comedy of deliverance is a fitting conclusion.

The inauguration of Purim as a permanent festival of

Judaism is an apt institutionalization of Esther's story. The comic spirit finds its most congenial home in carnival. Thus Esther's story of dramatic reversal in Jewish fortune, transforming terror into joy and tears into laughter, becomes perpetually reenacted in the festive events of Purim. In Purim comedy becomes carnival, celebrating deliverance from death, and exulting in the triumph of good over evil. Indeed, the explicitly carnivalesque spirit of Purim confirms and extends the comic form and communal festivity of the story itself.[66]

That medieval Judaism further developed Purim as the carnival season par excellence should not therefore be surprising. Arthur Waskow offers a vivid commentary on the vitality of Purim during the Middle Ages, showing thereby the intersecting lines of the carnivalesque spirit:

In medieval Europe . . . an already lively Purim was quick to enhance its own hilarity by borrowing the carnival masquerades and mystery plays. Jews costumed as Vashti and Moses, Solomon and Mordechai, would stroll the streets to sing and shout . . . The Purimshpiel or Ahashverosh-spiel – a burlesque of the Purim story itself – became a staple of the celebration, sometimes sexually obscene enough that the rabbis tried to stop them . . . So Purim became a Jewish version of the widespread custom of a season for relaxing the rules, even for making fun of the serious parts of life. Nor was this alien to its beginnings. For if indeed the Book of Esther was a fictional tale explaining a spring revel, then the Scroll itself was in a sense the first Purimshpiel, the first act of Purim-Torah.[67]

---

[66] Note Greenstein's pertinent observation on text and context of Esther: "the scroll was not canonized and read in the synagogue except as the Purim text. Whatever its inception, the biblical story of Esther was never heard except in the context of Jewish communal festivity. Accordingly, there was virtually no circumstance wherein a Jew might hear the scroll's words without simultaneously experiencing the strong influence of the surrounding carnival-like Purim scene." (See "A Jewish Reading of Esther," p. 226.) After I had completed this chapter, I came across the recent study by Kenneth M. Craig, *Reading Esther: A Case for the Literary Carnivalesque* (Louisville: Westminster/John Knox Press, 1995). Craig offers a stimulating interpretation of Esther from the perspective of Bakhtin's category of the "carnivalesque."

[67] Arthur I. Waskow, *Seasons of Our Joy: A Handbook of Jewish Festivals* (New York: Summit Books, 1982), p. 118.

CONCLUDING REFLECTIONS ON THE COMIC VISION IN EXODUS AND ESTHER

As indicated in the introduction to this chapter, it is my conviction that the parallels between Exodus and Esther are sufficient to warrant the pairing of these two biblical books as two interrelated "comedies of deliverance." First, they are similar in that they both use the powerful weapon of ridicule and satire to undercut the authority and stature of the reigning kings of the alien lands in which the Jews found themselves. Satirizing Egyptian Pharaoh and Persian king, the narrators resort to a typical instrument of survival by oppressed, subordinate people.[68] When the "wrong king is on the throne," one can satirically depict that king as a foolish, arrogant, stubborn ruler whose words and actions inevitably lead to his defeat and the ultimate triumph of the Jewish people. Hence God raises up the Pharaoh to "make a fool of him," to "make sport of him" (Ex. 10:2) in order to show the Jewish God's greater power and glory. The contest between Yahweh and Pharaoh ultimately is "no-contest." But the Exodus narrators use a very complex, varied form of satirical humor, resorting also to satire in order to show the weakness and folly of Moses, Aaron, and the Israelites – still another way to enhance God's glory. What is perhaps most startling is that even God is satirized on occasion, emerging as a capricious, fickle God who can go out of control in the pursuit of his goals. Thus God is a God full of surprises, who can sometimes threaten to kill Moses (Ex. 4:24–26) or even the whole people (Ex. 32), but who can be dissuaded by timely intervention or intercession. Ironically, it is perhaps only the women characters who appear more consistently in the best light, playing limited and yet crucial roles as sympathetic albeit subversive savior figures at the beginning in the birth stories (see Ex. 1–2), as knife-wielding rescuer at the middle with the rite

---

[68] Again, I refer the reader to the convincing analysis presented recently by Athalya Brenner, "Who's Afraid of Feminist Criticism," pp. 38–55.

of circumcision, and then finally as impassioned celebrants of deliverance in the climactic victory at the Red Sea (see Ex. 15). The contrast between the would-be powers of the world and the unlikely female saviors is most striking in the comedy of redemption we see in Exodus.

Esther takes another tack in its use of satire. The narrator no longer wants to resort to the sharp contrast between the all-powerful God and human pretenders, explicitly eliminating direct divine involvement in the story. Yet satire plays a significant role from start to finish. What emerges is perhaps a more subtle form of satire which allows a witless, easily swayed Ahasuerus to make a fool of himself without even requiring any divine intervention. The narrator depicts this Persian king as victim of his own excessive desires, his love of pompous display, his forgetfulness and muddle-headedness, and his dependence on the directives of others. He does not experience utter defeat himself, as happens in Yahweh's confrontation with Pharaoh and the gods of Egypt; no longer does the old theme of the battle between gods directly manifest itself in Esther, unless it be a subtle parody about the ironic reincarnation of Marduk and Ishtar in the Jewish(!) heroes named Mordecai and Esther. But God himself is not directly present in Esther, though interpreters have tirelessly wanted to find his "absent presence" behind the scenes in Esther. It is preeminently human protagonists who carry the action. Thus indirect, more subtle forms of satire subvert the powers arrayed against the Jewish minority in the vast Persian empire. By exposing the king as relatively weak and witless, too easily manipulated by others who are more savvy, the narrators enable two well-placed Jews in the court – a loyal courtier and a wise queen – to win over the king to their side. The vain Haman is tripped up when Esther resorts to a skillfully contrived waiting game, trapping Haman in a counter-plot designed to expose him as the arch-enemy of the Jews. The skilled deployment of such satirical humor becomes a weapon for Jewish survival in exile. Indeed, as Fox elegantly expresses it,

Humor, especially the humor of ridicule, is a device for defusing fear. The author [of Esther] teaches us to make fun of the very forces that once threatened – and will again threaten – our existence, and thereby makes us recognize their triviality as well as their power. 'If I laugh at any mortal thing,' said Byron, 'tis that I may not weep.' Jews have learned that kind of laughter.[69]

I would only add that Jews had already learned this ability to laugh in their foundational story in Genesis and Exodus, an ability brilliantly continued and further demonstrated in Esther, Daniel,[70] and other diasporic literature.

Both Exodus and Esther share still another feature of the comic vision – namely, a U-shaped plot-line where the crises and complications of the downward arc of the story serve to intensify the dramatic action, showing the perils of living as an oppressed minority while illustrating at the same time the possibilities for survival. Strategic intervention of heroic figures enables the Jews to be delivered from danger, with community solidified and strengthened, leaders honored and memorialized, and security insured for the future. Both narratives drive ineluctably upward to a "happy ending" celebrated in rite and liturgy. Hence Passover and Purim – separated by a month in the Jewish liturgical calendar – become linked together in Jewish tradition, two festivals which dramatically reenact comic forms of Israel's deliverance.[71] The resonance between these two stories of deliverance and their accompanying rituals helps to confirm and deepen the comic spirit that animates both the literature and liturgy. Hence liberation becomes wedded with laughter in these two comedies of deliverance.

Both Exodus and Esther highlight a form of comic

---

[69] Fox, *Character and Ideology in the Book of Esther*, p. 253.
[70] Robertson, *The Old Testament and the Literary Critic*, p. 16.
[71] Note the fascinating observation from Elie Wiesel: "for years and years – and centuries – we lived under the impression that Purim is Purim and Passover Passover. We were wrong. In the Talmud the events occur not in the month of Adar but one month later: the thirteenth, the fourteenth and the fifteenth of Nissan during Passover. In other words, Purim was Passover." See his *Sages and Dreamers: Portraits and Legends from the Jewish Tradition* (New York: Simon & Schuster, 1991), p. 135.

incongruity that revels in paradox and reversal. Who would think, for example, that a little child abandoned on the waters of the Nile would be adopted by an Egyptian princess and would then grow up to be the leader of the exodus in the name and power of a little known Hebrew god? Who could imagine that an adopted Jewish girl would be chosen as queen of the vast Persian empire and be able by her strategic and brave decisions to deliver her people from genocide – ironically all without any direct divine help? Fox puts his finger on this vital comic impulse of Esther (and his words ring true for Exodus as well): "The book's incongruous humor is one of its strange hallmarks. It mixes laughter with fear in telling about a near-tragedy that is chillingly reminiscent of actual tragedies."[72] It is this sense of incongruity, this sharpened awareness about ironic reversal, which gives insight into that narrow boundary between life and death, a comic sensibility that perceives the rhythms of life as sometimes surviving and even flourishing amidst the terrors of death and darkness.

[72] Fox, *Character and Ideology in the Book of Esther*, p. 251.

CHAPTER 4

Jonah as joke: a comedy of contradiction, caricature, and compassion

[I]n Jonah . . . we have the finest example of satiric humor in the Bible and one of the finest in any literature. Jonah is at once a deadly serious and a very funny book.[1]

(Roland M. Frye)

It is from the inspired duplicity of the prophet's task that the tale of Jonah derives its intellectual comedy.[2]

(George Steiner)

What . . . is inseparable from the comic is an infinite geniality and confidence capable of rising superior to its own contradiction.[3]

(Hegel)

A joke releases the tension, says the unsayable, any joke pretty well. But a true joke . . . has to do more than release tension, it has to *liberate* the will and the desire and to *change the situation.*[4]

(Robert M. Polhemus)

INTRODUCTION: ON DISCOVERING COMEDY IN JONAH

Jonah continues to have a reputation as an "odd" or "strange" book in the Bible. For example, it has been described as "the

[1] Roland M. Frye, *The Reader's Bible: A Narrative* (Princeton: Princeton University Press, 1965), p. xiii.
[2] George Steiner, *After Babel: Aspects of Language and Translation* (Oxford: Oxford University Press, 1975), p. 147.
[3] G. W. F. Hegel, *The Philosophy of Fine Art*, cited in *Theories of Comedy*, Paul Lauter, ed.(Garden City, NY: Doubleday and Co., 1964), p. 351.
[4] Robert M. Polhemus, *Comic Faith: The Great Tradition from Austen to Joyce* (Chicago: University of Chicago Press, 1980), p. 327.

odd one out"[5] in terms of its standing in the Minor Prophets, being the only one that is strictly a narrative as opposed to a collection of oracles. Moreover, Elias Bickerman included it among his "Four Strange Books of the Bible."[6] Yet paradoxically the book's unusual character should not be construed to mean that it lies outside the mainstream of the Hebrew Bible; in fact, in a curious yet compelling way, the book stands within a major trajectory in biblical literature, linking up intertextually with such obviously central books as Genesis and Exodus, on the one side, and Psalms and Job, on the other, with significant prophets like Elijah, Joel, and Jeremiah coming in between. Thus Jonah has a symbolically suggestive placement as the central chapter in this book. It serves to crystallize crucial comedic dimensions that refocus the comedy of Genesis and Exodus and to anticipate a part of the dramatic dialectic of "The Comedy of Job" which will be our next chapter.

Jonah has evoked a wild variety of interpretations, though an increasing number of recent scholars argue that Jonah represents some species of comedy – whether parody or satire or comic novella.[7] Of course the particular type of comedy is most debated, and a part of my task will be to delineate how Jonah might be appropriately approached as an incarnation of the comic vision, as a brilliant instance of a profound joke – to echo my title. Wolff in his well-known commentary on Jonah eloquently represents the book as a prime instance of comic art: "the unique beauty of the story and its liberating power is to be found in its *comedy* [emphasis his]. In no other book of the Bible do we find all the different varieties of the comic style so richly developed as here."[8] Our primary task

---

[5] The phrase is Golka's in the volume written by George A. F. Knight and Friedemann W. Golka, *Revelation of God: A Commentary on the Books of The Song of Songs and Jonah* (Grand Rapids: Wm. B. Eerdmans Co., 1988), p. 70.

[6] Elias Bickerman, *Four Strange Books of the Bible: Jonah/ Daniel/Koheleth/Esther* (New York: Schocken Books, 1967).

[7] See the discriminating survey in Jack M. Sasson, *Jonah: A New Translation with Introduction, Commentary, and Interpretations: Anchor Bible* (New York: Doubleday, 1990), pp. 331–334.

[8] Hans Walter Wolff, *Obadiah and Jonah: A Commentary*, trans. Margaret Kohl (Minneapolis: Augsburg Publishing House, 1986), p. 84.

and goal will be to test the viability of Wolff's claim about the comedy of Jonah and then to tease out the implications in reading this strange book as a comic work.

A few voices continue to argue vigorously, but unconvincingly in my view, against a comic treatment, asserting that Jonah is too "serious" or "earnest" for comedy whatever its precise type or affiliation. Adele Berlin, for instance, in an otherwise forceful critique of John Miles' essay on "Jonah as Parody," unfortunately appeals to the correlation of Jonah and Yom Kippur as a basis for rejecting Miles' interpretation: "Jewish tradition regards the Book of Jonah with such reverence that it is read at the afternoon service of the Day of Atonement, hardly the appropriate occasion for a parody of the Bible."[9] Craig's recent literary study of Jonah, which is filled with insightful analyses, offers a dismissive sentence about the case for Jonah's comedy: "a number of difficulties arise when the book is interpreted as parody or comedy. As we experience Jonah's thoughts and feelings first hand, we discover that the story is too earnest for laughter."[10] These remarks by Berlin and Craig display a failure to recognize that comedy and parody can in fact be compelling strategies in the service of religious faith. Such a dismissal of comedy from religious life and literature illustrates once more a superficial awareness of the range and depth of the comic vision which can profoundly engage topics that are "deadly serious" as well as "very funny." Indeed, comedy can serve powerfully as an apt and compelling vehicle for dealing with serious themes, especially in the realm of the sacred or religious.

PLOTTING A STORY: THE SIGNIFICANCE OF STRUCTURE

Though Jonah's generic affiliation and identification continue to be debated, virtually all interpreters agree that Jonah

---

[9] Adele Berlin, "A Rejoinder to John A. Miles, Jr., with Some Observations on the Nature of Prophecy," *Jewish Quarterly Review*, Vol. LXVI/4 (April, 1976), p. 227.

[10] Kenneth M. Craig, *A Poetics of Jonah: Art in the Service of Ideology* (Columbia: University of South Carolina, 1993), p. 142.

stands out as an artistic masterpiece where style matches substance in finesse, sophistication, and evocative power. For example, its structure reveals striking parallelism and symmetry, yet jarring dissonance, disruption, and an all but perpetual sense of surprise emerge, all of which already begin to suggest the presence of the comic spirit. Attention, therefore, to structure may serve as a fruitful entrance to the rich comic field of Jonah.

The plot structuring of this little story initially commands our interest, because the very symmetry that comes immediately to view takes some strange twists and turns. What on one level is a very simple plot – a prophet is divinely ordered to announce the destruction of a wicked city which then repents and is delivered from divine wrath – becomes marked by deviation from the norm and reversal of expectation. The complications and contradictions create, in my view, a finely drawn comic tale. Moreover, the characterization of the major protagonists provides comic heroes (or anti-heroes) known from a variety of ancient and modern literatures. Indeed, I will argue that the interplay between plot and character furnishes all the ingredients we customarily find in the comic vision.

As I have intimated, Jonah contains a basic plot-line as old as prophetic narrative, a plot which features prominently a structure of divine command and prophetic response. So Jonah's tale begins conventionally with a divine commission ("The Word of Yahweh came to Jonah: 'Go to Nineveh and preach against it'"). Whereas most prophetic stories then describe the compliance to the divine command, Jonah shatters this expectation not simply by showing reluctance (which even famous prophets like Moses and Jeremiah could do), but by an act of blatant disobedience. Instead of going east to Nineveh and doing the Lord's bidding, Jonah books passage on a ship that is going west to Tarshish. It is this fundamental conflict or contradiction between divine will and human willfulness that gives the story of Jonah its special character.

A whole series of oppositions or contradictions reflect the comic genius of the narrator in order to force deeper awareness about the nature of divine-human relationships, especially in regard to the role of prophecy and its paradox of the reversibility of a divinely decreed future coupled with such a corollary theme as the interplay and tension between justice and mercy in the divine disposition toward humanity.

Although recent studies of Jonah have shown an intricacy and complexity of design that reveals different structural possibilities,[11] the structure of the whole book at its most basic level unfolds in two major movements, the second dialectically and dramatically paralleling the first. The first major movement consists of Jonah's *disobedience* to a divine commission and its consequences (1:1–2:10), and the second involves Jonah's *obedience* to a divine commission and its consequences (3:1–4:11). Paradoxically, disobedience and obedience both lead to acts of deliverance grounded in divine mercy. A first contradiction – disobedience to the divine command – eventuates in a twofold act of compassionate rescue: both the innocent sailors and the guilty prophet experience deliverance which is vividly expressed in the sailors' rites of vows and sacrifice (1:16) and celebrated in Jonah's song of thanksgiving (2:1–9). In the second major movement, Jonah is put back on track and obeys the reiterated commission (3:1 ff). Wesley Kort shrewdly remarks that "at the beginning of chapter 3, midway in the story, we are no further along than we were at the beginning of the story, and the opening words of chapters 1 and 3 are virtually identical."[12] Thus the first "half of the book is given over to detour."[13] This fascinating detour or deviation, however, creates a necessary background for the second major movement, which rectifies the prophet's course and leads to deeper revelations of the opposition between Jonah and Yahweh, ending with a denouement rich in ambiguity.

[11] See, e.g., George M. Landes, "The Kerygma of the Book of Jonah," *Interpretation* 21 (January, 1967), pp. 3–31; Norbert Lohfink, "Jona ging zur Stadt hinaus (Jon 4, 5)," *Biblische Zeitschrift* 5, pp. 185–203, especially pp. 200–202; Jonathan Magonet, *Form and Meaning: Studies in Literary Techniques in the Book of Jonah* (Sheffield: The Almond Press, 1983), pp. 55–63.

[12] Wesley A. Kort, *Story, Text, and Scripture: Literary Interests in Biblical Narrative* (University Park: The Pennsylvania University Press, 1988), p. 35. [13] *Ibid.*

Indeed, what illuminates the basic plot is the image of detour in its double sense of deviation and delay, that is, a spatial sense of being deflected from the most direct route, of swerving from the main path as well as a temporal sense of losing time, of deferring fulfillment, of forcing the future to be perpetually open. Jonah's detour is initially of his own making: he disobeys the divine mandate, trying to flee from the presence of Yahweh. Clearly Jonah does not want the task of being a messenger of doom, but his precise motivation is not clear. Is he "tender-hearted" like Abraham (Gen. 18)[14] and thus concerned over the fate of innocent Gentiles, or is he simply afraid to venture into dangerous territory with a word of doom (recall the typical fate of a messenger of bad news in antiquity)?[15] At this point we do not know, but Jonah's deviation from his expected course creates the mood of uncertainty about this messenger who tries to escape from God.

The narrator underscores that Jonah is a fugitive from Yahweh who does fit at least partially into an old tradition of the reluctant prophet, but there are differences which suggest the presence of parody. First, other famous prophets like Moses or Jeremiah or even Isaiah shrink back from the prophetic task, but they express their unease with sometimes elaborate and ironically eloquent speeches (cf. Ex. 3–4; Isa. 6; and Jer. 1, 15, 20). Jonah is unique in saying nothing (at least as reported here), and simply attempting the impossible: fleeing from God's presence (cf. Ps. 139). Second, the other samples of reluctant prophets are typically motivated by their sense of inadequacy (cf. Ex. 3–4 and Jer. 1), whereas Jonah, though initially silent about his motivation for resisting, ultimately reveals that his disobedience stems from his perception of God's consistency which the prophet deems to be an inadequacy in his character (see 4:2). Third, other prophets might resist, but they do not blatantly disobey direct

---

[14] Meir Sternberg, *The Poetics of Biblical Narrative: Ideological Literature and the Drama of Reading* (Bloomington: Indiana University Press, 1985), p. 318.

[15] Cf. David M. Gunn and Danna Nolan Fewell, *Narrative in the Hebrew Bible* (Oxford: Oxford University Press, 1993), p. 130; note, too, Jack M. Sasson, *Jonah*, p. 87.

commands from God. Some kind of caricature of a prophetic rebel seems to be involved.

Yahweh, however, is not to be denied, and he shows his power as creator by hurling a "great wind upon the sea" which causes a mighty storm. The combination of God, wind, and sea echoes the images of Genesis' creation language (Gen. 1 and 6) as well as Yahweh's victory over the Egyptians at the Red Sea (Ex. 15), but in contrast to God's action to create the universe or to rescue Israel, here his resorting to his super powers serves simply to interrupt the flight of a single rebel.

The ship's captain and crew enter the scene as a foil for the major protagonists – Jonah and Yahweh. A disobedient Jonah appears in a bad light compared with the action of the innocent, generous sailors who desperately try to save the ship by crying to their different gods and jettisoning the cargo. In contrast, Jonah apparently at the first sign of the divinely sent tempest (or even earlier if this text represents a "flashback") continues his pattern of descent by going down into the hold of the ship and falling fast asleep. The captain finds him and says to him, "What are you doing sound asleep?" (1:6a). Some form of satire seems to be in play. Prophets could fall into a "deep sleep" to receive divine revelation as in the case of Abraham in Genesis 15 (cf. also Job 33), but it is an open question whether this is Jonah's situation (cf. also Adam in Gen. 2 and Eliphaz in Job 4:13).[16] Here the closest analogue seems to be Elijah who had fallen asleep under a bush in the midst of his flight from Jezebel's wrath, though here exhaustion seems to be the case (see I Kgs. 19).[17] If we grant that Jonah's action does fit the model of a prophet who is surrendering to the divine will and thus is now awaiting a divine word, we might wonder whether the narrator is parodying this prophetic procedure by having Jonah ironically hear at first only pagan voices that rudely wake him up to urge him

---

[16] Cf. Sasson, *Jonah*, pp. 101–102.

[17] Magonet, *Form and Meaning*, pp. 68–69; Jack Miles, "Laughing at the Bible: Jonah as Parody," *Jewish Quarterly Review* 65 (1975), p. 177. Sasson asserts that it is only "superficially similar to I Kgs 19:5," arguing that Jonah has made himself "ready to receive the divine message" (see his *Jonah*, p. 102).

to call upon his God and then interrogate him and demand some accounting for his actions. Is he really awaiting "to receive the divine message"?[18] Is his descent to the lowest parts of the ship not only a continuation of his descent to lower and lower depths but also suggestive of his death-wish? On any reading, the irony seems to be painfully clear: Jonah continues to be out of place and the narrator intensifies the pattern of deviation from the normal expectation. Either of McAlpine's possibilities – a prophet who is rendered "oblivious to YHWH's current action" or succumbs to a deep sleep anticipatory of eternal sleep or death – could be in play.[19] But the contrast alone between the feverish, futile activity of the sailors and the utter passivity of Jonah is sufficient to justify calling the scene satiric in design and effect.[20]

When the captain rebukes Jonah for sleeping, he does so with the urgent demand for him to "rise and call" to his God (1:6), thus echoing parodically Yahweh's initial commissioning of his rebellious prophet (cf. 1:2).[21] Apparently unaware at this point that Jonah had refused his prophetic mission, the captain anticipates how the storm is to be calmed and his ship and crew saved: "Get up, call on your god! Perhaps the god will spare us a thought so that we do not perish" (1:6).

Meanwhile the terrified sailors decide to cast lots, a time-honored way to decide who is guilty; the lot predictably falls on Jonah whom the sailors then interrogate. Already one may perceive incongruity between the studied quality of the questions and the desperate straits of the sailors who are panic-stricken in the midst of a raging storm. Is such a set of biographical questions appropriate at such a perilous time? Probably not – so an ironic intent may well be present.[22] In any case, Jonah only answers the last question, identifying

---

[18] Sasson, *ibid*. See, however, Thomas A. McAlpine's nuanced suggestions for the understanding of "sleep" in Jonah in his *Sleep, Divine and Human, in the Old Testament* (Sheffield: JSOT Press, 1987), p. 58. Sasson notes McAlpine's observations, but criticizes him for failing to see the implications for Jonah (*Jonah*, p. 102, note 5).   [19] McAlpine, *Sleep, Divine and Human*, p. 58.
[20] Wolff, *Obadiah and Jonah*, p. 113.   [21] Magonet, *Form and Meaning*, pp. 25–26.
[22] Good, *Irony in the Old Testament*, p. 44.

himself as a "Hebrew," and then adding "I fear Yahweh, the God of heaven, who made the sea and the dry land." Interpreters are too quick to drain the Hebrew word *yr'* of its sense of fear or dread and translate "worship," thus differentiating radically the meaning of the verb that three times is coupled with the Gentile sailors in a progressively deepening sense of fear.[23] This translation is a mistake, for it loses the ironic interplay and tension among the several uses of the verb (1:5,9,10,16). A confession of Jonah's fear of Yahweh is made rather perfunctory and empty in contrast to the genuine, albeit multi-faceted fear of the sailors who at first are terrified before the storm (1:5), a terror heightened when they hear Jonah's confession (1:10), but a terror sublimated into an awe before Yahweh after the sea becomes calm. Jonah is again implicitly condemning himself by testifying to fear before the creator, when he has attempted to flee from such a powerful God. The comic irony of his futile attempt to escape in light of his confession is all too apparent: why and how did he ever expect to run from the creator of heavens and dry ground? (Ps. 139). What kind of authentic fear did he manifest before such a God in doing something so inherently contradictory and dangerous?

Jonah makes what seems to be a magnanimous gesture in proposing to the sailors that they should throw him overboard as the only solution to the divinely sent tempest, but some have read his offer as a continuation of his death-wish. So one should not take too seriously his offer, which has a measure of an almost stoic acceptance of inevitability. In any case, after further unsuccessful efforts on the crew's part to reach shore, the sailors cast Jonah into the stormy waters. Before they do so, however, they pray that God not hold them accountable for "innocent blood" – an understandable desire on their part, though it serves to heighten the irony. After all, they are the innocent victims of the guilty prophet's action. Wolff rightly calls attention to the ironic contrast with

---

[23] See Magonet, *Form and Meaning*, pp. 31–32; note, too, Sasson's observations on this point (*Jonah*, pp. 97–98).

Jeremiah's words to his captors: "know for certain that if you put me to death, you will be bringing innocent blood upon yourselves . . ." (Jer. 26:15).[24] Moreover, the sailors conclude with a motive clause which shows their surrender to the divine will: "for you, Yahweh, have done as it pleased you." That the storm immediately ceases comes as no surprise to the reader – nor to Jonah, but brings relief to the terrified crew. Their "fear" changes into a "great fear before Yahweh" and fittingly climaxes the various states and stages of "fear" in the narrative, an intensifying accent that shows both the theological concern and the artistic skill of the story-teller. That thank-offerings and vows consummate the acts of worship is appropriate, demonstrating the sailors' acknowledgment of Yahweh's presence and power. The sailors thereby show themselves to be quick learners of Yahwistic practices (Lev. 7:12; Pss. 22:22; 50:14; 66:13,16; 107:22). Rescue and its proper recognition in festive rites bring a happy ending to this surprising tale of disobedience, desperate flight, and double deliverance.

The good and generous sailors provide a strongly satiric contrast with the foolish Jonah, who alone knows the will of God even though disobedient, and who becomes ironically both the reason for the danger and the revealer of the mode of deliverance; his futile flight marks a sharp deviation in the movement of the plot, bringing a storm in his wake and a near calamity to his ship-mates. A strange figure this rebel with a cause, who becomes both comic hero and comic victim: a hero in the sense that he is willing to rebel against God to follow out his own conviction; but also a victim who becomes manipulated by divine power and voluntarily offers himself up to appease the God whom he fears but disobeys and whom the sailors come to fear and acknowledge in acts of worship.[25]

But Jonah has not been forgotten, and the god who controls the storm and sea "appoints" a great fish to "swallow up

[24] Wolff, *Obadiah and Jonah*, p. 120.
[25] Cf. Sasson's suggestive remarks in his characterization of Jonah as "Comic Dupe" and "Comic Hero" in his commentary on *Jonah*, pp. 245–250.

Jonah" in order to provide a dark haven for three days and three nights (1:17–2:1). The prose frame for Jonah's strange, submarine journey through the sea consists of the report of God's action of first appointing a great fish to "swallow up" Jonah and then secondly commanding the fish to "throw up" Jonah on the dry ground. Again, it is in the style of a comic writer to take the old motif of heroes who are devoured by marine monsters and then miraculously survive the sojourn in the monster's belly, but in Jonah's case the manner of ingestion and especially regurgitation finds a ridiculous portrayal that can best be called comic. It is particularly the mode of the fish's compliance with the divine command to deposit Jonah on dry ground that heightens the humor of the story: the fish is to vomit up Jonah as the undignified means of expulsion of the fugitive. The Hebrew verb in question – *qy'* – consistently refers to "images that rouse disgust."[26] What a way to deal with a rebel prophet: to give him a lengthy ride in a sea monster that finally vomits him up on dry ground. One notes also that God acts silently during the whole episode. It is surely ironic during and after this scene of a fantastic submarine ride that Yahweh speaks to Jonah only after he has spoken to the fish. All in all it is a scene that shows a hilarious comic touch that probably evoked laughter in its ancient context.[27]

A more subtle interplay takes place within the frame of the fish's actions of swallowing Jonah and then vomiting him up. The initial verb about Yahweh's appointing the fish is used of employing servants, a verb suggestive of Yahweh's playful designation of a sea creature to perform a service.[28] The next verb, "swallow up, devour" always connotes "danger" (Jer. 51:34; Pss. 21:9; 35:25; 69:15; 106:17; 124:3; Lam. 2:2, 5, 8, 16). One initially imagines that the prophet is being duly punished for his disobedience, becoming one who experiences death not by drowning but by being devoured by a huge fish. But then suddenly, we note another deviation in

---

[26] Wolff, *Obadiah and Jonah*, p. 139.   [27] See also Sasson, *Jonah*, p. 222.
[28] See Wolff, *Obadiah and Jonah*, p. 132.

our expectation, another delightful twist in the plot. Instead of a horrifying death, the prophet lives, and even breaks out in a beautiful, seemingly heart-felt prayer which suggests an inner spiritual transformation. This sudden disruption in the narrative with its shift in mood and focus from a narrative of disobedience and dire punishment to a poetic expression of thanksgiving and praise for deliverance from death initially surprises us, yet paradoxically when read from the perspective of the whole book is curiously appropriate. That is, we have a plot movement that features deliverance as its dominant motif, but strange and marvelous modes of deliverance. Thus the sailors' deliverance adumbrates not only Nineveh's deliverance from destruction, but even Jonah's. In keeping with the dominant mode of comedy, nobody gets seriously or permanently hurt; it is a comedy where everyone ultimately is rescued, where various sorts of happy endings prevail – though for Jonah his final notes will be singularly unhappy. But that is getting ahead of our story.

For modern literary critics, the psalm of thanksgiving in 2:3–10 continues to evoke the greatest amount of debate, and they still remain divided whether it is original or not. For a comic reading of Jonah, the psalm receives different interpretations depending on whether we attribute it to the narrator or to a later interpolator: if it belongs to the original narrator, then it can be read as a self-conscious attempt to introduce incongruity that heightens the parody of prophetic behavior; if a later redactor is responsible, then it either is an awkward ploy to inject some piety into a rebellious prophet or it is an ironic, albeit perceptive intrusion which resonates at a profound level with the images of the prophet from the surrounding context. For example, the verb *yrd* ("descend") appears in the psalm (2:6), echoing the downward movement vividly expressed in chapter 1:3, 5.[29] We have now the deepest descent of the prophet, as he sinks into the depths of the marine underworld.

For the purposes of a comic reading, it really makes little

---

[29] Magonet, *Form and Meaning*, p. 17.

difference how we answer the question of the psalm's originality. The text now belongs to the story, and it heightens the comic dimension in the present form. The resonances of the text with its surrounding narrative have often been observed.[30] What is striking for a comic reading is both the psalm's strategic placement in its narrative context and its inner form and content. Since it comes between the swallowing up by the gigantic fish and the unceremonious expulsion when the fish vomits up the prophet on dry ground, it is hard to see how one can read this pious prayer with a straight face. Innumerable critics have seen the incongruity between the so-called "old Jonah" of the prose story and the "new Jonah" of the thanksgiving. Typically they have used this as one argument against its right to belong to the primary level of the tradition, yet a comic reading that revels in a constantly changing perspective should warn us not to be too concerned about the lack of fit: it is precisely the interplay and tension between the fit and no fit of psalm and story that feeds into a comic reading. In fact, the picture of the pious prophet yearning to see again the Jerusalem temple jars with the image of the fugitive who is trying to escape from God's presence, but the jarring of images is a way to heighten the parody. The prayer expresses the desperation of a drowning man: who wouldn't cry for help in such a time and then express thanksgiving for rescue?

Moreover, since the poem consists of a pastiche of psalmodic cliches, self-conscious parody becomes a possibility, as the narrator mixes up old and new to create a grotesque image of a praying prophet swallowed by a huge fish, miraculously surviving for three days and three nights, and then being vomited up on shore. I would highlight only three effects of the poem as pastiche and parody. First, we have the sudden shift in the beginning which starts off on the note of a lament – surely an appropriate beginning of a desperate prayer from a disobedient prophet who finds himself in grave

---

[30] *Ibid.*, pp. 49–54; Magonet especially emphasizes the ironic interplay between the psalm and its tradition (pp. 52–53).

danger – but then the psalm changes into the more dominant note of thanksgiving which presupposes that the rescue has taken place.[31] Second, the descent into the depths of the sea continues the quest for death revealed in the prophet's moves in his flight from Yahweh,[32] but the poet dramatically expresses the reversal of fortune in 2:6: "I went down to the land whose bars closed upon me forever; yet you brought up my life from the Pit." Third, the prophet's last word in his prayer, "Deliverance belongs to Yahweh" (2:9b) can stand as a motto for the whole book, looking back at the two acts of deliverance from the sea's power involving both the sailors and Jonah, and anticipating the astounding deliverance of all the Ninevites in the next chapter. A "happy ending" comes to the desperate flight of the prophet when he is rescued by a great fish. That the prophet echoes the sailors' acts of offering sacrifice and making vows (1:16) in his pious pledge before his affirmation of divine deliverance heightens the ironic contrast between the Hebrew prophet and the Gentile sailors.

The graphically humorous expulsion of the prophet from the fish serves both as an amusing response to the prayer and an ironic commentary on the utter freedom of Yahweh to effect his will. Yahweh speaks to the fish who obeys; then he speaks again to the prophet with a repeated word of commission to get on the road to Nineveh; no wonder that Jonah immediately complies the second time around. That Yahweh speaks to the fish before he speaks to the prophet in this sequence reminds one of Yahweh's allowing himself to be seen by Balaam's donkey before Balaam's eyes are opened to see Yahweh (cf. Num. 22).[33] Both prophets must be put in their place by Yahweh's employment of the two animals in these fables. Humorous satire that is more gentle than bitter seems to be present in both cases.[34]

---

[31] Cf. Wolff, *Obadiah and Jonah*, p. 133; Sasson, *Jonah*, pp. 154–155.

[32] Magonet, *Form and Meaning*, p. 17.

[33] As Sasson observes, we have only one other occurrence when God speaks directly to an animal – namely, the divine curse against the serpent of Eden (Gen. 3:14); see his *Jonah*, p. 219.   [34] Miles, "Laughing at the Bible," p. 176.

At long last the detour of the disobedient prophet is over. Whether Jonah has learned fully his lesson remains to be seen, but in any event he has at least learned that it is better to obey than oppose Yahweh who is the "God of heaven who made the sea and the dry land" (1:9). In the briefest of reports the narrator tells us that Jonah "began to go into the city, going a day's walk; and he cried out, 'Forty days more, and Nineveh will be overthrown!'" (3:4). What follows is a report of the most stupendously successful mission in the history of prophetic preaching: "The people of Nineveh believed God; they proclaimed a fast, and everyone, great and small, put on sackcloth" (3:5).

The whole city responds in an astounding expression of faith in Yahweh, an action whose report reaches all the way to the throne, evoking royal participation both in the king's individual response and his proclamation of a decree to insure the fullest conceivable compliance from all the populace including the animals. Although participation of animals in such ceremonies is attested by various sources from antiquity, the gesture here seems exaggerated for effect and fits into the pattern of comic hyperbole. The prescribed domestic animals dutifully decked out in sackcloth join their human owners and cry out mightily to God. In contrast to this ludicrous scene with its circus of penitent animals, the portrait that Joel paints of suffering animals may be seen as a compelling and even poignant representation of the solidarity between humans and animals in the disastrous conditions of a drought: "Even the wild animals cry to you because the watercourses are dried up, and fire has devoured the pastures of the wilderness" (Joel 1:20). How very different is this image from the royal decree for humans to deprive the animals of food and drink as a part of an exaggerated call for total participation in penitential rites: "By the decree of the king and his nobles: No human being or animal, no herd or flock, shall taste anything. They shall not feed, nor shall they drink water. Human beings and animals shall be covered with sackcloth, and they shall cry mightily to God . . ." (3:7–8). Moreover, the puns on two key roots enhance the humor (*ta'am*="taste" playing on *ta'am*="decree"; *ra'a'*="to be evil" and *ra'ah*="to graze"). The punning connection coupled with what appears to be a motif in the ancient world – the participation of animals in pivotal rituals of humanity – heightens the comic effect. Whereas Joel offers us a reminder of the intimate links between animals and humans during so-called natural disasters like severe drought, Jonah presents a ludicrous image of pentitent animals all covered in sackcloth. The hyperbolic humor of the latter should be all too apparent, revealing a fantastic and even funny image.[35]

The King of Nineveh then continues to demonstrate his keen insight into the ways of the deity, manifesting the proper blend of diffidence and fragile hope that divine mercy might be granted: "Who knows? God may relent and change his mind; he may turn from his fierce anger, so that we perish not" (3:9). That the king expresses a question similar to Joel's (2:14) illustrates once again the interplay between Joel and Jonah, each voice serving as a counterpoint to the other. For Joel, it represents a prophetic invocation of the old Israelite covenantal tradition and thus contains the hope that God will turn away from his anger and leave "a blessing behind him" (2:14) in response to the people's repentance; but for Jonah, it ironically attributes a sharp awareness to a foreign king concerning the conditional nature of God's dealings with his creatures. The King of Nineveh knows not only what to do in proclaiming his decree of national penitence, but he also reveals a sensitivity about the existential uncertainty whether God would react positively. His diffident "Who knows?" expresses a time-honored way of expressing human surrender to the mysterious and sovereign freedom of God to act as he will, echoing in his rhetorical question a sentiment similar to the anxious "perhaps . . . we perish not" of the ship's captain (1:6). The king's question heightens the sense of mystery as to what God will do especially after his prophet has announced the message of doom.

---

[35] See Wolff, *Obadiah and Jonah*, pp. 152–153; the satiric interpretation is challenged by Sasson (*Jonah*, pp. 255–258).

Nineveh's massive repentance evokes from God an act of reciprocal repentance: "When God saw what they did, how they turned from their evil ways, God changed his mind about the 'evil' that he had said he would bring upon them; and he did not do it" (3:10). Here we find an application of the Deuteronomic-Jeremianic teaching about repentance as a key to the averting of divine punishment of evil. Jeremiah gives it classic formulation: "At one moment I may declare concerning a nation or kingdom, that I will . . . destroy it, but if that nation . . . turns from its evil, I will change my mind about the disaster that I intended to bring on it" (18:7, 8). For the Ninevites, this change in God's mind offers a wonderful reversal of fortune, presenting another example of deliverance in this comedy of multiple deliverances. Such deliverance is heavily laden with irony, since it either stands as a sharp contradiction to Jonah's oracle of doom or it can be more subtly read as an ironic fulfillment of the key word of the oracle: the city is "overturned" – not in the way of its fabled forebears Sodom and Gomorrah (Gen. 19–25), but in the "turning" of repentance which evoked a divine change from doom to deliverance.[36] Typically, such a deliverance would be expected to bring a song of jubilation (e.g., as in Ex. 15 or in Jonah's song of thanksgiving). But no such song appears here. Nor does a more prosaic fairy tale ending appear. Of course the divine decision to turn aside the decree of destruction is not guaranteed to be viewed with equal favor by Israelites who saw Nineveh as an incarnation of evil and worthy of total destruction, a view that is presented with rare and awe-ful power in the brilliant poetry of Nahum.

To Jonah this radical turn-about in God's will concerning Nineveh makes him deeply unhappy: "But this was very displeasing to Jonah, and he became angry" (4:1). What sharpens the intensity of his reaction is to reflect on the Hebrew behind the words "very displeasing," which render *wayyer'a ra'ah gdolah* (="it was evil, a great evil"). As is obvious to even a cursory reader of the Hebrew text of Jonah, the narrator

---

[36] See Sasson, *Jonah*, pp. 234–235, 237, 295–296.

adroitly interweaves the word *ra'ah* (="evil") into the story
from start to finish. Thus the initial divine commission to
speak against Nineveh was motivated by its "evil" (1:2).
Likewise, the same word appears again in the story of
Nineveh's repentance of their "evil ways" (3:8,10) and then
reciprocated in God's turning away from the "evil" he
planned against them (3:10). Now in this climactic
encounter we hear once more the word "evil," applied this
time to Jonah's emotional disturbance (thus he is variously
described as "very displeased," "terribly upset," etc.). The
advantage and power of the same Hebrew word is to highlight
a chain reaction that is emphatically inscribed by the multiple and diverse uses of the same root: "evil" begets "evil" in
the linguistic chain, with each new context shading into
different nuances of an inter-related experience. In fact, "the
repeated catchword does not merely accentuate Jonah's
opposition to God's judgment; it also stresses that Jonah and
Nineveh have actually exchanged roles. That it should be
God's very mercy that brings 'great wickedness on Jonah' is
both dramatic and satiric."[37]

The precise cause of Jonah's particular disturbance
remains somewhat enigmatic, but crucial to a plot filled with
surprises is to discern another deviation of the plot beneath
the parallelism and symmetry between chapters 2 and 4.
Typically we expect celebration for deliverance as revealed
satirically in Jonah's own psalm of thanksgiving or stirringly
in the oracles of joyous salvation we read in Joel 2 which
follow on the beneficent response to the call to penitence.
But in Jonah 4 instead of an "ode to joy" we find a palpably
upset prophet who is bitterly angry – anger both turned
against himself (as expressed by his twofold death-wish) and
against God (his complaint). Thus when Jonah "prays" (using
the same word that typically begins a complaint as in Jon. 2),
he justifies his action in his initial act of disobedience. He
lodges the grounds of his opposition to the divine marching
orders in the very character of God, as he now divulges in his
second prayer to God:

[37] Wolff, *Obadiah and Jonah*, p. 165.

O Yahweh! Is not this what I said while I was still in my own country? That is why I fled to Tarshish at the beginning; for I knew that you are a gracious God and merciful, slow to anger, and abounding in steadfast love, and ready to relent from punishing. And now, O Yahweh, please take my life from me, for it is better for me to die than to live. And Yahweh said, 'Is it right for you to be angry'? (4:2–4).

For the first time in Jonah we hear a report of a dialogue between Jonah and Yahweh, whereas before we heard Yahweh's direct command (1:2) and of course Jonah's first prayer to Yahweh: but there was no genuine dialogue until the closing scene. Questions of course have run through the whole narrative, but now the two main protagonists exchange questions and counter-questions. At last dialogue moves into the space, helping to "bridge distance but not defiance."[38]

Jonah's question comes in the form of a "flashback" where he supplies a verbal explanation for his act of disobedience. So he is not out of step with the other resistant prophets who principally spoke their opposition to Yahweh's will. This delay or deferral of Jonah's verbal response to Yahweh's commission both supplies a reason for his earlier precipitous flight and subverts the seeming transformation that can be deduced from his song of thanksgiving. It shows that a prophet who began in resistance remains resistant, invoking one of the most fundamental confessions we have in the Hebrew Bible, a confession, however, now used in a context expressly contrary to its usual usage. For example, in the archetypal Exodus 34 text, we hear what is apparently Yahweh's own self-proclamation of his special name and his special character: "Yahweh, Yahweh, a God merciful and gracious, slow to anger, and abounding in steadfast love . . . keeping steadfast love for the thousandth generation, forgiving iniquity . . ., yet by no means clearing the guilty, but visiting the iniquity of the parents upon the children . . ." (34:6,7). In this famous context, Moses uses this divine declaration as the basis for his intercession on behalf of "his stiff-necked

---

[38] Phyllis Trible, *Rhetorical Criticism: Context, Method, and the Book of Jonah* (Minneapolis: Fortress Press, 1994), p. 215.

people" in order to find "pardon for our iniquity and our sin" (34:9). His prayer is answered and Yahweh renews the covenant with Israel.

In contrast to Moses' use of the tradition, Jonah invokes it as the basis for his resistance to Yahweh's extension of his mercy to the Ninevites. It is one thing to invoke Yahweh's gracious character in relationship to Israel, but quite another matter to extend it to foreigners. It is also significant that Jonah leaves out the negative part of the confession – namely, that Yahweh can punish the sins of the fathers to the third and fourth generations – thus underscoring the beneficent, gracious side of the deity who from Jonah's viewpoint can too easily and generously "relent from punishing." Jonah does not so much condemn Yahweh for caprice in manifesting his mercy as criticize him for too characteristically changing his sentence from doom to unmerited deliverance. What appears as caprice is in fact a kind of deeper consistency in the divine makeup: as connoisseur of the covenantal tradition Jonah knows about God's habit of changing his mind because of his compassionate nature. We hear no explicit word of reference to Nineveh's repentance (*nḥm*) as a motivation for God's change of mind, though the root *nḥm* does appear as an echo; the radical alteration in the divine will is simply rooted in the generosity of compassion. Whether Jonah is condemning the revelation of mercy to the Ninevites or simply expressing his displeasure at being left out of the action is open to debate, though most interpreters favor the first alternative.[39] What is perhaps most striking is that Jonah uses the tradition both to justify his disobedience and to criticize God. He ironically uses a tradition that had consistently been invoked to elicit mercy and pardon as the grounds for his petition to die. He therefore inverts the tradition, converting it from a basis for an appeal for pardon to grounds for his death-wish. Here too the allusion to Elijah's death-wish

---

[39] See Sasson's nuanced representation of Jonah's complex perspective which stresses the prophetic complaint about how Jonah feels about God's failure in not "giving his prophet a role to play in the reversal" of God's intent to punish Nineveh; cf. his comments in *Jonah*, pp. 296–297.

heightens and confirms the parody: Elijah not only is reeling
from apparent defeat but is fleeing the threat of death issued
by Jezebel.

In sum, Jonah is foreshadowed by both Moses and Elijah,
taking their language to subvert their different motivations
for prayer. Whereas Moses makes positive use of Yahweh's
attributes to appeal for Israel's life, Jonah construes the same
categories negatively to defend his earlier flight, to undercut
God's compassion for a foreign people, and to petition for his
own death. Whereas Elijah faces failure in his mission and
thus has greater grounds for his death-wish, Jonah paradoxically has enjoyed tremendous success in his mission. Hence
Jonah narrows his vision to his own egocentric interests,
unable to encompass an extension of divine mercy to another
people. The narrator creates a caricature of a prophet, whose
parody of famous prophetic words and images intensifies the
satirical effect.

Jonah indeed prays, but his posture provokes divine
response which comes in the form of a question that focuses
on relative "rights": "Is it right for you to be angry?" a query
Jonah does not verbally answer, though his exit from the city
can be read as his reaction to God's query: "Then Jonah went
out of the city and sat down east of the city, and made a booth
for himself there. He sat under it in the shade, waiting to see
what would become of the city" (4:5). There is no need either
to relocate the text or to read it as a "flashback."[40] We have
earlier examples of how Jonah sometimes responds to a
divine commission by deeds, not words; thus it is fitting to
construe Jonah's exit as his answer to Yahweh's question.[41]
Apparently, Jonah still harbors the hope that the decree of
destruction might yet be fulfilled. Moreover, still another
reason for his desire to be outside the city has traditio-
historical grounding: if the word "overthrown" in his oracle
of doom does evoke the memory of Sodom and Gomorrah
which perished in a fiery conflagration, then his wish to

---

[40] See Sasson's cogent argumentation: *ibid.*, pp. 287–290.
[41] Here I am following Magonet's suggestion; cf. *Form and Meaning*, p. 58.

depart from the city is understandable; like Lot he needs to get out before it is too late. Again, if images from Genesis are in view, Jonah possibly mimics Abraham's action of observing the fate of the cities on the plain (Gen. 19:27–28). Finally, Jonah's exit from Nineveh represents still another sample of his persistent deviations, thus fitting into a major dynamic of a book that proceeds often by means of detours. If this reading contains merit, then once again Jonah's resistance to the divine will is illustrated, and particularly his persistent, if not stubborn, adherence to his own perspective: God has seen that Nineveh has changed and he changes his decision to destroy the city; now Jonah will see for himself what in fact happens to the city.

Just as Yahweh earlier had reacted to Jonah's act of disobedience by creating a storm at sea, so again Yahweh resorts to an indirect means to confront his troubled and troublesome prophet: a series of inter-linked divine actions playfully create a game which contains an object lesson for the resistant prophet. First he provides or "appoints" a bush for Jonah which miraculously grows up overnight "to give shade over his head, to save him from his discomfort" (4:6a). Not only do we have a catchword connection in the seemingly redundant provision of extra source of shade (which now potentially comes from both the booth and the bush), but the wonderful plant is expressly designed to embody the key theme of the book – salvation or deliverance from evil, shaded here to mean physical discomfort. Just as the divinely appointed fish served as a comic means of deliverance in Jonah's sea journey, so the divinely given plant provides a better means to illustrate God's purpose for Jonah than the booth. The narrator even supplies an artful pun to cement the relationship between the plant's "shade" (*sel*) and its capacity to "save" (*hasil*). As a consequence of the plant's comforting presence, Jonah "enjoyed a great joy" (*wayyismah simhah gedolah*); the second appearance of a cognate accusative both matches the idiom of the first verse (*wayyera' ra'ah gedolah*="and it was evil – a great evil") and radically alters Jonah's mood from extreme distress to extreme joy. In relentless succession Yahweh then "appoints" a worm to attack and kill the plant (4:7), and quickly follows by "appointing" a searing east wind to intensify the burning sun that beats upon the head of Jonah and makes him faint (4:8a); once more Jonah petitions God to let him die since "it is better to die than to live" (4:8b). The swiftness of Jonah's mood swings, the exaggeration of his different emotional states, and the disproportion between cause and effect in his sudden changes – all combine to produce a striking parody. The specific allusion to Elijah who lies down under a bush and wishes to die heightens the parody, since Elijah has much more substantial reasons to give up on life.[42]

What Yahweh has engineered is a kind of "play within a play" in order to script a profound joke on Jonah in this climactic scene. The plot has rather bumpily converged to this point, averting once again any sort of traditional happy ending in order to have a denouement which raises the stakes in the game. We indeed have "move/countermove"[43] as the dynamic of the chapter, a dynamic intensified because of the questions which typically have no answer – or at best an indirect answer. Thus dialogue dominates, but dialogue which is ambiguous and open-ended. Dialogue is a word impregnated with different possibilities. First, as Trible observes, the dialogue bridges the distance between God and prophet, focusing the debate in the intensity of direct and angry exchange. Second, what has been implicit in the structure and movement of Jonah – gaps which invite and provoke multiple readings – now emerges with sharper focus, yet ambiguities and enigmas continue to challenge our interpretive skill. Third, since the denouement unfolds dominantly in dialogue, where two voices are heard in point and counter-point, the story moves into the realm that Bakhtin aptly describes as the "dialogic imagination," a zone of the imagination that has the potential to be brilliantly comic in its double-voiced qualities.[44]

---

[42] See Miles, "Laughing at the Bible," p. 180.
[43] The phrase is Sasson's: it serves as the title for his analysis of 4:1–6 in his *Jonah*, pp. 270–298.   [44] See Bakhtin, *The Dialogic Imagination*, pp. 324–330.

As we have seen, Jonah justifies both his present distress and his past disobedience by a rhetorical question that strikes to the heart of the divine nature (4:2). In invoking a central covenantal confession, Jonah "complains" that God can be too easily counted on to be "slow to anger and abounding in steadfast love." Hence the love and mercy are somehow wrongly directed and given to an undeserving recipient. His charge is that God can be reliable in displaying his gracious character, but he construes this sometimes hidden face of God as a fault, not a virtue. God is therefore duplicitous, commissioning a prophet to pronounce an oracle of destruction, but then concealing the alternative of gracious deliverance. As Steiner well observes, it is this very duplicity that creates the conditions for "the intellectual comedy" of Jonah.[45] What a profound irony in Jonah's take on the tradition! He is most unhappy to the point of desiring death after deliverance comes to a "great city" because of the divine decision to show mercy; then he becomes most happy in the next scene when a divinely provided plant offers him temporary deliverance from the evil of a burning sun; but when he loses his protective shade he is plummeted again into despair – despair unto death. What the narrator first describes as Jonah's repeated death-wish, he confirms by quoting Jonah's direct speech: "It is better for me to die than to live" (4:8b). The changes of mood are almost dizzying in their rapidly shifting character.

The whole series of events provides a rather contrived means to maneuver Jonah into a position to be challenged by God's renewed interrogation: "Is it right for you to be angry about the bush?" (4:9a), to which Jonah sharply retorts, "Yes, angry enough to die!" (4:9b). Here it is obviously an issue of the prophet's "right" to his anger, an issue frontally presented as the two protagonists face one another in their exhange of question and counter-question. God, however, poses the final question which becomes the provocative punchline of this complex joke: "You are concerned about the bush, for which

[45] Steiner, *After Babel*, p. 147.

you did not labor and which you did not grow; it came into being in a night and perished in a night. And should I not be concerned about Nineveh, that great city, in which there are more than a hundred and twenty thousand persons who do not know their right hand from their left, and also many animals?" (4:10–11). Yahweh's pointed question with its "lesser to greater" argument forces Jonah (and the reader) to confront the stark contrast between Jonah's "concern" for a plant that lasted only a day and God's "concern" for a plenitude of people and animals.

The irony is also clear: Jonah is hardly concerned for the plant, but in reality continues to focus on his own narrow needs. The plant was a source of comfort and joy; when it suddenly disappeared as quickly as it appeared, Jonah's mood was so resonant with the rhythm of the plant's brief cycle of life that his joy was replaced by abject sorrow. The fickleness in Jonah's moods so dependent on external circumstances often of a trifling nature is jarringly juxtaposed with God's capacious and consistent nature as a compassionate creator whose care embraces all creatures including ignorant, helpless humans and defenseless animals. Transcending the reciprocal action of repentance, God concludes his case by arguing for his right to show concern for all his creatures. This final question once more attempts to persuade Jonah by its appeal to a love that transcends a rule of reciprocity. How Jonah and all the subsequent "Jonahs" of later communities answer the question is not disclosed, leaving the question perennially open. The lack of closure is the final dissonant note in a pattern of detours, deviations, and delays. Perhaps, however, an unanswered question is ultimately the most compelling ending in a dialogue that might indeed bridge distance,[46] but does not automatically erase the difference between patient deity and disenchanted prophet. The form superficially is a rhetorical question, but in function it is a real question which serves to keep the issue open. We think – or perhaps hope – that Jonah (and we) will answer "Yes!", but at

---

[46] Trible, *Rhetorical Criticism*, p. 215.

bottom we are not fully certain. God does have the last word, symmetrically matched even in word length of thirty-nine words by Jonah's self-justifying speech (4:2–3),[47] yet the unanswered question remains to alter the pattern of formally balanced speeches and finish with the dissymmetry of an inconclusive conclusion. The joke may be on Jonah, but perhaps in the end that is not an ending the narrator plays a joke on those of us who constitute the ongoing audience for this prophetic short story.

If, as Mary Douglas suggests, a joke "brings into relation disparate elements in such a way that a once accepted pattern is challenged by the appearance of another which in some way was hidden in the first," then Jonah may be construed as a profound joke.[48] Its unceasing pattern of duplicity, deviation, and deferral forces us to confront contradictory possibilities of thought. The most congenial home for such provocative plays on language and tradition is the comic vision with its delight in ambiguity, duplicity, and contradiction.

CONCLUSION: ON READING JONAH AS A PROFOUND JOKE

Jonah stands in a central position within the biblical heritage and particularly performs a pivotal role in the Bible's comic vision. First, its comic form emerges in its pattern of contradiction, a pattern that shows the collision of divine and human wills. This clash of wills can sometimes take on tragic dimensions, but in Jonah's case the contradiction between divine and human purposes is used to play with the different possibilities that inhere in the relationship between God and his creatures. It is remarkable to note that no one gets hurt in Jonah (if we exclude the hapless plant that served as object lesson). Thus all God's creatures human and animal might be

---

[47] Sasson has convincingly demonstrated the symmetry in Jonah 4; cf. *Jonah*, p. 317.
[48] Mary Douglas, "The Social Control of Cognition: Some Factors in Joke Perception," *Man*, n.s. III (1968), p. 365. I owe this reference to Jonathan Z. Smith, "Good News is No News: Aretalogy and Gospel," in his *Map is Not Territory: Studies in the History of Religions* (Leiden: E. J. Brill, 1978), p. 206.

threatened by evil forces, yet no one perishes. In fact, to my knowledge, apart from the Song of Songs, it is the only book in the Hebrew Bible where no one dies.

Conflict between creator and creatures is an old theme which emerges primordially in Genesis, though again we argue that contrary to the usual more tragic readings Genesis is more aptly characterized as comic in its persistent drive to new life. Any tragic component gets "trumped" by the presence of comic affirmation.[49] Moreover, in Exodus we also see a comedy that deals with contradiction, this time more glaringly between God and Pharaoh, but also between God and his people. Both Genesis and Exodus must deal with the presence and power of death, but they do so within a comic vision that celebrates deliverance and delights in the birth of new life. Like Genesis and Exodus, Jonah deals with the continued conflicts between God and his often rebellious, recalcitrant creatures. In particular, the Jonah narrator focuses on the conflict between Yahweh and his prophet who is initially disobedient to the divine commission and who remains troubled by God's actions all the way to the end of the book. Using the pattern of multiple deviations, the narrator shows how God maneuvers his reluctant prophet into a series of confrontations, first with the innocent, unsuspecting sailors amidst the divinely sent storm, then with God in the coming of the storm and the encounter with the giant fish, then with the evil Ninevites to whom he must announce an oracle of doom but who against all expectation repent and are divinely spared, and finally once again he must contend with God, this time directly in a dialogue. In the end, God seems to be playing a huge theological and practical joke on Jonah, a joke that forces him to move from self-centered concern to an inclusive embrace of the alien "other" who also can be a recipient of divine mercy (see again 4:10–11).

The series of confrontations is an elaborate ruse designed to reveal deeply interlayered and contradictory motivations in God's dealings with his creatures who are themselves

---

[49] The image of trumping comes from Miles, *God: A Biography*, p. 405.

contradictory – being both evil and ignorant, willfully disobedient and innocent, pathetically helpless and strangely
responsive. Perhaps what is most deeply disturbing is that
God emerges as a God of contradiction, who can be charged
with caprice and duplicity. A comic form is most fitting in
dealing with the contradictory tendencies that confront the
reader of this dramatic story. Indeed, we have appealed to the
genre of a joke in order to get at the play on form that Jonah
represents, a play that provokes thought, expands the
horizon of possibility, and revels in contradiction and
paradox. To continue with the dynamic of a joke, I invoke
once more the insightful analysis of Mary Douglas: "The joke
affords opportunity for realizing that an accepted pattern has
no necessity. Its excitement lies in the suggestion that any particular ordering of experience may be arbitrary and sub-
jective."[50] That Jonah becomes the unwilling butt of God's
joke is necessary to shatter traditional expectations about the
extension of divine mercy to a consummate enemy.

We have also named Jonah as a "comedy of caricature,"
including all those elements of parody and satire that are
close relatives of caricature.[51] In my view, Jonah's satiric
humor is deft and decisive, intensifying the play of contradiction and subverting traditional prophetic forms. The satire
especially emerges in a series of striking parodies – a prophetic commission undercut by resistance and deviation, a
lament for the dying transformed into thanksgiving for
deliverance, an oracle of doom changed by a ritual of reciprocal repentance, and a pardon for a "great city" that evokes
prophetic displeasure. At every significant moment from his
outright disobedience to his reluctant compliance, Jonah
emerges as a caricatured prophet, a victim of satire whose
most striking images stem from parodied comparisons with
Moses, Elijah, Jeremiah, and Joel. The satiric humor inter-

[50] Quoted in Smith, *Map is Not Territory*, pp. 206–207.
[51] In addition to the literature cited earlier, note John C. Holbert's essay,
"'Deliverance Belongs to Yahweh!': Satire in the Book of Jonah," *Journal for the
Study of the Old Testament* 21 (October, 1981), pp. 59–81; see also the critical review
of various attempts at satirical interpretations in Sasson, *Jonah*, pp. 331–334.

weaves a subtle, self-destructing series of prophetic forms that strike to the heart of Yahweh's conflict-ridden relationships with his prophets, his people, and indeed his whole creation. Ultimately, the fundamental point focuses on the incalculable freedom of the divine will to save.[52] Just deserts set out in a rigid and mechanistic calculus do not offer a fool-proof system. Thus the ritual and rule of reciprocity (I'll repent if you do – or if you change your behavior I'll change my mind) only deals with a part of the problem. God may indeed follow that script (so 3:10), but there is never a guarantee, and the "perhaps . . . we do not perish" spoken by the ship's captain (1:6) and the "Who knows? God may relent and change his mind . . . so that we do not perish" (3:9) uttered by Nineveh's king stand as a reminder of the mystery of divine freedom. To be sure, the acts of divine deliverance involving the innocent sailors (ch. 1), the guilty prophet (ch. 2), the repentant Ninevites (ch. 3), and the angry, despairing prophet as well as the helpless humans and numerous animals (ch. 4) create a spectrum of diverse, even contradictory, possibilities for divine and human reconciliation (ch. 4). But the freedom of God to deliver appears amidst a thicket of puzzling contradictions which can never be fully resolved. The final note struck in Jonah heralds the power of unmerited compassion born in the heart of divine freedom. Once more Jonah is best construed as an elaborate joke, but a most profound and provocative one. Lastly, as already suggested, Jonah reveals the compassion of God as the most mysterious motivation for his action toward his erring creatures. At this point Jonah takes his stand within different stories of divine deliverance or restoration stretching from Genesis and Exodus to the prophets and even the Book of Job – a vital, varied tradition in which God as Creator continues to delight in the feverish rush of life and to celebrate the birth of new life even in the midst of ever-threatening death. Perhaps it is symptomatic and symbolic of the comic vision that no one dies in Jonah –

[52] Cf. Joseph Blenkinsopp, *A History of Prophecy in Israel: From the Settlement in the Land to the Hellenistic Period* (Philadelphia: The Westminster Press, 1983), p. 273.

thus the fragile hope of the "Who knows?" spoken by an
anxious king is realized. The hope is grounded in a mystery
of divine grace that sometimes might appear to be capricious,
contradictory, and wonderfully unpredictable, yet at a deeper
level it might indeed be strangely consistent with an illogical
compassion, a generosity that goes beyond calculation.
Perhaps Hegel is right when he asserts that the comic cannot
be separated from its "infinite geniality and confidence
capable of rising superior to its own contradiction."[53] Such
geniality and confidence can only reside in a comic sensibility rooted in an expansive vision of compassion and mercy
and love. Hence compassion that transcends guilt or innocence, mercy that goes beyond the rule of reciprocity, and
love that embraces all creatures great and small enable the
comic spirit to prevail in Jonah. Whether this spirit ever fully
triumphs remains an open question, and God's unanswered
question to a silent prophet lingers in our minds to provoke
us and even to haunt us.[54] Jonah's comic vision remains
enshrouded by the riddling play of unresolved ambiguity –
"Who knows?"

[53] Hegel, *The Philosophy of Fine Art* in Lauter, ed., p. 351.
[54] See the recent article by Walter B. Crouch, "To Question an End, To End a
Question: Opening the Closure of the Book of Jonah," *Journal for the Study of the
Old Testament* 62 (1994), pp. 101–112.

CHAPTER 5

The comedy of Job: creation, chaos, and carnival

The Book of Job is the great reservoir of comedy.[1]

(Christopher Fry)

THE UNENDING QUEST FOR THE GENRE OF JOB

The book of Job, like all literary masterpieces, has the power to evoke radically diverse interpretations; its ambiguity continues both to challenge and frustrate interpreters in their ongoing quest for solutions to its enigmas. No part of the interpretation of Job is more clouded with uncertainty than the identification of genre. The parallels offered do not quite fit, and most scholars end up by concluding that Job belongs to no literary category: it simply is! To be sure, there is no dearth of suggestions: Job has variously been called a "wisdom disputation," an "answered lament," a "trial," a "theodicy," an "epic", etc.[2] It is not necessary for my purpose to repeat the various arguments pro or con for these alternatives, or to enumerate other possibilities which have been proffered. Suffice it to say that many of these proposals are outgrowths of an exercise of one type of literary criticism – legitimate in itself – which reconstructs different stages in the book's development and applies a generic label to each stage, especially that of the alleged autograph of the original

---

[1] Christopher Fry, "Comedy," p. 17.
[2] See the standard Old Testament introductions. Unless otherwise noted I will use Pope's translation; see M. H. Pope, *Job: The Anchor Bible* (Garden City, NY: Doubleday, 1965).

Job.[3] I am in full agreement with Good's wise comments on the pitfalls that await the literary critic who seeks to find the autograph and then tries to interpret it as the authentic Job.[4] That the book of Job experienced several stages of growth is no doubt true, but that fact does not exempt the interpreter from the responsibility of coming to grips with the book's final form. One of the strengths of Polzin's structural analysis of Job is that he takes seriously the necessity and importance of interpreting Job's present form.[5] It will likewise be my starting-point to take the book as it stands and interpret the totality of its parts.

I now return to the problem of the overarching genre of the book of Job. As mentioned, one long-standing position claims that Job is a tragedy. At least as far back as Theodore of Mopsuestia, scholars have observed affinities of Job with Greek drama.[6] The tragic view of Job received its most extreme statement in Kallen's book in which he argues for an explicit dependence of the Joban poet on Greek tragedians – Euripides in particular – and then proceeds to rearrange and rewrite Job à la Euripidean tragedy.[7] The deficiencies of Kallen's approach have been amply demonstrated, but the view of Job as tragedy persists. Terrien, for example, argues that Job is a "festal tragedy" in which the poet articulates two interwoven and controlling mythical patterns: first, the theme of royal expiation that centers in the vicarious suffer-

---

[3] For a recent vigorous defense of the older style historical analysis of various stages, see the stimulating study of Bruce Zuckerman, *Job The Silent: A Study in Historical Counterpoint* (Oxford: Oxford University Press, 1991), pp. 7–9. Zuckerman wants to argue that the original Joban poem is best construed in its "grand design" as "parody" (p. 136), thus confirming prior insights into the role of satire and parody in Job that other scholars including myself have long argued for. See my earlier essay, "The Comedy of Job," *Semeia* 7 (1977), pp. 9, 13, 15, 16, 19, 23, 27. In contrast to Zuckerman, I want to argue that comedy supplies the grand design of the whole book with parody supplying one of the key ingredients.

[4] Edwin M. Good, "Job and the Literary Task: A Response," *Soundings* 56 (1973), pp. 471–475.

[5] Robert Polzin, "The Framework of the Book of Job," *Interpretation* 28 (1974), pp. 182–200.

[6] I owe this reference to A. B. Davidson, *The Book of Job* (Cambridge: Cambridge University Press, 1962), p. xv.

[7] H. M. Kallen, *The Book of Job as a Greek Tragedy Restored* (New York: Moffat, Yard & Co., 1918).

ing of the king; second, the rhythm of the seasons with the accent on the renewal of the earth through the life-giving rains of autumn.[8] Early in the exile (c. 575 BCE), an Israelite poet experimented with cultic forms and forged his masterpiece "as a para-cultic drama for the celebration of the New Year Festival."[9] The Joban poet used diverse genres – e.g., lament, hymn, judicial discussion, wisdom dispute, prophetic vision, onomasticon, theophany – to create a new genre, "the festal tragedy."

Terrien's interpretation is stimulating and suggestive. He goes far towards explaining the presence of certain tragic elements long noted in Job, and he does so with full awareness of the traditional genres and motifs embedded in Job. But in limiting himself to the poem of Job, Terrien exemplifies once again a literary criticism that restricts the genuine poetic production to a given stage and then interprets that stage in terms of genre, setting, and intention. As indicated above, this mode of criticism fails to pay sufficient heed to the whole book of Job. In contrast to Terrien, it is my thesis that once the poem is set in its full and final literary context, replete with prologue and epilogue as well as the Elihu speeches, the most apt and compelling generic designation of the book of Job is *comedy*.[10] In my judgment, the broad, overarching cate-

---

[8] Samuel Terrien, "The Yahweh Speeches and Job's Responses," *Review and Expositor* 58 (1971), p. 507.

[9] *Ibid.*, p. 509.

[10] When I first broached this thesis in a lecture over twenty-five years ago, I was keenly aware that it represents a rather lonely position in biblical scholarship. However, while I was reading in the area of comic theory, I was delighted to come across an enticing observation by the playwright Christopher Fry that "Job is the great reservoir of comedy." (See his essay, "Comedy," p. 17.) Needless to say, I was pleased to know that I was not completely alone in my opinion, but Fry's remark is in a general discussion of the relationship between tragedy and comedy, and he is not concerned to argue the case for Job. I also discovered that another Frye – this time the well-known literary critic Northrop Frye – also describes the book of Job as technically a comedy (1965). The two Fry(e)s have been an encouragement and a stimulus for me to continue my research into the comic dimensions of Job, and their insights have helped to deepen both my perception into comedy in general and the comedy of Job in particular. After I had completed this essay I discovered a collection of short, popular essays by J. C. McLelland in which he sets Job and other biblical narratives in the context of comedy. See *The Clown and the Crocodile* (Richmond: John Knox Press, 1970).

gory of comedy is able to illuminate best the wealth of disparate genres, formulas, and motifs (including those construed
as tragic) which are now interwoven in the total structure of
the book.

At first blush, many will recoil from the suggestion that Job
is comedy and will dismiss my thesis as downright crazy or a
bad joke in the worst tradition of gallows humor. How can a
book so filled with agony and despair, so dominated with the
images of suffering and death, be considered a comedy? This
type of reaction is rooted in the identification of comedy with
laughter and light humor. I would only counter that literary
criticism has long recognized that it is a mistake to make an
easy and absolute equation between comedy and laughter.[11]
Comedy can be profoundly serious; in fact, it has often served

---

[11] For convenience, see the collection of essays edited by Corrigan, *Comedy* (especially the comprehensive essay by Sypher, "The Meanings of Comedy," pp. 19ff.).
Don Saliers' comments are indicative of an emerging consensus in comic theory
about the subtlety and the wide, complex range of comedy: "When we ask what
constitutes the 'comic' or the 'comic vision . . .,' we come to a vast tract of inquiry.
What at first seem to be clearly demarcated pathways become, in closer approach,
tangled, ill-defined thickets. On the surface, we are inclined to regard what is
comical as more homogeneous than it actually is, perhaps because we think of the
comical primarily in terms of laughter . . . What strikes us as comic and funny
depends, of course, upon the evaluative perceptions we make of the matter at
hand." "When it is said," he continues, "that the comic is not as homogeneous as
it may first seem, I am not referring simply to the range of laughter – from the
tenuous inner smile of recognition and sympathy through the brilliant quick-
witted burst of intellectual laughter, to the uproarious guffaw. The psychology of
laughter is another tangled inquiry; related, but not directly relevant. No, we are
being reminded that one person's comedy is another person's pathos. Which is
to say again, the comical is *relational.* It springs from the way we value and from
the way we can distance ourselves from what is grave or valued or sacred. Thus,
what constitutes the comical is as variegated as communities of perception are; or
at least as variable as the publicly sharable capacities for seriousness or detachment are." (See Don Saliers, "Faith and the Comic Eye." *Andover Newton Quarterly*
13/4 [1973], pp. 259–276.) In an essay on the irony of Job, J. G. Williams makes
the following admission which illustrates the difficulty of determining what is
'funny': "At times, may I admit, I think the whole thing [i.e., the book of Job] is
terribly funny. But irony is never really funny, is it? For what kind of universe must
Job now live in? A meaningless universe mismanaged by a chaotic, capricious,
jealous Tyrant." (James G. Williams, "'You Have Not Spoken Truth of Me': Mystery
and Irony in Job." *Zeitschrift für die altestestamentliche Wissenschaft* 83 [1971], p.
247.) Although I question why irony cannot sometimes be funny, I think this
quotation aptly shows the problem highlighted in Saliers' reflections on comedy
and laughter.

as one of the most compelling strategies for dealing with chaos and suffering, the most obvious example being so-called "dark comedy."[12] Moreover, as we have observed from the outset of our exploration, critics have long perceived a subtle and powerful interplay between comedy and tragedy. So my interpretation of Job as comedy does not depend on elements we might consider to be funny. Also, how does one accurately define what might be considered funny? Thanks to Freud and others we are all aware of the difficulty of defining laughter in our own context – let alone a context distant from us in time and tradition.[13] Thus we do not exactly know what might have elicited laughter from the ancient Israelites or any of their contemporaries in the Near East. From the evidence of Near Eastern and biblical texts, we might be surprised at the degree to which some of this literature was able to evoke laughter from its original audiences.[14]

In any case I wish to avoid an oversimplified equation

---

[12] J. L. Styan, *The Dark Comedy* (Cambridge: Cambridge University Press, 1968).

[13] For a balanced and discriminating study of the interplay and tension between comedy and laughter, see Neil Schaeffer, *The Art of Laughter* (New York: Columbia University Press, 1981), pp. 3–16.

[14] We are too often wont to think of Aristophanes' *Comedies* as the unique and determinative exemplar of ancient comedy. In my judgment, however, the whole subject of comedy in the Near East and Israel has been seriously neglected. Over the years a few books and essays have appeared to begin to fill the gap, but the subject still awaits complete exploration (see my introduction above). To be sure, we cannot overlook some of the pioneering efforts already published. In addition to the works cited in my introduction to this volume, I would single out for attention E. Speiser's brilliant thesis that the so-called "Dialogue of Pessimism" from Mesopotamia is not "pessimistic" at all, but is rather a humorous, farcical satire; in short, it is one species of comedy. (See Ephraim Speiser's *Oriental and Biblical Studies*, J. J. Finkelstein and Moshe Greenberg, eds. [Philadelphia: University of Pennsylvania Press, 1967], pp. 344–368.) Other seminal works especially focused on the broader domain of the ancient Near East are: B. R. Foster, "Humor and Cuneiform Literature," *Journal of the Ancient Near Eastern Society of Columbia University* 6 (1974), pp. 69–86; B. Van de Walle, *L'Humour dans la Littérature et l'Art de l'Ancienne Égypte* (Leiden: E. J. Brill, 1969); Franz Rosenthal, *Humor in Early Islam* (Leiden: E. J. Brill, 1956); Howard M. Jackson, "The Shadow of Pharaoh, Your Lord, Falls upon You: Once Again *Wenamun* 2.46," *Journal of Near Eastern Studies* 54 (1995), pp. 273–286. From evidence presented in such studies, scholars are beginning to make an increasingly impressive case for a much richer comic tradition in the Near Eastern and Mediterranean world than has hitherto been recognized. I hope that the present volume will contribute to the ongoing discussion of this important topic.

between comedy and laughter and want to utilize that complex, flexible vision of comedy which I have delineated in the course of this book (see again the introduction). As we recall, the comic vision typically contains four central ingredients: first, its use of the U-shaped plot-line that leads ultimately to the happiness of the hero and his restoration to a serene and harmonious society; second, its conventional character types such as a boaster, buffoon, and fool; third, its exploitation of various literary strategies such as caricature, irony, parody, and satire – strategies designed to highlight incongruity and ridiculousness; fourth, its dual intention of both subversion of the status quo and celebration of life and love – all in the service of transforming perceptions and affirming hope and the possibility of renewal.

THE QUESTION OF STRUCTURE: THE SIGNIFICANCE OF THE PROSE FRAMEWORK (JOB 1–2 & 42:7FF)

Now I want to look at the overarching structure of Job and argue more precisely my case for the comedy of Job. It is important initially to observe that the poet has framed his poetic speeches with a prose narrative, now broken up into a prologue (Job 1–2) and epilogue (Job 42:7ff.). It is a long-held view that the poet borrows a didactic folktale or legend – i.e., a prose narrative that describes the fall and ultimate restoration of a folk hero in the days of yore. A number of literary conventions and typical motifs show that the narrative is best construed as a folktale. It has the customary "once upon a time" fairy-tale beginning: "There was a man in the land of Uz, whose name was Job" (1:1). The setting in a non-Israelite locale, the vaguely defined land of Uz, heightens this dimension. The stylized numbers – seven sons and three daughters, seven thousand sheep and three thousand oxen – contribute further to the folktale flavor, as does the adroit use of repetition (a two-fold test, a four-fold series of disasters each of which is laconically reported by an anonymous messenger, two-fold audience between Yahweh and the Satan). Moreover, the characters are stylized, being defined by formulas and motifs typical of folktales. So Job is the best of men, "the greatest of all the people of the east" (1:3b). He always does the right thing at the right time – whether in prosperity or adversity (cf. 1:5, 20–22; 2:10). His response to his traumatic trials is exactly what we would expect from such a figure and is comparable to that of Abraham in the story about the sacrifice of Isaac (Gen. 22). Lastly, and important for our purposes, the plot is not only similar to that of other folktales, it is also typical of comedy. In such stories, the hero is usually subjected to a test from which he comes out on top only by the utmost effort and the demonstration of his prowess. So it is with Job, who endures his sufferings with unflinching faith, and in the end is restored to a harmonious relationship with God and humans. He has all his possessions doubled, he receives a new set of children, and his daughters are renowned far and wide for their beauty. He himself lives 140 years after his trial and dies a fulfilled and satisfied man. Such a story follows the plot-line of many comedies. To cite again the useful observation of Northrop Frye: "Comedy has a U-shaped plot, with the action sinking in to deep and often potentially tragic complications, and then suddenly turning upward into a happy ending."[15]

It is important to stress that the poet has retained the basic plot of the folktale, even though he has altered the old tale by cutting it in two parts and making it into a prologue and an epilogue. The genre and intention are thereby transformed. By breaking the tale in two and inserting the long poetic speeches as the literary centerpiece, he has fractured the integrity of the original narrative and forced it to serve dual functions: it supplies the framework in which the poetic dialogues unfold, and at the same time it provides the fundamental story line. The intention of the frame story lies on multiple levels: (1) It describes "what is to be considered the normal and 'right' condition of the world and the characters."[16] (2) It gives the reader decisive information which is

---

[15] N. Frye, *Fables of Identity*, p. 25.
[16] Amy Shapiro, *The Myth of Job* (Pomona College: Unpublished Senior Thesis, 1975), p. 54.

kept from the protagonists of the story but which defines and conditions their actions and words. (3) It provides the "U-shaped plot" for the whole book.

Significantly, the prologue contains presuppositions and questions that trigger the movement of the entire book. First, by taking a figure famed for his righteousness, the poet intensifies and authenticates the agony of the innocent sufferer. Moreover, by stating explicitly that Job's suffering is in no way due to sin, the poet puts his readers in a privileged position: we know what neither Job nor his counselors know – that Job is afflicted because of a chain of events that occurred in a mysterious divine council. This fact throws the whole ensuing dialogue into extreme tension and creates one of the fundamental incongruities of the entire book. The knowledge gained in the prologue shows the major debate to be misplaced and wide of the mark; this perspective is sharpened by skillful use of repetition in which Job's antagonists keep on giving wrong answers with thudding monotony. Incongruity – which at least is potentially comic – stands at the heart of the main course of the dialogues.

Second, the prologue foreshadows the theme of God's ambiguous personality, a theme richly developed in the poem (cf. chs. 7, 9, 12). Even if we accept Edwin Good's explanation that the Satan's self-curse and not a wager *per se* motivates God's action against Job, ambiguity still colors the representation of God.[17] Good is probably correct in pointing out the way this curse by necessity elicits the divine response, but we still have Yahweh's potentially self-incriminating acknowledgment: "you have incited me against him / To destroy him without cause" (2:3b). This theme of divinely caused suffering that capriciously strikes innocent and guilty alike will reappear: "'Tis all the same . . .,'" Job later asserts, "'guiltless as well as wicked he destroys'" (9:22). So an aura of ambiguity hovers over the old tale, an aura that will penetrate the later dialogues.

Third, an age-old mythical motif – the determination of human fate in the divine council – is used in the prologue,

---

[17] Good, "Job and the Literary Task," pp. 475ff.

only to come under attack in the poem. The poem unveils this vision of mythical action in order to challenge its ultimate adequacy. Such a God may still have the power to determine a person's destiny, but already the question is implicit whether this kind of God is still righteous and trustworthy.

Fourth, Job's wife's impatient intervention with her brief but brutal counsel – "Do you still maintain your integrity? Curse God and die" (2:9) – anticipates the course that Job takes in the poetic dialogues. Though he never curses God directly, he comes very close: not only in the opening curse of his birthday (see below), but in his intensifying attack against God in his complaints (see chs. 6, 9, 12, 23, etc.). Ilana Pardes rightly calls our attention to the key role that Job's wife plays in setting us up for Job's dramatic reversal: "Job's wife," suggests Pardes, "prefigures or perhaps even generates the impatience of the dialogues."[18] Pardes goes on to argue that "Job's wife thus opens up the possibility of suspending belief, of speaking up against God."[19] Job's wife, therefore, functions in a way comparable to Eve, displaying a similar kind of initiative when she decisively intervenes and thereby serves as an agent who helps to activate the process leading to a dramatic transformation of the major characters. Again, to cite Pardes' illuminating words: "Much like Eve, . . . Job's wife spurs her husband to doubt God's use of his powers, but in doing so she does him much good, for this turns out to be the royal road to deepen one's knowledge, to open one's eyes."[20] Though Job rebukes his wife, calling her a "foolish woman," he ironically raises the key issue of the book in a rhetorical question, "Shall we accept good from God and not accept evil?" (2:10). Given here in the spirit of piety and resignation, Job's words anticipate his later radical doubts about the justice of a God who unleashes evil against good people. In sum, though her appearance is all too brief, Job's wife performs a vital function in creating the conditions for the transformation of Job from pious, patient sufferer into radical rebel who challenges the justice and the mercy of the creator God.

The epilogue is equally crucial for understanding the total

---

[18] Pardes, *Countertraditions in the Bible*, p. 147.   [19] *Ibid.*, p. 148.   [20] *Ibid.*, p. 151.

literary work and cannot so easily be set aside as many literary critics have suggested. By retaining the restoration scene in the epilogue, the poet suddenly shifts the direction of the whole poem and returns to the prologue's vision of the idyllic society into which the main protagonists are now reintegrated. To be sure, in the journey through the dramatic dialogues, Job experiences ultimately a vital re-vision of his world and a transformation in his vision of God. In any event, there is a restoration of the hero's fortunes, which resembles formally at least the traditional upturn found in the happy ending of comedy.

JOB'S CRY FROM THE ASHHEAP: A VOICE OF
DESPERATE CHALLENGE (JOB 3)

The poetic speeches open with Job's soliloquy (ch. 3) which begins on a dark, discordant note totally dissonant from Job's pious words in the prologue. The hero has fallen! His dramatic curse of his birthday represents a sudden, sharp downturn into despair. As Good has noted, the self-curse of the Satan that evokes the action of the prologue and expects a curse from Job has been partially effective, though it is not as clearly directed as the Satan had claimed.[21] Job's curse is ambiguous: does it only concern Job's own existence? – "Damn the day *I* was born" (3:3a); or is it also implicitly a curse against the Creator? Robertson answers the latter question affirmatively,[22] but I share Good's reluctance to be so sure as to the ultimate thrust of the curse.[23] It does seem clear, however, that Job hurls a curse and a challenge against the whole creation. This intention is epitomized in Job's appeal to mythological tradition: "May those who curse Yam curse it, those skilled in rousing Leviathan" (3:8). Job calls the old creation myth to mind in order to reverse its effects; he apparently desires to throw all of creation back into primordial chaos. So whether or not Job indirectly curses God, the

---

[21] *Ibid.*
[22] David Robertson, "The Book of Job: A Literary Study," *Soundings* 56 (1973), pp. 449–450.   [23] Good, "Job and the Literary Task," p. 476.

incongruity between the Job of the prologue who blesses and the Job of the poem who curses is sharply drawn. The Satan was at least partially right in his assessment of the situation. To be sure, ironically the Job that is now cursing his birthday is doing so precisely in the name of maintaining his integrity.

Job's soliloquy reveals still another attack on normative Hebraic tradition. Job goes counter to the Hebraic preference of life over death and reverts to what seems to be more compatible with the Egyptian expectation of the afterlife where restful ease greets the one who is fortunate enough to find his way to the grave (3:13, 22). In fact, it is not inappropriate to call this reversal of tradition a parody of the usual Hebraic emphasis on life over against death – an emphasis found especially in the Complaint Psalms (cf. Ps. 88). Later on in his discourses Job will return to the more normative Hebraic view of death as a grey, gloomy form of existence (cf. 7:9f.; 10:21, 22; 14:1ff), but for now at least death seems better than life.[24]

In sum, Job 3 represents on the one hand a jarring contrast to how Job was initially portrayed in the prologue, but on the other hand it sets a fundamental tone for the succeeding speeches. That Job's outburst counters elements in more normative Hebraic tradition and thus stands in an incongruous relationship to that tradition witnesses to its radicality and newness.

THE FOLLY OF WELL-MEANING FRIENDS: JOB'S CARICATURE OF HIS "WISE" COUNSELORS (JOB 4–31)

After the bitter curse in chapter 3, the three friends now begin to offer their contribution. The friends are initially presented in a favorable light; they are sensitive and compassionate to Job: "When they saw him from afar, they could not recognize him, and they raised their voices and wept; each

---

[24] Note how Yahweh in his magnificent whirlwind speeches will answer Job's preference of death over life by asserting the fundamental drive to life built into creation (Job 38–39). (See further below.)

tore his robe and sprinkled dust on his head. They sat with him on the ground seven days and seven nights, and no one said a word to him, for they saw that his anguish was very great" (2:12–13). The friends engage in customary mourning rites, and one should understand their silence primarily from this point of view. But when one remembers Job's later sarcastic wish, "Oh that you would keep silent, and it would be your wisdom!" (13:5), it is not remiss to suggest that this initial period of silence in retrospect is represented incongruously as their finest hour.

Although the friends' speeches can be read on several different levels, it seems that the poet has created a magnificent caricature of the wise counselor. Eliphaz's opening speech has typical elements which are carried through the ensuing speeches of the friends. Decades ago Fullerton pointed to the presence of "double entendre" in this speech.[25] And Eliphaz indeed evokes an ambivalent response, as Robertson has argued.[26] On the positive side, Eliphaz appears to be motivated by a genuine concern for Job. He begins very solicitously: "If one ventures a word with you, will you be offended?" (4:2a). Moreover, he seems convinced that Job is what he claims to be – an innocent sufferer. Nowhere in his first speech does he resort to direct accusation or name-calling. He explains Job's present misfortunes by an appeal to a dramatic visionary revelation about the inherent and thus inevitable sinfulness of humankind (4:13ff.). Job is only implicated because he is a member of the human race, not because of any particular sin he has committed. Finally, even though Eliphaz was not privy to the proceedings of the divine council, he seems on one level to have Job's situation analyzed fairly well. Job's suffering is a disciplinary test; so Job has only to hang on to his integrity and trust in his piety and his God. If Job therefore commits his cause to God, "who does great things and unsearchable, marvelous things without number," then he may expect full restoration, replete with his possessions,

[25] Kemper Fullerton, "Double Entendre in the First Speech of Eliphaz," *Journal of Biblical Literature* 53 (1934), pp. 321–349.
[26] Robertson, "The Book of Job," pp. 451–452.

numerous descendants, and the expectation of dying "in ripe old age" (cf. 5:24–26). In fact, Eliphaz accurately, albeit ironically, predicts the final denouement of the whole book, as will also his two companions (cf. 8:5–7; 11:13ff.).

But Eliphaz's speech can be viewed from another angle, which gives a negative slant to his words. Eliphaz and his two cohorts rely heavily on their accumulation of proverbial wisdom gained from traditional lore as well as their own personal observation; thus they strike the pose of exemplary sages. Eliphaz even goes beyond the usual ambience of the sage when he describes an awesome night vision in order to authenticate his wise counsel, though there is a curious incongruity between the elaborate portrayal of the vision and the rather commonplace information contained therein (cf. 4:14ff.). So on another level Eliphaz comes across as a rather pompous, pretentious counselor, who must in the end resort to general maxims which simply fail to apply in this specific situation (cf. 4:8–11; 5:2–4) even though these maxims be clothed in the language of a mysterious visionary experience.

Though Bildad and Zophar by no means may be considered carbon copies of Eliphaz and sometimes formulate their arguments differently (e.g., Bildad especially emphasizes the authority of the fathers whereas Zophar appeals to the impenetrable mysteries of the divine nature), they both begin with the same basic premise as Eliphaz: there is a necessary and universal correlation between suffering and sinning. It is no surprise therefore that their essential advice is the same: repent and trust God (cf. 8:5–7; 11:13ff.).

In the second and third cycles of speeches the friends resort more and more to stereotyping as they indulge in long, lurid portrayals of the grim destiny of the wicked (cf. chs. 15, 18, 20, 22, 27:13ff.). In behaving thus the friends become increasingly ludicrous as they engage increasingly in repetition. "Exaggeration," remarks Bergson, "is always comic when prolonged and especially when prolonged."[27] To put it

[27] Henri Bergson, quoted by Roger Cox, "The Invented Self: An Essay on Comedy," *Soundings* 57 (1974), p. 141.

another way: "In ridiculing [they] become ridiculous"[28] –
which is a fundamental ingredient of comedy. From the
outset both Job and the reader, albeit on different levels of
knowledge, are keenly aware of the utter incongruity between
the friends' speeches and Job's situation. The friends become
cruelly and grotesquely comic as they strive with increasing
dogmatism to apply their faulty solutions to the wrong
problem – and the wrong person.

Job's sarcastic and satirical rejection of the friends and
their irrelevant advice is sharp and bitter, but not unmerited:

> No doubt you are the gentry;
>   and with you wisdom will die.
> But I have a mind as well as you;
>   I am not inferior to you.
> Who does not know such things?   (12:2–3)

> Ask the beasts, they will teach you;
> The birds of the air, they will tell you.   (12:7)

> Galling comforters are you all.
>   Have windy words a limit?
> What move you to prattle on?
>   I, too, could talk like you.
> If you were in my place,
>   I could harangue with words,
> Could shake my head at you.
>   I could strengthen you with my mouth.
> My quivering lips would soothe you.   (16:2b–5)

> How you have helped the powerless,
> Aided the arm that had no strength!
> How you have counseled the unwise,
> Offered advice in profusion!
> With whose help have you uttered words,
> Whose breath came forth from you?   (26:2–4)

According to Roger Cox in a fine essay on comedy,
Schopenhauer classified pedantry as a form of folly and says
that "the pedant, with his general maxims, almost always

---

[28] *Ibid.*, p. 155. The whole quotation is noteworthy: "At the bottom literary comedy
rests upon a paradox which no human being can either solve or avoid: in ridiculing we become ridiculous" (p. 155).

misses the mark in life, shows himself to be foolish, awkward, and useless!"[29] In Schopenhauer's sense, Job's comforters may be termed pedants, who though claiming to be wise in fact emerge as fools. Job's cutting retort to his friends dramatizes this perception: "Your maxims are ashen aphorisms / Defences of clay are your defences" (13:12). In his article Cox goes on to argue that moralizing leads toward incongruity for several reasons, not least of which is that it usually takes the form of universal statements: "Obviously universal statements gather so many things under a single heading that there is almost bound to be incongruity among the things brought together under the heading."[30] Cox ends his discussion with an observation that strikingly bears on the Joban poet's parody of the wise comforter: "The pedant with his general maxims is simply a caricature of the basic comic character, who strives constantly . . . to justify and preserve his invented self against the onslaughts of the realities he encounters."[31]

In conclusion, the poet has created a brilliant, biting caricature of the friends in their role as wise counselors, who indeed say some "right things about God," but who ultimately become ridiculous in their approach to Job because of the irrelevance of their counsel. The would-be wise men become fools, the mockers become a mockery. The friends resemble the classical comic figure of the *alazon* – the impostor, the offender, and finally the enemy of God (cf. 42:7).[32] As impostors the friends are finally reduced to silence and confusion. Elihu's words, though self-serving, nevertheless illuminate what happens to the friends in the course of the debate and anticipate Yahweh's condemnation of the friends: "I paid close attention to you, but none of you confuted Job. None of you answered his words" (32:12); "Dismayed, they answer him no more: Words have forsaken them" (32:15). According to Sypher this result is typical of what happens to the *alazon*: "In the course of the comic debate the supposed wisdom of the *alazon* is reduced to absurdity, and the *alazon*

---

[29] *Ibid.*, p. 139.   [30] *Ibid.*, p. 148.   [31] *Ibid.*
[32] Cf. Aristophanes' famous parody of Socrates in *The Clouds*.

himself becomes a clown."[33] Thus in the end, the friends
become comic characters, and their pretentious pose vis-à-vis
Job and God is exposed and ridiculed.

Job's case against his friends and his God (Job 6–31)

When one examines Job's speeches, it is all but impossible to
find any systematic and orderly progression – despite the best
efforts of scholars. Rather the poet has built a rambling discursiveness into the dialogues which seems to heighten the
sense of chaos that is so terribly threatening. I want to highlight two facets of this discursiveness. First, one notices that
the poet has built into Job's responses to his friends the stylistic feature of delayed reaction: Job often seems to ignore
the immediately preceding speech in order to deal with an
earlier argument of one of the comforters (cf. 9:2 which is the
answer to Eliphaz in 4:17). Thus a certain incongruity is
present in the very structuring of the speeches. The various
speakers are sometimes portrayed as talking past one
another. Second, Job's speeches sometimes shift addressees
in midstream, often without forewarning; suddenly Job is no
longer speaking to the friends but is addressing God (cf.
7:7ff.; 13:20ff.; 17:3f.). This observation reveals how Job
keenly knows that he is fighting a battle on two fronts against
two different adversaries: his erstwhile human friends have
become his enemies (cf. 6:14ff.; 19:19), and God, likewise his
one-time friend (29:4), has become his foe. Throughout the
entire course of the dialogues Job confronts first one adversary and then another without always explicitly informing the
reader. Job's speeches, therefore, operate on different levels,
a fact which heightens the ambiguity of the dialogical situation.

To Job, however, it is his second adversary – God – who presents the most awesome threat. Job moves from his own plight
to a radical and comprehensive indictment of God and a
frontal challenge to God's justice in the universe. As interpreters have long argued, what began as a trial of Job has now

---

[33] Sypher, "The Meanings of Comedy," p. 42.

turned into a trial of God; thus the moral vision of the universe comes to stand under a severe and searching scrutiny. Since Job is convinced that his suffering is not due to any particular sin, he senses that his misfortune is symptomatic of a grave and general disorder of the universe. His language of attack against God is probably the most searing in the Hebrew Bible. God often emerges as a grotesque, demonic deity, a cosmic bully and tyrant. The following is a typical catalogue of divine terrors:

> His anger rips and rages against me;
>   he gnashes at me with his teeth;
> My enemy whets his eye against me.
> God puts me in custody of the vicious;
>   tosses me into the hand of the wicked.
> I was at ease and he crushed me;
>   grabbed me by the neck and mangled me.
> He sets me up as his target;
>   his archers ring me round.
> He stabs my vitals without pity;
>   pours out my guts on the ground.
> He rends me rift upon rift;
>   rushes at me like a warrior.   (16:9, 11–14)

To Job the contest is grotesquely unequal; yet God persists in treating Job not as a piece of frail flesh, but as some primordial monster of the deep (cf. 7:12). If one is looking for the dark comedy of the grotesque, Job is indeed a fertile field.

It is possible to view Job's speeches as a collage of brilliant parodies, where at almost every crucial juncture Job takes up diverse parts of his traditional heritage only to twist them and make them ludicrous.[34] Job's parody of Psalm 8 is the most

---

[34] Bruce Zuckerman has offered the most comprehensive argument that the original Joban poem represents a sustained series of brilliant parodies: "So we see that the relationship of the Poem of Job to the legend of Job is a contrapuntal relationship between a parody and its conventional tradition" (*Job The Silent*, p. 49). For his elaboration of parodied genres or themes, see especially pp. 93–135. Zuckerman has presented a fine study, combining his own reconstruction of the different stages of the book's growth with a discriminating study of the multiple faces of parody. I would simply counter that the parodied elements (many of which have been long noted) may be seen appropriately as an important component of the overarching comic vision which in my view still accounts best for the final form of the book.

frequently quoted example (7:17–18). But he bitingly parodies the complaint genre time and again (cf. chs. 3, 7, 14).
His speeches reach a crescendo of bitter irony when he catalogues examples of the pervasive chaos in creation under the
generic pattern of the hymn of praise:

> Truly I know that it is so:
> > But how can a man be just before God?
> If one wished to contend with him,
> > one could not answer him once in a thousand times.
> He is wise in heart, and mighty in strength –
> > who has hardened himself against him and succeeded? -
> he who removes mountains and they know it not,
> > when he overturns them in his anger;
> who shakes the earth out of its place,
> > and its pillars tremble;
> who commands the sun, and does not rise;
> > who seals up the stars;
> who alone stretched out the heavens,
> > and trampled the waves of the south;
> who does great things beyond understanding,
> > and marvelous things without number.
>
> > > > (9:2–10 in the RSV translation)

It should not be missed that this speech answers Eliphaz
and not the immediately preceding Bildad; it also parodies
elements in Eliphaz's speech (cf. 4:17 and 9:2; 5:9 and 9:10).
What results is an ironic parody of the doxological hymn,
which is invoked only in order to twist its intention and
convey an opposite meaning; it no longer serves to praise
Yahweh as just and merciful in his role as Creator, but rather
portrays him as a God of terror who revels in destruction.
When Job concludes his hymnic catalogue of divine attributes with an almost verbatim quotation of Eliphaz's earlier
lines ("who does great things beyond understanding and
marvelous things without number" [5:9 and 9:10]), he brings
to a fitting climax his sardonic song to the God of chaos.

But Job is not finished with his parody of the hymn of
praise, for in 12:13–25 he once again invokes the image of
the powerful creator God who creates only to destroy. The
text delights in satire and sarcasm as Job delivers his diabol-
ical doxology:

With him is wisdom and might;
His are counsel and understanding.   (12:13)

If he withholds the waters, there is drought;
Or lets them go, they engulf the earth.   (12:15)

Earth's counselors he makes foolish;
Judges he makes mad.
He loosens the belt of kings,
And finds a rag on their loins.
He makes priests go bare,
Overturns the well-established.
The confident he deprives of speech,
Takes away the reason of elders,
Pours contempt on princes,
Loosens the girdle of the mighty,
Reveals from darkness mysteries,
Brings forth dense darkness to light,
Makes nations great and then destroys them,
Expands nations and leads them away,
Deprives leaders of intelligence,
Makes them wander in a pathless waste.
They grope in darkness with no light.
He makes them stagger like a sot.   (12:17–25)

One finds here an inversion of almost all the typical motifs of Yahweh's vaunted wisdom as the creator: instead of order, chaos; instead of justice, violence; instead of light, darkness. Job's reveals a world where God revels in destruction more than creation, and the parody of the hymn of praise dramatically features God's savagery in his orgy of violent acts. What kind of God rules the world?

Throughout his arguments Job continually reverts to the certainty of his innocence and integrity as the cornerstone of his case (cf. 9:3ff). If there be any justice in the universe, Job is convinced that he must be vindicated. So early on in the dialogue Job calls for a cosmic trial, where he will be the defendant and Yahweh the plaintiff. If he can at all get a fair trial, God must acquit him. But no sooner has he broached this idea than he realizes that he is sure to lose. God will rig the trial and overpower Job with his superior strength and wisdom and especially his rhetorical prowess (cf. 9:14–23).

So the dominant and guiding metaphor of a trial has a "self-destruct" mechanism.[35] To the Joban poet a trial simply is not sufficient to deal with the case of Job versus God; the two adversaries are unequal in a direct encounter.

It is because of Job's fears which are born of his sense of inequality that he conceives of having a mysterious third party who might possibly ensure a just and fair trial. The first time we hear such a figure, Job promptly negates the notion: no such arbitrator really exists (9:32,33). But the second time Job is more confident, and he has also modified the character of the mediatorial figure; the umpire or arbitrator has become one who will vouch for Job on high and guarantee a fair trial (16:19). This theme reaches its climax in the famous "Redeemer" passage (19:23ff.). Although no one pretends to understand this text completely (it is next to impossible to translate it!), what clearly stands out is that Job is absolutely confident that his redeemer/vindicator/avenger lives.[36] Job is therefore assured of some sort of ultimate vindication, but what exactly is entailed in this vindication is unclear. Robertson has proposed the most extreme interpretation: Job conjures up here the image of one who will vindicate him by murdering God.[37] Though a rather grotesque thought, it is a possible interpretation given the semantic range of the word *go'el*.[38] What is interesting for my purpose is that in Job's dramatic confrontation with Yahweh

---

[35] "The legal debate is not presented straight . . ., but 'self-destructs' along the way, both in the language used and in the over-all architecture of what is said and when." Shapiro, *The Myth of Job*, p. 56.

[36] For a masterful delineation of the interpretive possibilities, see the magnificent new commentary on Job by David J. A. Clines, *Job 1–20*. Word Biblical Commentary *17* (Dallas: Word Books, 1989), pp. 455–470. Clines proposes that the mysterious mediatorial figure is best construed as Job's own protestation of innocence; that is his cry of the righteous sufferer becomes personified as his "witness" on high, his living "champion" that will vouch for his innocence before the God who has so afflicted him: "this is not the cry of faith it has been commonly thought to be. Yet it is a cry of faith – of faith in himself, which is, in the circumstances, when his innocence is being denied by everyone, perhaps more an act of pure faith than the most reverent piety toward God" (p. 470). Clines' view is a most suggestive interpretation and goes a long way toward solving this famous crux.

[37] Robertson, "The Book of Job," p. 460.

[38] See the nicely balanced assessment in Norman C. Habel, *The Book of Job: A Commentary* (Philadelphia: Westminster Press, 1985), pp. 302–309.

there is ironically no mediator in view except that we do meet again the term "umpire" (*mokiah*) now applied to Job (40:2), which heightens the irony of the absence of any bona fide mediator.[39] At any rate, the absence of the mediator negates Job's utter sense of confidence in 19:25–26. To be sure, Job does experience the fulfillment of his utmost desire to "see God" (42:5) and to realize a form of divine vindication on earth (42:10, 12). Clines rightly calls our attention to the "irony" in this unexpected form of fulfillment of words so filled with desire intermixed with despair.[40] What to many interpreters is the high point in Job's odyssey of faith finally finds its place in the sea of incongruity and irony that surges through the book.

Job concludes his appeal for a trial in chapter 31, where he utters an oath of clearance in the form of a series of self-curses. This oath serves as a most effective means of forcing God's hand to ensure that he shows up for Job's trial.[41] It now becomes necessary for God to make a personal appearance. Job's final challenge to God is rather comically Promethean:

O that someone would listen to me! Behold my signature, let Shaddai answer me. Let my opponent write a document. I would wear it on my shoulder, I would bind it on like a crown. I would tell him the number of my steps; I would approach him like a prince (31:35–37).

Once again Job uses royal language in order to make his strongest appeal: he will be like a prince in his proud entrance before the deity. Yet the scene contains comedy; as Habel has well observed, "the image of Job, the disheveled victim rising from his ashes to parade with a 'paper crown' as the new attire marking his innocence . . . is both colorful and comic."[42]

---

[39] I owe to Good the observation concerning the ironic application of the term "umpire" to Job in 40:2. He kindly called this text to my attention after I had delivered an earlier form of this chapter at the 1974 Annual Meeting of the Society of Biblical Literature.   [40] Clines, *Job 1–20*, pp. 462–463.

[41] Cf. Robertson, "The Book of Job," p. 461; also Edwin M. Good, *In Turns of the Tempest: A Reading of Job* (Stanford: Stanford University Press, 1990), p. 314.

[42] Habel, *The Book of Job*, p. 439.

THE INTRUSION OF AN ANGRY YOUNG MAN: THE EXPOSTULATIONS OF ELIHU (JOB 32–37)

When we turn from Job's heroic challenge to God for personal encounter, we are primed for a dramatic visitation of God; we are taken aback by the appearance of the young interloper – Elihu. It is this sharp sense of disconnection with what precedes and follows, coupled with stylistic and linguistic differences, which has led the vast majority of scholars to relegate Elihu's speeches to the heap of secondary and inferior materials. Such overblown, bombastic language, so the argument runs, could never be the work of the poet of the authentic Job![43] Perhaps this is correct, but then again perhaps it misses something. As Rowley points out, "Whoever wrote the Elihu speeches probably deliberately put banal lines into his mouth, since his purpose was rather to expose this type of character than to exalt it."[44] I think Rowley is on the right track with this remark, but he does not go far

---

[43] Bruce Zuckerman is one of the latest to argue for the secondary character of the Elihu speeches, criticizing in particular the attempt to perceive the presence of satire and parody in the representation of Elihu as a young fool. Suffice it to say I fail to find Zuckerman's remarks convincing. He has an overly narrow perspective on what constitutes appropriate parody or satire which has "subtlety" when it is from the artistically skilled poet responsible for the "Poem of Job," whereas in the Elihu speeches the parody is simply too crude to be from the hand of the same poet. This kind of critique unduly limits the poet. Indeed, some of Job's speeches in particular are rather blatant in terms of the sarcastic sharpness and directness of the satirical attack (cf. chs. 6, 9, 12), whereas the self-parody of the friends becomes subtly heightened because they are so blindingly unaware. In brief, parody can parade in all kinds of colors depending on the intention of the poet: sometimes subtle, sometimes brutally direct. See Zuckerman, *Job the Silent*, pp. 146–157.

[44] H. H. Rowley, *Job* (Ontario: Nelson, 1970), p. 268. Note, however, Pope's counter opinion in his discussion of Elihu's opening speech: "This sample of Elihu's rhetoric may strike the modern reader as ridiculously pompous and verbose. There is, however, no ground for supposing that this effect was intended by the author" (Pope, *Job*, p. 213). Contrast the opinion of Skehan on the major intention of Elihu's opening speech in ch.32: "The poem is . . . a formal rhetorical exercise, with a caricature of its ostensible protagonist inherent in its hesitations and its outbursts; if it has more words and more structure than the contents would seem to deserve, this is quite deliberate (Patrick W. Skehan, "I Will Speak Up," *Studies in Israelite Poetry and Wisdom. Catholic Biblical Quarterly Monograph Series I* [Washington, D.C.: Catholic Biblical Association, 1971], p. 87). Such sharply contradictory views from equally reputable scholars illustrate how far we are from a consensus in interpreting the book of Job, though I argue that those interpreters who find caricature, parody, and satire in Elihu's speeches have the more compelling case.

enough with it. In my opinion, a reading of these speeches in the whole context of Job shows that Elihu is a comic character whom the writer seeks to expose by the timing of Elihu's appearance and the type of language he uses.[45] From everything that precedes Elihu's entrance, the reader surely expects Yahweh to appear; but instead of the mighty God young Elihu steps brashly onto the scene. Elihu appears as the "Johnny-come-lately, who pops up from nowhere in ch. 32, disappears after ch. 37, and is never heard from again."[46] The effect is an ironic reversal of expectation and a jarring example of incongruity. We expect God – and we get Elihu! Once again the poet uses the tactic of delay and digression, to catch the reader by surprise.

Elihu emerges as the proverbial and prototypical "angry young man" who attempts to speak to God and to straighten out his elders. His long, verbose introduction sets the tone for his whole contribution:

I am young in years, and you are venerable men;
So I recoiled and was afraid to declare my knowledge to you.
I thought, 'Days should speak,
Many years ought to teach wisdom.'
But it is the spirit in man, the breath of Shaddai gives insight
Seniors may not be sage, nor elders understand right.
So I say, 'Listen to me, I too state my view.'
I waited for you to speak, I gave ear to your arguments while
    you tested words.
I paid close attention to you, but none of you confuted Job.
None of you answered his words.

I will now say my piece; I will declare what I know.
For I am brimming with words, wind bloats my belly.
My belly is like unvented wine, like new wine-skins ready to
    burst.
I must speak and get relief, open my lips and reply
                                        (32:6b–12, 17–20).

---

[45] The opinion about the possible comic dimension in the depiction of Elihu is by no means original with me; I would simply note that such a view has found sufficient currency to find its way into the explanatory comments of *The New Oxford Annotated Bible.* "The ludicrous boastfulness of Elihu's introductory remarks may have been introduced as a comical element, to relieve tragic tension" (p. 644). See also Habel, *The Book of Job,* pp. 444–445; similarly, Habel finds "wry humor" in the poet's depiction of Elihu (p. 444).   [46] Good, *Irony in the Old Testament,* p. 208.

After such windy words one would imagine that Elihu is finally ready to begin his subject. But he continues on a similar note in verses 1–7 of chapter 33 which he directs more particularly to Job. "It has pleased the author," remarks Dhorme, "to depict the new speaker as interminably prosy."[47] Is not this one sort of first-class parody – to put banal, verbose lines in the mouth of a pretentious interloper who is so unaware about his unwitting self-subversion? According to Davidson and Toy, many ancient scholars branded Elihu as a buffoon, "a boastful youth whose shallow intermeddling is only to be explained by the fewness of his years, the incarnation of folly, or the Satan himself gone amumming."[48] From a comic perspective, Elihu, like the three friends, seems to play the role of the *alazon* or buffoon, and it seems that the author's intent is to expose him as such. Just as we find a caricature of the friends in their role as "old" sages, so we have a caricature of the "angry young man" who now aspires to be the one who would defend the ways of God. Though there may be "no fool like an old fool," Elihu, as a young fool, comes close. He not only reiterates and expands essentially the same views of disciplinary suffering first mentioned by Eliphaz (5:17), though Elihu modifies it by combining it with a mediatorial figure (33:23–24); he also anticipates some of the themes of the Yahweh speeches (cf. esp. chs. 36:22–37:19). In the first instance he basically repeats the tired arguments of the friends, which were based on the premise that Job's suffering must be tied to his sinfulness; and in the second, he shows how different it is when a brash young man speaks on God's behalf from when God himself speaks out of the awesome whirlwind. So Elihu emerges in the total context of the book as a comic figure whom the author exposes and ridicules. Like the friends, Elihu appears to be wise; indeed, he says many things that are theologically

---

[47] Edouard Dhorme, *A Commentary on the Book of Job*, trans. Harold Knight (Ontario: Nelson, 1967), p. 485.

[48] A. B. Davidson and C. H. Toy, "Job," in the *Encyclopaedia Britannica* (1911), reprinted in *The Voice of the Whirlwind: The Book of Job*, Ralph Hone, ed. (San Francisco: Chandler Publishing Co., 1960), p. 99.

correct, but he ultimately misses the mark since he fundamentally misconstrues what is involved in Job's particular
situation.

JOB'S CONFRONTATION WITH GOD: THE DIVINE INTERROGATION FROM THE WHIRLWIND (JOB 38–42)

Most interpreters rightly consider the Yahweh speeches to be
the climax of the book of Job. That the speeches are laced
with irony is widely held; but what kind of irony is the debated
issue. The speeches side-step the questions posed by Job – or
at least they offer no clear-cut answers. At any rate ambiguity
seems intrinsic to the speeches. How one finally resolves the
problem of the Yahweh speeches and Job's responses supplies
one important key to a comprehensive interpretation of the
book of Job.

The most common view takes the Yahweh speeches at more
or less face value and interprets Job's repentance as genuine.
Job had become pretentious, even arrogant, stepping way
beyond his limits (cf. 40:1–8); so the divine interrogation was
eminently appropriate. In his confrontation with God, Job
became aware of the hugeness of creation and the presence
of a divine mystery that transcends human understanding.
The overpowering theophany unveiled to Job not only the
majestic Creator God, but the wonders of creation; he
responds with a sense of awe:

I know you can do all things; no purpose of yours can be thwarted
... I talked of things I did not know, wonders beyond my ken ... I
heard of you by hearsay, but now my own eyes have seen you. So I
recant and repent in dust and ashes (42:2, 3b, 5, 6).

With such a vision Job's repentance appears to be the
appropriate and authentic response. What then, according to
this view, is the intention of the Yahweh speeches and Job's
responses? Von Rad's answer is typical:

The purpose of the divine answer in the book of Job is to glorify
God's justice towards his creatures, and the fact that he is turned

towards them to do them good and bless them. And in the intention of the poem that is also truly an answer to Job's question. If Job's holding fast to his righteousness was a question put to God, God gives the answer by pointing to the glory of his providence that sustains all his creation. Of course this justice of God cannot be comprehended by man; it can only be adored.[49]

In a word, the incongruity at the root of creation is surmounted by the vision of the Creator and his creation; prayer and praise become the only fitting responses.

If von Rad's view is typical, Robertson has presented a highly atypical interpretation. Utilizing a peculiarly literary tack, Robertson has set the Yahweh speeches in the larger context of the book of Job and argued the position that they yield a fundamentally ironic sense.[50] For instance, in chapter 9 Job predicts what Yahweh would do in a face-to-face encounter: Yahweh would simply overwhelm Job with his awesome powers, and with his superior intellectual abilities he would pose questions that Job could not possibly answer (cf. especially 9:3ff.). Thus the Joban poet has "set up" God; we want and hope that God will not act as predicted, but when God does finally appear he in fact performs as Job says he would. To Robertson,

God's rhetoric, because Job has armed us against it, convinces us that he is a charlatan God, one who has the power and skill of a god but is a fake at the truly divine task of governing with justice and love.[51]

Moreover, argues Robertson, Job's repentance is "tongue-in-cheek," since both he and the friends had already predicted that Job would inevitably knuckle under in a show-down with God ("Though guiltless, my mouth would declare me guilty" 9:20a; cf. also 9:14–15).[52] So God becomes "the friends writ large" and is parodied as a blustery, false comforter.[53] God

---

[49] Gerhard von Rad, *Old Testament Theology: Volume I: The Theology of Israel's Historical Traditions*, trans. D. M. G. Stalker (New York: Harper and Bros., 1962), p. 417.

[50] Robertson, "The Book of Job," pp. 462ff.   [51] *Ibid.*, p. 464.   [52] *Ibid.*, p. 467.

[53] *Ibid.* It is noteworthy that Sypher brings out the ambiguous aspect of the *alazon* or impostor figure in classical comedy: "the Impostor, the enemy of God, is not only the alter ego of the ironist, he is, in Cornford's phrase, the very God himself" ("The Meanings of Comedy," p. 43).

himself in the end confirms this reading when he approves Job's words in the epilogue (42:7). Thus the meaning of the book of Job, according to Robertson, is that the poet, like "a medicine man," has developed a strategy for dealing with "man's fear of fate, his destiny, the unknown."[54] That strategy involves the curing of fear by "ridicule of the object feared."[55] "So we know of him what we know of all tyrants, that while they may torture us and finally kill us, they cannot destroy our personal integrity."[56]

In my judgment, it is possible to accept some of Robertson's insights into the irony of Job, but I think it is necessary to set them in the larger context of comedy. In this way the two diametrically opposed interpretations presented above may be brought together in a new and illuminating synthesis.

I would only underscore what Robertson says about the adroit use of irony in the book of Job; in fact, it is the type of irony the poet utilizes that leads me to suspect it is best interpreted from a comic perspective. As I have noted, time and again the irony often veers in the direction of the ludicrous and ridiculous. Comic incongruity and parody pervade the representation of Job's friends including young Elihu, Job's God, and *Job himself*. I think Robertson's interpretation, in fact, would have been strengthened had he not eliminated Elihu from his discussion and had he given more attention to the ironic portrayal of Job.[57] For example, are not the friends correct to a point in their estimate of Job's pride? And is it not the case that Yahweh's magnificent parody of Job's heroic posture has elements of truth?

> Gird your loins like a hero;
> I will ask you and you tell me!
>
> Have you an arm like God?
> Can you thunder with a voice like his?
> Deck now yourself with grandeur and majesty;
> be arrayed in glory and splendour.

---

[54] Robertson, "The Book of Job," p. 468.   [55] *Ibid.*   [56] *Ibid.*, p. 469.
[57] Robertson, *The Old Testament and the Literary Critic*, pp. 47–48.

> Let loose your furious wrath;
>> glance at every proud one and abase him;
> Tread down the wicked where they stand.
> Bury them in the dust together;
>> bind them in the infernal crypt.
> Then I will acknowledge to you that your own
>> right hand can save you!   (40:7, 9–14)

"[This] final challenge to Job," says Terrien, "parodies iron-ically the prerogatives and functions of the divine monarch in the ancient Middle East."[58]

Moreover, I think that even the irony in Job's predictions of how Yahweh would act takes a different turn from Robertson's description. It is true that Job declares that Yahweh would be physically and verbally overpowering to a mere mortal in a face-to-face encounter. But from the per-spective of comedy this kind of satirical questioning of the human hero is not at all out of place.[59] Also, in my opinion, there is an incongruity between the content of Job's predic-tions and the content of the theophanic vision: fulfillment does not quite match prediction. In Job's description of Yahweh's action, he caustically parodied the Creator God as one who brought chaos not order, darkness not light, death not life (cf. 9:5ff.; 12:14ff.). But the Yahweh speeches move in a different direction. Terrien is correct, I think, in dis-cerning at the heart of the Yahweh speeches a mythical pattern that appears in the seasonal changes with concentra-tion on the life-giving rains which do indeed sometimes fall on "no man's land" (38:2ff.).[60] But should not the rains fall there? Are not the creation and its needs bigger than human-ity with its more narrow vantage point on what constitutes superfluity and waste? The rhetorical questions concerning the emergence of *new life* bespeak the wondrous vitality of

[58] Terrien, "Yahweh's Speeches and Job's Responses," p. 507.
[59] See von Rad's intriguing interpretation of Job 38ff. as a satirical, ironical piece dependent on Egyptian prototypes: Gerhard von Rad, "Job xxxviii and Ancient Egyptian Wisdom," *The Problem of the Hexateuch and Other Essays*, trans. E. W. Trueman Dicken (New York: McGraw Hill Book Co., 1966), pp. 281–291.
[60] Terrien, "Yahweh's Speeches and Job's Responses," p. 508.

creation – they do not focus on death and disorder (cf. 39:1ff.).[61]

Finally, I think that it is not a misreading of the Yahweh speeches to hear a playful, festive note in the portrayal of creation.[62] The carnival of creation evokes joy and laughter. Hence the occasion of creation was when "the morning stars sang together, and all the gods exulted" (38:7). The pictures of the animals do not initially conjure up images of primordial chaos so much as they do images of freedom (the wild ass), awesome strength (the buffalo), majestic power (the horse), and grandeur of flight (the hawk and the eagle). Even the much-maligned ostrich is not so much a symbol of threatening chaos as ludicrous stupidity: yes the stupidity is God-given, but there are compensating features: "When up she spreads her plumes, she laughs at horse and rider" (39:18). She may be bizarre in looks, ridiculous in action, but she is a superb runner![63] Similarly even the mighty Leviathan, the most terrifying and truly monstrous creature in this "carnival of animals,"[64] is described somewhat sportively – at least from the Creator's view. The portrayal in Job 41:1ff. is not so distant or different from what we find in Psalm 104:26: "Leviathan you formed to make him play in it" (i.e., the sea) or as an alternative translation puts it, "Leviathan you formed to play with." "Yahweh," says Terrien, "permits himself to

---

[61] Harold Fisch makes a similar point in his powerful chapter, "Job: Tragedy is Not Enough," in *Poetry with a Purpose: Biblical Poetics and Interpretation* (Bloomington: Indiana University Press, 1988): "The speeches celebrate the *vitality* of the universe: abundant life and creation are their theme. In this, God responds to Job's first speech in chapter 3: life, not death is given. Crude, barbaric, even chaotic the creation may seem, but it is bursting with purpose" (p. 39). Though Fisch is critical of my comic interpretation (pp. 38–39), he still sees that any tragic movement is aborted in the Yahweh speeches.

[62] Since Habel criticized my overall case for the comedy of Job in an earlier version of the present chapter, I am happy to note that at least he agrees with my arguments about the comic notes of the Yahweh speeches: "Beyond the structure and function of the cosmic design appear elements which seem to exist for celebrative rather than pragmatic reasons. They point to the aesthetic, the playful and the comic in Yahweh's design." See Habel, *The Book of Job*, p. 533 (see also p. 535).

[63] Habel likewise finds the ostrich a "comic anomaly" (*ibid.*, p. 534).

[64] Terrien, "The Yahweh Speeches and Job's Responses," p. 501.

speak of these threatening realities with the detachment of the humorist, because he controls them."[65]

Moreover, as noted already in the case of the ostrich, the Creator builds into his creatures the capacity to laugh. Thus one hears the sounds of laughter from a number of the creatures that form the parade of animals in Yahweh's zoological discourse.[66] The wild ass laughs scornfully at the city's tumult (39:7), the speedy ostrich laughs triumphantly at the slower horse and rider (39:18), the undaunted horse laughs in the face of fear (39:22), the beasts of the steppe "laugh/play" even in the terrifying presence of Behemoth (40:20), and the proud Leviathan laughs fearlessly at the javelin's whirr (41:29). As Habel aptly observes,

the playful irony of the poet is reflected in his picture of wild animals 'playing/laughing' with Behemoth and his absurd scene where children 'play/laugh' with Leviathan as if he were a harmless pet bird (41:5). In the hands of Yahweh, it seems, the defiant laugh of this sea monster can be transformed into a giggle or a game (as in Ps. 104:26).[67]

The laughter varies in its tones, ranging from laughter mockingly defiant – laughing *at* – to laughter engagingly sympathetic and playful – laughing *with*. Moreover, the Joban laughter enhances and deepens the comic sensibility of the whole book of Job, highlighting the congeniality between the comic vision and the carnivalesque festivity and laughter of the Yahweh speeches. Thus the profundity and poetic power of the divine speeches include an element of playfulness, of exuberant laughter that revels in the comic rhythms of creation.

On still another level, I would argue that the irony and incongruity of the Yahweh speeches are best interpreted as elements in a comic vision. As interpreters have often noted,

---

[65] *Ibid.*, p. 504.
[66] After I had written an earlier form of my observations on the laughter theme in the Yahweh speeches, I was happy to discover that Habel offers a similar rendition – a point that I am doubly happy to acknowledge since he has been critical of my comic interpretation of Job. I enlist his insights as an independent confirmation of the comic elements of the speech from the whirlwind. See Habel, *The Book of Job*, p. 573.   [67] *Ibid.*

Yahweh's answer to Job is no answer – at least it is not an unambiguous answer. God sidesteps Job's persistent plea for his legal vindication in a court of law. Incongruity is involved, however one chooses ultimately to deal with that incongruity. Edwin Good seems to be correct when he argues that Yahweh decisively shifts the issue from the question of justice – Job's primary question in his legal brief against God – to the question of order.[68] That order involves justice is clearly a part of the Hebraic heritage, but it is an order that transcends narrow human views of justice and comprehends all creation. The issue is pinpointed in Job 40:8, which I believe Good correctly translates: "Would you even annul my order (*mishpat*), treat me as wicked so you can be innocent?"[69] Is it the case, Good asks, that either Job or God must be wicked and the other innocent? The answer in Good's opinion is "no!"[70] "What God demonstrates," argues Good, "is that moral presumptions are not the way the world is handled, that the question of order is another one entirely from the one Job put."[71] Thus if one examines carefully Job's speeches, the trial metaphor involving guilt and innocence becomes dominant; but the Yahweh speeches, though retaining the setting of a lawsuit, move more dominantly in the mythological metaphors of creation and thereby transcend the more narrow limits of the courtroom.[72]

Job's new perception, I would argue, is rooted in a comic perspective, which comes only when Job has a double view – i.e., a divine and human view – of himself and the world. This double view only becomes Job's through the theophanic vision. He sees God and through God's eyes he now sees the world; he sees the mysterious and marvelous interworkings of the universe; he sees the seeming superfluity which is nevertheless required for the larger needs of life in the cosmos; and he sees that humanity only constitutes a small part of the

---

[68] Good, "Job and the Literary Task: A Response," p. 480.
[69] *Ibid.*, p. 479.   [70] *Ibid.*, p. 480.   [71] *Ibid.*, p. 481.
[72] According to Cross, Job "repudiated the God of history whose realm is politics, law, and justice" and recalled rather the Creator God of the ancient myths. Frank M. Cross, *Canaanite Myth and Hebrew Epic: Essays in the History of the Religion of Israel* (Cambridge, MA: Harvard University Press, 1973), p. 344.

cosmos. Job becomes privy to the carnival of creation, where God takes him by the magic of visionary experience to the primordial beginnings of the cosmos and gives him a ring-side seat to see as God sees. He now beholds the grand sweep of creation which contains the wondrous excess and unrestrained laughter of a universe filled with bountiful, boundless life. As Terrien states:

Job is invited, in effect, to liberate himself from the microcosm of his egocentricity, to borrow the perspective of God without pursuing the mirage of self-deification, and to discover the broad horizons of the macrocosm of life on the grand scale.[73]

Stephen Mitchell puts it even more elegantly: "It is a God's-eye view of creation *before* man, beyond good and evil, marked by the innocence of a mind that has stepped outside the circle of human values."[74] In brief, the mystery and incongruity at the heart of the universe remain; they are now accepted and affirmed but not resolved.

After the initial theophanic speech the hero is silenced: "Lo, I am small, how can I answer you? My hand I lay on my mouth; I have spoken once, I will not reply; twice, but I will say no more" (40:4–5). On one level silence is a profoundly authentic response of the one who has become wise and this reaction is not to be denigrated. Yet there is a second divine speech and a second response. The seeming redundancy of the two speeches has perplexed interpreters for centuries. A common approach is to brand the second speech a secondary addition and then blend Job's two responses into one harmonistic account. I side with those who argue that the second speech lies on the primary stage of tradition; but whatever one's position on this question, it is still necessary to interpret the final stage of the text with its duplicated structure. As a rule when scholars have attempted to take the text as it stands and interpret the intention of the two speeches and the two responses, they have done so in theological and/or psychological terms: Job has been silenced, but he still needs to be repentant. Silence therefore is construed on

---

[73] Terrien, "The Yahweh Speeches and Job's Responses," p. 502.
[74] Stephen Mitchell, *The Book of Job* (San Francisco: North Point Press, 1987), p. xx.

a lower level in the hierarchy of appropriate responses. Terrien's interpretation typifies this approach:

Job no longer protests of his innocence, nor does he clamour for his rights. He is not yet ready to surrender his pride, nor can he exteriorize a confession in words. The poet stresses the negative aspect of Job's response to the First Speech (40:4–5). He may well be aware of the need for psychological suspense in view of the processes of man's conversion. The encounter must continue.[75]

One can find evidence to support this view. Although we find parallelism in form and content between the two speeches and the two responses, the parallelism is designed to be incremental and build to a climax. The introductory challenge – "Gird your loins like a hero; I will ask you, and you tell me" – is repeated from the opening speech (38:3), but the issue under debate is now more clearly stated in 40:8: "Would you annul my order, condemn me that you may be justified?" Moreover, the hero's arrogation to himself of the divine prerogatives, certainly present in the first speech, is sarcastically parodied in 40:9–14. Then, too, Behemoth and Leviathan play different roles from those of the animals in the first speech: both creatures take on mythological dimensions as monsters symbolizing chaos and evil that only Yahweh could control, yet though Job is no match for either monster, he is paradoxically likened to both mythical beasts. Like Behemoth, Job was divinely created (40:15); like even the fearsome, fire-breathing Leviathan, Job has been silenced (cf. 40:5 and 41:12). Earlier in the dialogues Job had likened himself to a mythological monster that God must watch and guard (7:12); now God himself is likening Job to such monsters. Ironically, Job was right, and God so acknowledges that Job had become an adversary comparable to Behemoth and Leviathan. Though perhaps one could accuse God of "overkill," since the comparison is ludicrous given that Job can hardly match these two mythical monsters in brute strength (though Job can wreak his own form of chaos and evil in the universe by his harsh parodying of God). The ludicrousness is heightened in the comic image of the mighty Leviathan, the

---

[75] Terrien, "The Yahweh Speeches and Job's Responses," p. 502.

king of the beasts, being likened to a pet that children can play with (41:5). God delights apparently in designing Leviathan as a plaything both for himself (Ps. 104:26) and for children (who do not parody God). But if Leviathan becomes a playful creature designed in part for levity, how can we take God or Leviathan or Job seriously? Hence the whole scene dissolves in a parody of parodies, in which God throws up on the screen what initially appears as a dreadful monster, but cuts it down to size through absurd images and comic ridicule.[76]

Nonetheless, the divine rhetoric is effective in eliciting from Job a second response, deepening his sense of awe as he recants and repents. Thus a climax is achieved in the second round of the encounter between the divine orator and the human protagonist. The hero's silence is both complemented and consummated by his repentance. Hearing the divine speech silences the human hero and seeing the divine presence – as opposed to simply hearing of God – triggers repentance. Though silence is often the mark of the truly wise and faithful person in Hebraic and Near Eastern tradition (cf. especially Egyptian wisdom), the two-stage movement in the book of Job seems to suggest that silence as a response is not sufficient; so silence must be coupled with and climaxed in repentance.

I think, however, that comedy helps to illumine and further explicate this movement of the text. The incongruity between the two speeches and the two responses has comic dimensions. Just at the moment readers finish the first speech and hear Job's response, they sense a climax has finally been reached – a climax already delayed once before by the entrance of Elihu. But again the poet shifts his ground and throws off his audience, for he has Yahweh break in and repeat virtually the same challenge to Job. Yet one detects

---

[76] Again, Harold Fisch recognizes how ill-fitting the Behemoth and Leviathan scenes are for a genuine tragic movement: "No more extraordinary anticlimax to a would-be tragedy could be imagined. The tragic mood is radically undermined in this 'carnival of animals.' The vision of Behemoth and Leviathan may not be strictly relevant to the questions raised by Job. But these chapters are utterly relevant to the artistic and structural questions that the book raises. They are part of the character of Job as antitragedy." I couldn't agree more. See his discussion in his chapter, "Job: Tragedy is Not Enough," *Poetry with a Purpose*, p. 40.

differences in the unfolding of the second divine speech. As indicated above, one hears a more clear-cut formulation of the issue involved (40:8) as well as a sharper parody of the hero. Moreover, though the theme of the "carnival of animals" is resumed, the two primordial and mythological monsters are cast up before our eyes in opposing images: they appear first as terrifying symbols of the powers of chaos and evil which Job can hardly expect to quell, but they also appear as mere playthings before God, because he alone as Creator controls them. So presumably the audience, like the hero, is caught off guard. What was thought to be the climax is not the climax; in fact, it is only a powerful prelude to the second and more decisive encounter between the hero and his God. The stylistic technique of structural parallelism serves to heighten the sense of incongruity in Yahweh's renewed challenge to Job and Job's second capitulation in the act of repentance. Thus commentators have been right in discerning an incongruity between the two speeches, but they have gone astray in seeking a solution by deletion or rearrangement, according to a logic that fails to catch that the poet effectively exploits the age-old Near Eastern literary convention of parallel structures in order to create a comic effect.

In conclusion, Job's second response of repentance does represent a climax, but its interpretation is profoundly ambiguous and suggests multiple levels of meaning.[77] In Robertson's ironic interpretation, Job's repentance is "tongue-in-cheek";[78] the hero bows his head but with a side-

---

[77] See Habel's summary of the different interpretations and his own balanced view in his commentary, *The Book of Job*, pp. 577–583.

[78] Robertson, "The Book of Job," pp. 466ff. Recently, Jack Miles has offered a vigorous critique of the traditional translation of "repentance" and a defense of the heavily ironic interpretation of the meaning of Job's final response (see his *God: A Biography*, pp. 323–328). Though I share considerable appreciation for the ironic perspective, I think that Miles, like Robertson, underplays the significance of the visionary experience to which Job testifies: seeing God does make a profound difference to the hero and his total vision of God which effects a re-vision of Job's sense of his place in the greater cosmic scheme. Moreover, such a re-vision does not at all undercut his stubborn conviction about his innocence and integrity which God never denies. "Repentance" as involving fundamentally "a change of mind" need not include contrition for sin; Job has embraced a more expansive vision of God and the cosmos and simply acknowledges ignorance not sin.

long glance to the audience he winks his eye. It must be admitted that Robertson's view is appealing and has textual support on its side (note again the sequence of chapter 9 in comparison with the sequence of Yahweh's speeches and Job's responses). Moreover, it is obviously easy to incorporate a "tongue-in-cheek" repentance into a comic view; it would be one more element in the "poet's ironic joke."[79]

I think, however, that the repentance can still be taken as an authentic response of the hero, because he has been granted the double view delineated above; it is too simple therefore to view it as "tongue-in-cheek." Thus Job's confession is genuine and becomes equivalent to the recognition scene in the comic plot: "I talked of things I did not know, wonders beyond my ken ... I had heard of you by hearsay, but now my own eyes have seen you" (42:3, 5). According to the poet, a crucial part of Job's vision is that he sees as God sees and paradoxically he sees that he as a mortal does not see! That he repents is expected because he now sees aright. His confession is authentic but paradoxical: his new wisdom is that he does not know all, his new perception is that he does not see all; but he now knows enough and sees enough. Of course it is still possible to construe this confession of new sight as ironic and tongue-in-cheek; but I think that the poet's portrayal of Job's vision of God makes a difference when one remembers that Job has complained, on the one hand, about his inability to see God (cf. 9:11; 23:8–9) and expressed, on the other, the confidence that in the moment of his vindication he would see God (19:26–27). So I would argue that Robertson underplays the significance of Job's vision of God when he concentrates on the ironic interplay between Job's prior speeches and the Yahweh speeches. To be sure, whether one interprets the repentance scene as tongue-in-cheek or authentic depends finally on whether or not one senses an incongruity between Job's predictions of how God would act in a confrontation and God's actual self-representation in the Yahweh speeches. In my view, as I argued earlier, there is an incongruity between prediction and fulfillment which the

---

[79] Robertson, *The Old Testament and the Literary Critic*, p. 54.

poet has Job himself confess. Thus I read the confession as genuine and Job's acknowledgment of his new perception into the ways of God and the world as authentic. Job as comic hero rediscovers his limits as a human being and repents before the creator God when he is allowed to see both the creator and the wonders of the creation. In this direct encounter with God, Job also perceives God's limits in his inability as creator to effect perfect justice for his sometimes innocent sufferers – at least in the vision of divine rule revealed to Job. Ambiguity, if not absurdity, still pervades this world so filled with wonders beyond human knowledge. But comedy can tolerate such ambiguity; indeed, comedy often revels in it.

AN IMPROBABLE HAPPY ENDING: RESTORATION AND REGENERATION IN A COMIC MODE (JOB 42:7–17)

That the restoration scene (42:7ff) follows immediately Job's repentance is explicable from the perspective of comedy; in fact, it is decisive to a comic movement according to numerous literary critics. Building on Cornford's classic analysis of Attic Comedy, Sypher argues that the movement from repentance to festivity is a necessary component of comedy, which shows among other things that comedy is a more complex form than tragedy:

In Cornford's opinion the dramatic form known as tragedy eventually suppressed the sexual magic in this canonical plot, leaving only the portrayal of the suffering and death of the hero, king, or god. Comedy, however, kept in the foreground the erotic action, together with the disorderly rejoicing at the rebirth or resurrection of the god-hero who survives his *agon*. In this sense comedy preserves the archaic "double occasion" of the plot formula, the dual and wholly incompatible meanings of sacrifice and feast, cruelty and festival, logic and license . . . Retaining its double action of penance and revel, comedy remains an "improvisation" with a loose structure, and a precarious logic that can tolerate every kind of "improbability."[80]

[80] Sypher, "The Meanings of Comedy," p. 35.

Critics have been correct in noting the "improvised," "improbable," and gratuitous quality of the restoration, but they have either missed or dismissed the significance of this part of Job within the totality of the book's structure. Here I part company with Terrien, Robertson, Good, and many other interpreters who in different ways tend to discount the importance of the epilogue. Good is typical: "The restoration of wealth is not a sign of divine pleasure but is simply something that happens, as far as Job cares."[81] I think this sort of interpretation overly psychologizes the hero and fails thereby to deal with the generic structure of the whole book. The restoration is not at all superfluous or surprising when one traces out the characteristic plot-line of comedy, where catastrophe is typically followed by restoration, penance by festivity, and alienation from society by reintegration into society. And one should note that this restoration includes not simply Job and his new family but Job's three friends as well. A crowning irony surely comes when Yahweh rebukes the friends and commends Job (42:7) – and then orders the friends to go to Job, offer sacrifice, and have Job intercede for them in order that they might likewise be restored to divine favor.[82] Yahweh's words of rebuke and commendation addressed to Eliphaz provide a wonderful turn-about in the movement of the book and offer at last a vindication of the fundamental "truth" of Job's case: "My anger burns against you and your two friends; for you have not spoken truth of me, as did Job, my servant" (42:7). Then, too, it is interesting that Job's restoration is apparently contingent on Job's intercession for his friends: "Yahweh accepted Job and restored Job's fortune when he prayed for his friends and increased what he had twofold" (42:9b–10). Thus reconciliation precedes full restoration.

Moreover, after sacrifice, intercession, and restoration, we

[81] Good, "Job and the Literary Task: A Response," p. 482.
[82] Robertson also focuses on the irony of the divine speech in 42:7 but gives it a different twist: "[God's] words in 42.7 mean exactly the opposite of what he wants and once intended them to mean. God is the object of the poet's ironic joke. And after this bit of irreverence on the part of the poet it is impossible for us to take seriously the solution to the problem of suffering offered by the folktale" ("The Book of Job," p. 468).

find festivity and fertility. Job's whole extended family and his former friends gather around Job for a festive meal replete with gifts for Job. Blessed with the proverbial double restoration, Job receives again bountiful flocks and above all his new children in the perfect proportions of seven sons and three daughters. Then comes a final reversal of conventional expectation: the daughters, not the sons, are named, given an inheritance, and singled out for their beauty. Perhaps this striking feminine presence is a last note of incongruity, compensating for the rather harsh rebuff of Job's wife in the prologue whose counsel is to "curse God and die." Job initially rebuked her but ultimately followed her counsel at least in part when he turned to complain against God. Though his wife plays no explicit role in this scene of reconciliation and restoration, their daughters are elevated to a starring role. Hence in an otherwise conventional ending, the narrator offers still another antithetical twist to normative expectations, subverting the patriarchal ambience of the scene and celebrating the charming names and famed beauty of Job's daughters. Stephen Mitchell captures the power of the scene most eloquently:

> There is something enormously satisfying about this prominence of the feminine at the end of *Job*. The whole yin side of humanity, denigrated in the figure of Job's wife, and in Job's great oath looked upon as a seductive danger, has finally been acknowledged and honored . . . It is as if, once Job has learned to surrender, his world too gives up the male compulsion to control. The daughters have almost the last word. They appear with the luminous power of figures in a dream: we can't quite figure out why they are so important, but we know that they are.[83]

In the fashion of a good domestic comedy, virtually all the crucial segments of the Joban society are therefore restored to a happy, harmonious relationship. The last word reverts to the formula we recall from the Genesis patriarchal stories, a formula that bespeaks a most satisfying conclusion to an

---

[83] Mitchell, *The Book of Job*, p. xxx. I am happy to acknowledge that I first came across this quotation in Pardes' fine book, *Countertraditions in the Bible*, pp. 151–152. Her whole treatment of Job's wife and daughters is most illuminating and has sharpened my overall interpretation (see pp. 145–156).

earthly life: "After this Job lived 140 years and saw his children and grandchildren to four generations. So Job died, old and satisfied with life" (42:16–17).

The happy ending of the book of Job illumines and helps to confirm the comic perspective I have tried to delineate. In fact, the happy ending, in my view, demonstrates the ultimate irony and comedy of Job, where the problems are not fully and satisfactorily resolved, where the contradictions and incongruities remain. Describing the book of Job as technically a comedy, Northrop Frye remarks:

> The author of Job has solved the moral problem of his play in the usual comic fashion, by cutting its Gordian knot. But we can accept this solution only by thinking of the world of Job's reward as a different world from the nightmare world of misery and boils and uncomprehending comforters.[84]

Although I owe an enormous debt to Frye for insights into comedy, I think his interpretation of the comedy of Job misses something. I would argue, first of all, that Frye does not give sufficient heed to the prior elements of comedy within the poem of Job (e.g., the pervasive presence of parody and satire); thus he depends too exclusively on the happy ending to define Job as technically a comedy. Moreover, as I read comedy, it seems that a major point is its perception of the incongruities of existence in which celebration and festivity occur side-by-side with evil and death. Thus the comic vision does not necessarily eliminate evil and death; it is not incorrigibly and naively optimistic; it does not shut its eyes to the dark, jagged edges of life in this world. In fact, many would argue that it is precisely because humans have experienced suffering that they have a sharpened awareness of comic incongruity.[85] Comedy therefore may incorporate rather

---

[84] Northrop Frye, *A Natural Perspective: The Development of Shakespearian Comedy and Romance* (New York: Harcourt, Brace & World, 1965), p. 129.

[85] "Man laughed only after the Exile, when he knew sin and suffering; the comical is a mark of man's revolt, boredom, and aspiration." Sypher, "The Meanings of Comedy," p. 26. If Sypher and other critics are correct in this insight (as I believe them to be), and if it is true that the book of Job was most likely born in Israel's exile, then one must deal seriously with the comic perspective in evaluating the different types of literature that emerged from Israel's experience of exile. In my judgment, the correlation of exile and comedy is one which needs to be explored

than ignore the haunting riddles of life. Thus even though
the happy ending does stand in an incongruous relationship
with the preceding poem, that does not mean it refers to a
different world; it simply affirms that a harmonious, prosper-
ous society is still most desirable in the midst of a world of
pain and death.[86] Such a dream, often so far from reality,
nonetheless energizes a suffering people and provides one
strategy for survival with a sense of meaning and hope.

That the book of Job fades out in a scene borrowed from
the world of fairy tale and romance not only helps to confirm
its comic mode, it also breaks off or at least alters its potentially tragic movement, which as we have noted has long been
a concern of commentators. Even here, however, one must
emphasize that the line between tragedy and comedy is fluid,
and a work as richly complex and ambiguous as Job can legitimately evoke both responses. Job can indeed be painted as a
tragic hero, as a Hebrew Prometheus who steadfastly holds to
his integrity and defiantly challenges God and the world. But
when Job has his theophanic vision, when he beholds God
and the world from a double view, when he sees cosmic
wonders that transcend logical and legal propositions, when
he perceives that the incongruities are not totally resolvable,
then he repents and is restored to an idyllic society.[87]

more fully in dealing with biblical literature (see my attempts to deal with this
theme in other chapters in the present volume).

[86] From a realistic perspective, one cannot imagine that the birth of new children
fully compensates for the unjust deaths of Job's first children; yet renewal of life
nonetheless offers consolation in the midst of ongoing grief (cf. the moving
account of David's mournful reaction to the illness and death of the unfortunate
first child of his union with Bathsheba, which is then followed immediately by the
report of his "comforting" Bathsheba in renewed sexual union and the resulting
pregnancy and birth of Solomon – see II Sam. 12). We must always recall the
world of fairy tales can look death in the face and yet partially neutralize its power
by affirming the triumph of goodness and the coming of new life.

[87] Cf. Polzin's conclusion as to the achievement of the book when one views its dominant structural movement: "The framework of the story . . . is a work of genius.
By means of its remarkable resources it takes the reader on a journey, the beginning of which may be described as equilibrium without insight and whose conclusion is appropriately equilibrium with insight. The genius of this journey is that
insight is conferred not by the avoidance of contradiction and inconsistency but
precisely by the courageous integration of contradiction and resolution." Polzin,
"The Framework of the Book of Job," p. 200. I would support this interpretation
of the fundamental movement of the book; I would only argue that it finds its best
focus and richest meaning in the comic vision.

The eminent playwright, Christopher Fry, captures well these multiple dimensions in his perceptive observations on the interplay between tragedy and comedy:

The bridge by which we cross from tragedy to comedy and back again is precarious and narrow. We find ourselves in one or the other by the turn of a thought . . . I know that when I set about writing a comedy the idea presents itself to me first of all as tragedy. The characters press on to the theme with all their divisions and perplexities about them; they are already entered for the race to doom, and good and evil are an infernal tangle skinning the fingers that try to unravel them. If the characters were not qualified for tragedy there would be no comedy, and to some extent I have to cross the one before I can light on the other. [But] a bridge has to be crossed, a thought has to be tuned. Somehow the characters have to unmortify themselves: to affirm life and assimilate death . . . Their hearts must be as determined as the phoenix; what burns must also light and renew: not by a vulnerable optimism but by a hard-won maturity of delight, by the intuition of comedy . . . The Book of Job is the great reservoir of comedy.[88]

The aura of ambiguity indeed remains to hover over the book of Job, but it is comedy – rich, full, celebrative of life despite its contradictions and riddles – that emerges as the final and dominant note in the Joban chorus of dissonant voices.

---

[88] Fry, "Comedy," p. 17. For a contemporary, comic adaptation of the biblical story of Job, see Neil Simon's play, *God's Favorite: A Comedy by Neil Simon* (New York: Random House, 1975; see also Elizabeth Swados, "Job: He's a Clown," in *Out of the Garden: Women Writers on the Bible*, Christina Buechmann and Celina Spiegel, eds. (New York: Fawcett Columbine, 1994), pp. 204–220. In her essay Swados describes what inspired her to write *Job*, "a live musical circus of clowns" (p. 204). The comedy of Job lives on in such contemporary dramatic and musical forms!

CHAPTER 6

Paradox and parody in the Song of Solomon: towards a comic reading of the Song of Songs

Is it not true . . . that erotic love makes a person ridiculous, if not in the eyes of others, at least in the eyes of the gods?[1]

(Kierkegaard)

I find it comical that all human beings are in love, and want to be in love, and yet one can never get any illumination upon the question what the lovable, i.e. the actual object of love, really is.[2]

(Kierkegaard)

Comedy blends insensibly into satire at one extreme and into romance at the other.[3]

(Northrop Frye)

ON HEARING COMEDY IN A LYRICAL KEY

Our current delight in ambiguity, indeterminacy, and multivalency may be a new mania of our so-called post-modern age, but the history of interpretation shows no reluctance to engage in spirited conflicts over how we should read the great texts of our tradition. The resulting interpretations are often wildly diverse, outrageously contradictory, and teasingly provocative. Perhaps no book in the Bible offers a greater diversity of readings than the Song of Songs. I wish to offer yet another way of interpreting a book that Pope calls "the sublime song of Solomon,"[4] a way that combines old and new

[1] Soren Kierkegaard, *Stages on Life's Way* (New York: Schocken Books, 1967), p. 49.
[2] *Ibid.*, pp. 48–49.   [3] N. Frye, *Anatomy of Criticism*, p. 162.
[4] Marvin Pope, *Song of Songs: The Anchor Bible* (New York: Doubleday, 1977), p. 1.

into a fresh combination. I want to look at the presence of paradox and parody in the Song in order to test the possibility of a comic reading.

Of course I am not the first to attempt such a reading. Athalya Brenner has recently rendered a suggestive, stimulating interpretation of the role of comic forms in the Song, focusing on 7:1–10 as a parody of the description of the woman's body and utilizing in particular a Freudian and feminist approach to deal with the motivation and intention behind such a parody of a long recognized genre.[5] I am also happy to note that one of my Pomona College students was the first to call my attention to the possibility of reading the descriptive catalogues as parody.[6]

Brenner and my Pomona College student, however, must take their place in a long line of interpreters who have suggested the possibility of finding comedic forms in the Song of Songs. Haimo of Auxerre, a noted ninth-century Christian commentator, asserts that the Song "is composed in a rather comic style."[7] Moreover, seconding this view, Cornelius à Lapide, an eighteenth-century commentator, emerges as another interpreter who made the comedic designation explicit, characterizing the Song as an "allegory written in comic and bucolic style."[8] Barbara Lewalski links him with commentators who follow Origen in emphasizing the Song's "dramatic elements and terming it an 'interlude,' in evident reference to its brevity and comedic form."[9] Lewalski also indicates that many Protestant exegetes interpreted the Song in terms of a comedic plot. She concludes that Milton "evidently intended the same emphasis when he contrasted the divine pastoral Drama of Canticles with the 'high stately Tragedy' of Revelation."[10]

It seems clear that complex continuities link Origen,

[5] Athalya Brenner, "'Come Back, Come Back The Shulamite' (Song of Songs 7:1–10): A Parody of the *wasf* Genre," in *On Humour and the Comic in the Hebrew Bible.*   [6] Edward Tessier, class discussion at Pomona College, 1987.
[7] E. Ann Matter, *The Voice of My Beloved: The Song of Songs in Western Medieval Christianity* (Philadelphia: University of Pennsylvania Press, 1990), p. 37.
[8] Cited by Barbara Kiefer Lewalski, *Paradise Lost and the Rhetoric of Literary Forms* (Princeton: Princeton University Press, 1985), p. 201.   [9] *Ibid.*   [10] *Ibid.*

Haimo, Cornelius à Lapide, and Milton in a variegated tradition in which a comic interpretation was represented, though it goes beyond the bounds of this study to trace out in any detail this interpretive trail. Suffice it to say this earlier comedic view illustrates once again the variety and vitality of the history of biblical interpretation. Whatever the merits of the case that these earlier commentators make for the presence of comedic elements in their allegorical interpretations of the Song, their assertion of a *comic* style of the book should intrigue and stimulate us, provoking us to rethink our own views of this perennially enchanting, enigmatic text.[11] What happens to our reading of the Song when we view its movement and its generic configuration from the perspective of comedy? How might the perception of a "comic style" illumine this most diversely interpreted biblical book? How might the comic vision in the Song echo or evoke various dimensions of comedy we have noted in Genesis, Exodus, or Job?

SOCIAL ROLES IN THE SONG: REVERSALS AND REVELS IN LOVE-MAKING

One can initiate a *comic* exploration of the Song of Songs with the roles of female and male in the Song, especially the characterization of the two lovers. Landy has called the "dominance and initiative of the Beloved [his term for the woman] the most astonishing characteristic of the Song."[12] In particular, the portrayal of the relative positions of the fabled Solomon and the unknown Shulamite highlights the subversive spirit of the Song, representing an inversion of cus-

---

[11] Apart from Brenner's new reading of the Song and its possible humor, one finds few contemporary interpreters who even raise the possibility of a comic reading. A spot check of recent monographs and commentaries on the Song yields meager results. For example, in Pope's mammoth Anchor Bible commentary, the index shows no entry under comedy; Francis Landy's splendid volume on the Song, *Paradoxes of Paradise* (Sheffield: Almond Press, 1983), contains only *one* reference to comedy, though it is a suggestive reference which I will pick up later. As I was revising the earlier essay form of this chapter, I was happy to discover that Jack Miles also puts the Song into the comic category (see his *God: A Biography*, p. 405).

[12] Francis Landy, "The Song of Songs," *The Literary Guide to the Bible*, p. 317.

tomary roles in patriarchal and royal society. Thus at the
beginning and ending of the Song, the unnamed woman
appears in the commanding and controlling position, inviting the king to kiss her and then sending away her lover at the
end with an imperious *berah*, "flee away" (8:14).[13] The ironic
and incongruous reversal in showing the commanding feminine presence dramatically shifts the focus from the typically
dominating male lover to the powerful role of an unnamed
country maid, a classic instance of an outsider known simply
but suggestively as the Shulamite (an echo possibly of a
goddess? or a feminine form of Solomon's name? or a veiled
reference to a woman from *Shunem* evoking perhaps the
image of the beautiful Abishag?). Whatever the exact
meaning of Shulamite, the woman's position as the central
protagonist of the Song puts the royal figure into a surprisingly subordinate role.

This paradoxical reversal of roles provides an occasion for
the use of parody and travesty. In fact, Gottwald, following
Gerleman's lead, calls these portrayals "travesties . . . in which
the lover is portrayed in a role deliberately outside – often
above but sometimes below – the social class or occupation to
which he belongs (e.g., the roles of 'king,' 'shepherd,'
'servant,' 'doorkeeper,' etc.)."[14] If travesty be an appropriate
word to describe this process of strategic displacement of
typical social roles, then it should not surprise us that the
Song contains paradoxical twists and turns as well as subtle
parodies. How paradoxical and incongruous is the passive,
subordinate position of the male lover when one recalls the
typical image of King Solomon in his relationship to women!
How comically ludicrous that Solomon, a legendary posses-
sor of a huge harem, is portrayed as an outsider looking in

---

[13] Roland Murphy sees this reply as an invitation to the man: "She invites him to
'flee' to the mountains of spice, i.e., to herself." Whichever way one takes the final
command of the book, my point is the same: at the beginning and ending of the
Song, the woman's commanding voice frames the words and actions of the whole
series of love songs. For the citation, see Roland E. Murphy, *The Song of Songs: A
Commentary on the Book of Canticles or Song of Songs*, S. Dean McBride, Jr., ed.
(Minneapolis: Augsberg Press, 1990).

[14] Gottwald, *The Hebrew Bible*, p. 547.

(2:9) or as one whom the woman commands to flee away at the end of the Song (8:14)!

To be sure, the fictionalizing of the lover as king can cut two ways: it can elevate the male; but it can also deflate him. Commentators have usually emphasized the first, stressing the lover as larger than life whether as king or god. But if we allow for the presence of parody whereby the exalted royal role may be subverted and undercut, then the opposite effect of deflation can be achieved.

Take, for example, the depiction of the royal wedding processional (3:7–11). On one level, one can read this text as a portrayal of a magnificent parade on the king's wedding day, a grand festal processional that no doubt has its roots in sacred marriage rites of the ancient Near East (see Psalm 45 for a beautiful rendition of the king's wedding day). Yet, on another level, one can discern here a parody of a royal processional, a parody whose rhetoric is designed to satirize an ostentatious display of royal pomp:

> There is Solomon's couch,
> Encircled by sixty warriors
> Of the warriors of Israel,
> All of them trained in warfare,
> Skilled in battle,
> Each with sword on thigh
> Because of terror by night.
> King Solomon made him a palanquin
> Of wood from Lebanon.
> He made its posts of silver,
> Its back of gold,
> Its seat of purple wool.
> Within, it was decked with love
> By the maidens of Jerusalem.
> O maidens of Zion, go forth
> And gaze upon King Solomon
> Wearing the crown that his mother
> Gave him on his wedding day,
> On his day of bliss.

"The Palanquin," remarks Landy, "is the scene of self-glorification, the gratification of Solomon's heart, the delusion of grandeur."[15] Hence Gerleman's suggestion that we find here another instance of "royal travesty" is compelling.[16] In sum, within the world of the Song, the poet has a way of undercutting royal pretentiousness by employing erotic love to level class distinctions.

A later scene mirrors parallel images of the royal entourage, but reverses and sharply alters the focus: now the Shulamite takes center stage:

> There are sixty queens,
> And eighty concubines,
> And damsels without number.
> Only one is my dove,
> My perfect one,
> The only one of her mother,
> The delight of her who bore her.
> Maidens see and acclaim her;
> Queens and concubines, and praise her.　　　(6:8–9)

The king's love for the Shulamite reveals the motive power for his exalted image of her. The same erotic power that undercuts and reduces royal pomp now elevates the country maiden to the dominant position both in the eyes of her royal lover and his harem. She stands alone in his court.

BODIES BEAUTIFUL IN PLAYFUL PARODY

Obviously the difficult, delicate task of a comic interpretation is to discriminate as closely as possible between what might appear comical and ludicrous to us in contrast to the perception of an ancient audience. The famous descriptive poems of the Song, those depictions of the gorgeous bodies of the two lovers, represent a case in point (4:1–7; 5:10–16; 6:5–7; 7:1–10). It takes little imagination to understand how these catalogues of physical attributes have provided a seedbed for imaginative allegorical treatment. Modern scholars continue

---

[15] Landy, *Paradoxes of Paradise*, p. 124.
[16] Gillis Gerleman, *Ruth. Das Hohelied. Biblischer Kommentar Altes Testament* (Neukirchen-Vluyn: Neukirchener Verlag, 1965), p. 137.

to engage in heated debate about the best way to read this genre. Interpreters often invoke ancient Near Eastern parallels, especially Egyptian love poems.[17] Pope offers a fascinating reading of these poems in light of their alleged superhuman, divine prototypes.[18] Most recently one of the most fruitful paths has been the exploration of the metaphoric configuration of the descriptive poems.[19]

The most extended poem in this genre appears in 7:2–6:

> How lovely are your feet in sandals,
> O daughter of nobles!
> Your rounded thighs are like jewels,
> The work of a master's hand.
> Your navel is like a round goblet -
> Let mixed wine not be lacking! -
> Your belly like a heap of wheat
> Hedged about with lilies.
> Your breasts are like two fawns,
> Twins of a gazelle.
> Your neck is like a tower of ivory,
> Your eyes like pools in Heshbon
> By the gate of Bath-rabbim,
> Your nose like the Lebanon tower
> That faces toward Damascus.
> The head upon you is like crimson wool,
> The locks of your head are like purple -
> A king is held captive in the tresses.
> How fair you are, how beautiful!

As I noted above, Brenner has offered a provocative interpretation of the descriptive poem of chapter 7, arguing that the poet has subtly parodied the genre.[20] She contends that the dancing figure of the Shulamite receives a parodied representation in which the poet departs from the conven-

---

[17] Michael Fox, *The Song of Songs and Ancient Egyptian Poetry* (Madison: University of Wisconsin Press, 1985).

[18] M. H. Pope, "Metastases in Canonical Shapes of the Super Song," in *Canon, Theology, and Old Testament Interpretation*, G. M. Tucker, D. G. Petersen, R. R. Wilson, eds. (Philadelphia: Fortress Press, 1988), pp. 312ff.

[19] Robert Alter, *The Art of Biblical Poetry* (New York: Basic Books, 1985), pp. 185ff.

[20] Brenner, "'Come Back, Come Back The Shulamite'," pp. 251–276.

tional norms and injects a *comic* element where "the tone is ribald and the humor is sexual."[21] For example, reversing the direction of the earlier descriptive poems in which the poet begins with the head and works down the body, the speaker starts here with the feet and moves upward. The poet sets aside conventional modesty and reverence and mentions every significant part of the body, "including an explicit reference to the dancer's vulva."[22] Brenner argues that a lighter tone appears, with sexual humor introduced. The portrayal is playful, with ludicrous touches such as a corpulent body, quivering breasts that are "like frolicking fawns, a nose like the tower of Lebanon." The female appears as a vital, energetic, full-bodied earth dancer whose physical charms may be in fact a "mixed bag" (Brenner's phrase), but whose sexual power is enhanced by her earthy, exaggerated features. In brief, according to Brenner, the "dancer of Chapter 7:1–10 cuts a comical figure."[23]

As a possible analogue, Brenner cites Shakespeare's 130th sonnet, "where the poet pokes fun at his love object. . .":[24]

> My mistress' eyes are nothing like the sun;
> Coral is far more red than her lips' red:
> If snow be white, why then her breasts are dun;
> If hair be wires, black wires grow on her head.
> I have seen roses damask'd, red and white,
> But no such roses see I in her cheeks;
> And in some perfumes is there more delight
> Than in the breath that from my mistress reeks.
> I love to hear her speak, yet well I know
> That music hath a far more pleasing sound:
> I grant I never saw a goddess go, -
> My mistress, when she walks, treads on the ground:
>   And yet, by heaven, I think my love as rare
>   As any she belied with false compare.

---

[21] Athalya Brenner, abstract of the above cited article, in *Abstracts* from the 1988 International Meeting of the Society of Biblical Literature, August 1–3, 1988, Sheffield, England, p.6.

[22] Brenner, "'Come Back, Come Back The Shulamite'," p. 260.

[23] *Ibid.*, p. 271.   [24] *Ibid.*

Brenner avers, "the protest against conventional, idolized, idealized images of love and of the female love object, similar to those expressed in love poetry of the *wasf* type and intentionality, speaks for itself."[25]

Brenner also appeals to Freud for support, offering a quotation that "sums up the question of 'sexual humour . . .'":[26]

the spheres of sexuality and obscenity offer the amplest occasions for obtaining comic pleasure alongside pleasurable sexual excitement; for they can show human beings in their dependence on bodily needs (degradation) or they can reveal the physical demands lying behind the claim of mental love (unmasking).

To Brenner, "these two quotations sum up the case for a comic/humorous tone of Song 7:1–10 admirably."[27]

Brenner has offered a daring, even dazzling new interpretation which I find imaginative and compelling. Yet I do not think she has gone far enough with her intriguing suggestion about the possible play of parody in the Song. First, I believe it is significant that we find three such poems focused on the woman (4:1–7; 6:5–7; 7:1–10) and only one on the man (5:10–16), another instance where the female lover stands more often in the spotlight. Second, I wonder whether we don't have parody also in Song of Songs 5:10–16, the sole description of the male lover?

> My beloved is clear-skinned and ruddy,
> Preeminent among ten thousand.
> His head is finest gold,
> His locks are curled
> And black as a raven.
> His eyes are like doves
> By watercourses,
> Bathed in milk,
> Set by a brimming pool.
> His cheeks are like beds of spices,
> Banks of perfume
> His lips are like lilies;
> They drip flowing myrrh.

[25] *Ibid.*, p. 72.   [26] *Ibid.*   [27] *Ibid.*

> His hands are rods of gold,
> Studded with beryl;
> His belly a tablet of ivory,
> Adorned with sapphires.
> His legs are like marble pillars
> Set in sockets of fine gold.
> He is majestic as Lebanon,
> Stately as the cedars.
> His mouth is delicious
> And all of him is delightful,
> Such is my beloved,
> Such is my darling,
> O maidens of Jerusalem!

Is not this still another sample of rhetoric that satirically deflates the image of the male who appears as bigger-than-life, standing somewhat awkwardly as a gargantuan, immobile, distant figure? The ostentatious display of divine-like attributes is especially striking, an ostentatiousness that easily suggests the presence of parody. Moreover, it is possible to discern here an incongruity in the female portrayal of her beloved, a discrepancy in representation that Landy captures well: "on his face, the expressive articulate part of his body, we find animate images of the woman; whereas the rest of his body, though appropriately formidable, is coldly metallic and disjointed. By a curious paradox that which is alive in him and relates to her is feminine."[28] Thus in his maleness the royal lover emerges as a static presence, larger than life but curiously immobile and lacking in sensuality.

In summary, the Song offers examples of an adroit, subtle use of parody both in order to subvert the conventional male dominance in patriarchal and royal society and to highlight and celebrate the erotic earthiness of the female dancer. It is comedy that reveals the cutting edge of satire,[29] but also comedy that unveils the playful, tantalizing power of eros.

[28] Landy, *Paradoxes of Paradise*, p. 90.
[29] Note the epigraph I have used at the beginning of the chapter: "Comedy blends insensibly into satire at one extreme and into romance at the other." See N. Frye's whole discussion of the relationship between comedy and satire in his *Anatomy of Criticism*, pp. 162 ff.

LOVE'S UNIONS AND REUNIONS IN COMIC PLAY

The Song contains still another staple of the comic vision: I speak here of the drive to integration and union. As Landy compellingly asserts, "the cardinal paradox of the Song is the union of two lovers through love."[30] Among its various themes the Song tells the tale of two lovers who represent the contrary worlds of country and city and who are able to overcome various obstacles in the path of love, coming together in a strong, mutual bond that is as strong as death. In this regard, Landy catches a glimpse of the comic potential of the Song. After developing sensitively the pastoral images of the Song in which the country maiden moves from her position as outsider to become the leader of "the daughters of Jerusalem," Landy offers the following suggestion: "If, as Northrop Frye . . . claims, comedy is essentially characterized as social cohesion, this induction [of the Shulamite into a position of leadership] presents the cooperation of country and city, thanatos and eros, innocence and purity, and all the contraries we have cited, in mutual dependence."[31] Landy wants primarily to delineate the rich interplay among different pastoral themes. He does not attempt to develop specifically how comedy might play itself out in the Song.

As I have already indicated, various interpreters from an early time have remarked the bucolic and comic aspects of the pastoral scenes in the Song. Moreover, interpreters have long noted that the oscillating pattern of separation and union functions as a structural hallmark, wherein the call for separation paradoxically represents the last word (8:14). Yet the two lovers revel in the moments of union and reunion, celebrating exuberantly the sweet times of consummation. After all, the Song is preeminently a song of springtime (2:11–13), an enchanting duet that bespeaks the seductive lure of eros and the promised delights of sexual union. The

---

[30] Landy, "The Song of Songs," p. 305.   [31] Landy, *Paradoxes of Paradise*, p. 147.

duet voices the lyrics of a community and cosmos alive with
the sounds of new love and life!

> My love spoke and said to me,
> Arise, my darling,
> My fair one, come.
> For, lo, the winter is past,
> The rain is over, gone.
> Blossoms appear in the land,
> Pruning-time has come.
> The voice of the turtledove
> Is heard in our land.
> The fig ripens her fruits,
> The vines in bloom give scent.
> Arise, come, my darling,
> My fair one, come away.   (Pope) (2:10–13)

Does not such a song of springtime echo the fundamental
drive of comedy whose season preeminently is spring?[32] Does
not this strange power of erotic love to overcome sharp differences and to engender the paradoxical union of two lovers
find its most congenial home in the world of comedy?

Once the equation of the Song's two lovers with God and
Israel was made, it is not surprising that these ancient lyrics
were connected with the celebration of God's love story with
Israel in the Exodus deliverance; hence the Song was read on
the final day of Passover services. Moreover, the Midrash drew
out intertextual connections between the Song and the Book
of Exodus.

THE SIGNIFICANCE OF SINGING LOVE'S SONG IN A COMIC KEY

I should now draw back and reflect on possible implications
of correlating the Song with comedy. In my view, comedy
offers genuine insight into the complex dynamics that
animate the Song, dynamics that show also the deep reso-

---

[32] See especially N. Frye, "The Mythos of Spring: Comedy", *Anatomy of Criticism*, pp.
163 ff.

nance between the Song and other instances of comedy in the biblical heritage.

First, as we have seen again and again in our biblical texts, comedy often *criticizes* social roles – it does not simply entertain, it can also undercut and subvert. Following the lead of other scholars (especially Brenner), I have suggested that the Song is a case in point, where the age-old comic strategies of satire and parody come into play, strategies directed principally against the fabled King Solomon and his royal court. The poet satirizes Solomon as an ostentatious king whose image as a master of a great harem is undercut. He finally disavows his huge entourage of women for his one and only (6:8, 9). Even the jaded Solomon can be smitten by eros: "You have captured my heart my sister, my spouse, you have captured my heart with one glance of your eyes" (4:9). Solomon breaks away ultimately from the static image of an immobilized, metallic king and becomes an incarnation of mobility and vitality: he is swift as a gazelle or a young stag bounding upon the mountains. But the parody also brings the woman lover delightfully down to earth, subverting statuesque, static imaging of the female body in the name and power of earthy, ribald sexuality. Thus the Song expresses a spirit of fun and frivolity in its poetic tale of two lovers.

Second, comedy characteristically *connects* divided parts of a community, driving toward integration, reconciliation, and union.[33] Thus in the Song, age-old antagonisms between country and city are at least temporarily overcome by the power of love; the Shulamite moves from being an outsider of the Jerusalem court to occupying the central position in the royal harem – and the royal heart. Here parody becomes an ally in the service of love, helping to effect this rapprochement precisely by clearing away obstacles between the two lovers. In fact, Martha Andresen suggests that in the Song "parody, undercutting and subverting of prevailing, exagger-

---

[33] *Ibid.*, p. 43: "The theme of the comic is the integration of society, which usually takes the form of incorporating a central character in it."

ated role types or role masks . . . is a phase *in* union, a step *towards* celebration."[34] Using parody in describing the bodies of the two lovers (notably in 5:1off and 7:1ff) helps to overcome the separation between royal and pastoral types "in order to achieve that essential naked humanness of erotic love."[35] In sum, parody becomes a key strategy in forging this paradoxical union of two opposites – man and woman, city and country, king and commoner. The Song of Solomon becomes also the Song of the Shulamite, a duet of two lovers united in a love stronger than difference and distance.

Third, as we have stressed, comedy typically *celebrates*: it can affirm love and life even in the midst of separation and death.[36] In the world of the Song as in the world of comedy, "love is strong as death" (8:6). The lovers may have to endure times of separation and loneliness, but they come together again in marvelous unions and reunions, in celebrative consummations that help to unite, even for a moment, the divided parts of community and cosmos. The Song therefore most appropriately unfolds within a comic vision that revels in an exultant drive to life. It is a vision aware of the threatening, terrifying shadows of loneliness and death, yet a vision at the same time vibrant with the desire for sexual union and its promise of new life.

Not surprisingly, the Song has often been connected with the book of Genesis in its celebration of love and life. In fact, there is an explicit echoing of the infamous line of Genesis 3:16 – "Your desire shall be for your husband, and he shall

---

[34] Martha Andresen, Department of English, Pomona College, Claremont, CA. (Private communication).   [35] *Ibid.*

[36] Once again I find N. Frye's remarks illuminating of the world of Solomon's Song as well as Shakespeare's comedies (*Anatomy of Criticism*, pp. 183–184): "The green world has analogies, not only to the fertile world of ritual, but to the dream world that we create out of our own desires. This dream world collides with the stumbling and blinded follies of the world of experience, of Theseus' Athens with its idiotic marriage law, of Duke Frederick and his melancholy tyranny, of Leontes and his mad jealousy, of the Court Party with their plots and intrigues, and yet proves strong enough to impose the form of desire on it. Thus Shakespearean comedy illustrates, as clearly as any *mythos* we have, the archetypal function of literature in visualizing the world of desire, not as an escape from 'reality,' but as the genuine form of the world that human life tries to imitate."

rule over you" – but an echoing designed to reverse and subvert the force of the original: "I am my beloved's, and his desire is for me" (7:11). Now erotic desire goes in the opposite direction, restoring the mutuality of the Edenic bond before it descends to bondage and domination. Trible has given striking rendition to this inversion:

> In Eden, the yearning of the woman for harmony with her man continued after disobedience. Yet the man did not reciprocate; instead, he ruled over her to destroy unity and pervert sexuality. Her desire became his dominion. But in the Song, male power vanishes. His desire becomes her delight. Another consequence of disobedience is thus redeemed through the recovery of mutuality in the garden of eroticism.[37]

Moreover, the Song of Songs has been construed as an "answer to Job," which it immediately follows in the Jewish Bible.[38] The love lyrics of the Song, with their fervent affirmation of the powers of eros, resonate especially with the drive to new life which the Yahweh speeches celebrate. Like Job, the Song does not allow the threatening forces of death to be the last word. Even while recognizing the risks of love, it revels in the life-enhancing wonders of a love sweeter than wine and as strong as death.

In conclusion, the Song of Songs claims by its title to be "the sublime song of Solomon,"[39] and its sublimity most fully realizes itself within the comic rhythms of a cosmos exuberantly alive with the pulsating power of eros. Different voices are indeed heard in the Song, but the voice of the female lover especially sounds the comic tones of love's erotic art. The mysterious Shulamite thus becomes love's celebrant and lyrical comedienne.

---

[37] Trible, *God and the Rhetoric of Sexuality*, p. 160.
[38] See the intriguing paper by Tamara Eskenazi, "Song of Songs as an Answer to the Book of Job." Presented at the Annual Meeting of the Society of Biblical Literature, held in San Francisco, December, 1981. More recently Jack Miles has also taken Song of Songs as a comic response to Job: "If the tragic climax at the end of the Book of Job is not somehow trumped, God's life will be over. Song of Songs is the trump card. It breaks the mood, changes the subject, and saves the Lord's life." See *God: A Biography*, p. 405.   [39] Pope, *Song of Songs*, p. 1.

Conclusion: towards a comprehensive view of biblical comedy

> With one attitude comedy sees the failure of the world, morally, ethically, socially; it ridicules, condemns, corrects, uproots, and subverts. With the opposite attitude it sympathizes, celebrates, accepts, confirms, and embraces. The comic attitude is a restless one: it disrupts the norm even as it creates one; it disturbs our values even as it delights.[1]
>
> (Alice Rayner)

THE DUAL FACES OF COMEDY

The epigraph captures well the Janus-faced character of comedy as it emerges in the Hebrew Bible. The subversive and celebrative sides of comedy often appear in the same biblical book, with the polarized "comic attitude" set within a dynamic interplay and tension, thus unveiling a comic vision that oscillates between attack and affirmation, corrective and celebration, ridicule and revel. In their different ways all six biblical books we have examined reveal such polarization and oscillation.

Genesis and Exodus, for example, as the foundational texts of the Bible, show a deft use of parody and satire designed to subvert foreign kings, magicians, patriarchs, prophets, priests, and even God – no one is completely spared. Adam appears as comically passive over against the bold, decisive Eve, and the serpent, a classic seducer and trickster, raises

---

[1] Alice Rayner, *Comic Persuasion: Moral Structure in British Comedy from Shakespeare to Stoppard* (Berkeley: University of California Press, 1987), p. 165.

278

some uncomfortable, penetrating questions about God's motivations. Esau plays the classic simpleton ridiculed as a hairy hunter who is none too bright. His younger twin Jacob plays the wily schemer, tricking his way through life, though often paying a high price when he too is tricked, whether in his marriage bed or in the cruel deception involving his favorite son Joseph. Both patriarchal figures – paradoxically opposite in their twinness – nonetheless receive somewhat similar treatment as they are satirized in their fraternal struggle over the prized blessing.

Aaron in his role as Moses' associate and founding priest in Israel is parodied in the Golden Calf incident when he gives a lame and comical rationalization of how the calf got made. Moses himself as the leader of the Exodus – indeed as archetypal embodiment of Israel – also has his blind spots revealed in the lengthy parody of his prophetic call in which we see the "unmaking and remaking" of a prophetic hero – or perhaps better an "anti-hero" who paradoxically becomes a hero in spite of himself.

Job and Jonah are showcases for the art of parody, subverting traditional ideals of patriarchal and prophetic existence. In Job's case the parody especially becomes damning when the Creator fails at the bar of justice. Only an appeal to a mysterious order that goes beyond good and evil partially mitigates the harsh verdict against the Creator God; even then the irony lingers to haunt the reader, evoking highly ambivalent responses.

Finally, royalty receives brilliant and sometimes subtle satire in Esther and Song of Songs, each author operating in a world where God is absent and where the imagery of royal power and presence is particularly stressed. Each one wields a satirical knife against the royal protagonist, the poet of the Song against the Israelite Solomon and the narrator of Esther against the Persian Ahasuerus, in order to deflate royal pretension. The paradox of this powerful use of subversive strategies is that both Israelite and foreign figures receive similar treatment.

In summary, all these notable characters become satirized

in order to show their weaknesses, foibles, and all too human failings. They are creatures of dust whose comic types feature the conflicts, fears, and anxieties of the offspring of Adam and Eve, yet ultimately they all perform pivotal roles in the human struggle for a share in the divine blessing.

Most remarkably, God often receives parodied representation, highlighting the ambiguous character of the deity whose dividedness and inner contradictions become all too evident in the unfolding biblical story. Hence from Genesis and Exodus to Job and Jonah, God reveals his conflict-ridden sides: is he omnipotent creator or bungler, tyrant or friend, warrior or healer?[2] The various narrators display all these dimensions and more in their parodied descriptions of a multi-faceted deity. What kind of a God is Yahweh-Elohim? Is God a deeply flawed, out-of-control creator who simply does what he will, inflicting unjust injury on his erring human creatures in what some would call a tragic universe? Or is God a benevolent comedian who orchestrates a sometimes hilarious carnival, with all the contradictions and catastrophes detailing how and why creation can be construed as an elaborate cosmic joke?

The Bible characteristically does not stop with subversion, for the texts usually drive on toward an affirmation of life and a celebration of the wonder and hopefulness of creation. Thus each of the biblical books I have analyzed shows the basic rhythm of comedy, a rhythm that finds expression in "an art form that arises naturally wherever people are gathered to celebrate life, in spring festivals, triumphs, birthdays, weddings, or initiations."[3] So again and again we have beheld Genesis' generative drive toward new birth and fertility even amidst barrenness and death; Exodus' wedding of liberation and laughter in celebrating Yahweh's victory over the Egyptians and in founding a covenantal community; Esther's depiction of the collaboration of Mordecai and Esther in

---

[2] The most comprehensive delineation of the contradictory personalities of God as character is now found in Jack Miles' *tour de force, God: A Biography.*

[3] Langer, "The Rhythm of Comedy," p. 124.

delivering a Jewish community from genocide and the resulting carnival celebration in Purim; Jonah's powerful punchline in the form of a question which affirms the sometimes capricious Creator's compassion for all creatures great and small; Job's song of creation in the carnival of morning stars and animals, a song that reveals a larger cosmic theater than Job's limited vision can perceive and leads to his re-vision of the universe which in turn results in his repentance and restoration; and finally, the Song of Songs' duet of two young lovers who delight in the wonders of wild gazelles and lush gardens as compelling images of their joyous participation in the spring-time of new love.

In sum, subversion and celebration typically belong together in a comprehensive view of biblical comedy: subversion often serving to undercut and clear away obstacles to the realization of fertility and forgiveness; and celebration finding expression in festivals of freedom and hope.

WOMEN OF WIT AND WISDOM IN BIBLICAL COMEDY

A hallmark of biblical comedy is the surprising roles that women often play over against the male protagonists. Beginning with mother Eve, women especially live by wit and wisdom to fulfill their function as symbolically captured in the pun involving Eve (*havah*="life") who is the prototypical "mother of all living" (*hay*). Hence, as already noted, Eve is counterposed as the strong, active one over against the passive, compliant, comical Adam. The various women of Genesis, Exodus, Esther, Job, and the Song of Songs continue to embody this drive to give birth to new life and then to nourish and protect it. We can draw a comic arc among Eve's daughters that stretches from Sarah who laughs with embarrassed skepticism at the promise of life but who then laughs joyfully over the birth of her son "Laughter," to the mother and sister of Moses who conspire together with Pharaoh's daughter in defiance of her father's decree to save Moses from a watery grave, to Esther who plays the clever and coura-

geous heroine who rescues her people from Haman's genocidal plan and helps to institute the festival of Purim, to Job's
wife and daughters who play peripheral, albeit striking roles
in the story of Job, and finally to the fabled Shulamite who
becomes the more dominant speaker and lover in the Song
of Songs, a woman who both playfully subverts the domi-
neering presence of the royal lover and powerfully affirms
the "love that is strong as death" (8:6).[4]

In these decisive roles of key women characters we see once
again how comedy displays its Janus face: namely, its subversive, disruptive power that culminates in its celebration of
the miracle and mystery of life. Recent studies of women and
their special kinds of humor and comedy may suggest there
is nothing accidental about the presence of such notable
women of comic wit among the stories and poems which are
so fundamental to biblical literature. Perhaps the special
powers of comedy are particularly invoked by those who are
marginalized and subordinated. It is no surprise, therefore,
that comedy becomes a part of the repertoire for survival
among oppressed, exiled, and enslaved people. One scholar
has singled out the humor of recent North American native
writing as having the status of "a survival skill, a tool for
acknowledging complexity, a means for exposing or subverting oppressive hegemonic ideologies, and an art for
affirming life in the face of objective troubles."[5] If this generalization also be applicable to the biblical women I have cited
(as I think it to be), then the congeniality between various
forms of comedy and women's life-giving and life-saving per-
formances in society should not be surprising: standing on

---

[4] According to Julia Kristeva, the Shulamite is "the first common individual who,
on account of her love, becomes the first Subject in the modern sense of the
term." See her *Tales of Love*, trans. Leon S. Roudiez (New York: Columbia
University Press, 1987), p. 100.

[5] M. M. J. Fischer, "Ethnicity and the Post-modern Arts of Memory," in *Writing
Culture: The Poetics and Politics of Ethnography*, J. Clifford and G. E. Marcus, eds.
(Berkeley: University of California Press, 1986), p. 224. Cited in Linda Hutcheon,
Irony's Edge: The Theory and Politics of Irony (London and New York: Routledge,
1994), p. 26.

the margins of society, women are able to deconstruct the dominant power structures and to recharge the forces of life.[6]

COMIC FORMS AND RITUAL EXPRESSIONS

The striking resonance between comedy and ritual needs to be highlighted. As we have observed, it is most revealing that the books that we have deemed comic play crucial roles in the most significant holy days in the Jewish liturgical calendar. Hence the intimate coupling of Exodus and Song of Songs with Passover, the vital connections between Esther and Purim (the carnival day par excellence among Jews), and even the reading of Jonah on the afternoon of *Yom Kippur*, illustrate vividly the correlation of the comic spirit with crucial rituals.

Ironically, as we noted earlier, one scholar has used the fact that Jonah accompanies *Yom Kippur* as an argument against a comic interpretation of Jonah. This strange argument suggests a fundamental misunderstanding of the role of comedy as a serious strategy for dealing with the most profound problems of human existence. In my view, the fact that the rabbis chose Jonah for the holiest day of the Jewish year demonstrates their keen insight into the necessity of invoking the comic spirit for ceremonies that define life and death in terms of atonement and forgiveness. Parody supplies the "corrective of laughter" and injects the solemnity of *Yom Kippur* with the satiric spectacle of a petulant prophet who must learn through a parable and its haunting question the mystery of divine love that embraces both humans and animals. That the rabbis deemed *Yom Kippur* as "no happier day" is apt testimony to the appropriateness of coupling a parody about an angry prophet with the holy day that celebrates penitence, purgation, and forgiveness.

Hasidic Judaism demonstrates still another striking linkage

---

[6] For a most illuminating exploration of women's wit, see the fine book by Juhasz, Miller, and Smith, *Comic Power in Emily Dickinson*.

between the day of atonement and the carnival spirit of parody in creating a provocative word-play: *yom kippurim-yom kepurim* ("day of atonement" [*kippurim*] – "day like [*ke*] Purim").[7] The pun is suggestive, providing special insight into a fundamental perspective of the comic vision. Given the prominence of puns in the Hebrew Bible, how appropriate for Hasidism to use a pun to suggest a secret affinity between the holiest day of the Jewish liturgical calendar and the most hilarious day: Day of Atonement and Festival of Purim seem to be opposites, yet they become nonetheless paradoxically and profoundly alike. Thus sanctity and gaiety, solemnity and festivity, join hands in this "odd couple" to give a stunning condensation of two vital parts of the comic vision: atonement that brings forgiveness and deliverance celebrated in laughter and revelry. The English verbal play found in the variant spellings of holy day/holiday says it all: *Yom Kippur* becomes the holy day par excellence and Purim the holiday of holidays. Holiness and hilarity thus combine to express a deeply felt comic sensibility.[8]

---

[7] I owe this observation to Tamara C. Eskenazi.

[8] Cf. Waskow, *Seasons of Our Joy*, p. 125; he suggests that one reason for the similarity between the two days may lie in the common image of lots: "For on Yom Kippur lots are cast between the goats: one for sacrifice, one for sending into the wilderness. Purim gets its name from the lots cast by Haman, as the day on which to destroy the Jews, the most propitious day for himself and the least propitious for the Jews. Another similarity between the days is that both remind us that chance has an important role in the world, but does not rule the world." Note also Deborah Simon's fine paper, "Unmasking the Masquerade: Doubt and Faith in Purim," unpublished essay (Claremont, CA: Pomona College, 1979). Simon offers the following astute remarks: "This proverb . . . is used in two divergent ways. On Yom Kippur, the proverb is moralistic, reminding one, like Isaiah (56:14–58:14 – the Haftorah reading for the day) that shows of penitence and great piety are but a masquerade. On Purim, its use is part of the general apologetics of Purim which elevate and justify the holiday, saying, the reality of Yom Kippur (its seriousness) is farce, whereas the reality of Purim is the true piety of its celebrants" (p. 1). After I had completed this manuscript, Tamara Eskenazi kindly called my attention to a new essay by Rachel Adler, "A Carnival at the Gates: Jonah and Laughter on Yom Kippur," forthcoming in Judith A. Kates and Gail Twersky Reimer, eds., *Beginning Anew* (New York: Ballantine Books, 1997). Adler gives an incisive, compelling argument for the intimate affinity between Purim and Yom Kippur and their correlative texts Esther and Jonah. She offers a striking confirmation of the vital role of comedy and laughter within the liturgical life of Judaism. "Viewing Purim as the inverse of Yom Kippur brings us closer to under-

TRAGEDY AND COMEDY IN THE HEBREW BIBLE

History is radical, and passes through many phases when it carries an old form to the grave. The last phase of a world historical form is as comedy. The gods of Greece who had already been tragically wounded in Aeschylus' Prometheus Bound, had to die again comically in the dialogues of Lucien. Why this course of history? So that humanity could part from its past gaily.[9]   (MARX)

Throughout the book we have returned again and again to the question of the interplay between tragedy and comedy in biblical literature, an interplay that haunts the course of history. In fact, if Marx is correct in the provocative claim of the epigraph, the movement of history is intimately caught up in the sequence of tragedy and comedy, a sequence that he couples enticingly with the Greek tradition. I would argue that the Hebrew biblical tradition also involves movement from tragedy to comedy. This movement, however, is not simply sequential but includes a dialectical interplay between tragedy and comedy with comedy typically having the last word. In particular, I have raised this important issue in conjunction with Genesis and Job which resonate with one another in suggestive and subtle ways, particularly in the symbolic relationship between Abraham and Job as archetypal patriarchs who represent polar opposites in the biblical tradition.[10] For instance, as Jack Miles has pointedly observed, the

---

standing their likeness, for an inversion is merely a likeness reversed. Yom Kippur is a fast preceded by a feast, while Purim is a feast preceded by a fast. Purim is a celebration tinged with somberness, whereas Yom Kippur is a solemn occasion pervaded by celebration" (pp. 1–2 of the unpublished manuscript).

[9] Cited in Susan Buck-Morss, *The Dialectics of Seeing: Walter Benjamin and the Arcades Project* (Cambridge, MA: The MIT Press, 1989), p. 257. In the context of her discussion, Buck-Morss couples Marx's view with the play and place of surrealistic humor in Benjamin's complex thought: she quotes Benjamin, "Surrealism is the death of the last century through farce."

[10] Amos Funkenstein offers a penetrating assessment of the inter-linkage between Abraham and Job: "Abraham and Job are the biblical paradigms of a trial of the faithful, and the latter is a conscious reflection of the former. What, then, is the difference between them? Abraham, it seems, is the realization of the maximum of 'faith' in the biblical sense of the word, which is trust. Job represents the minimum of faith to which a person can hold and still withstand his trial.

God who begins with a magnificent speech in Genesis finishes his speaking with the eloquent whirlwind speeches in Job 38–42. The silence of God after Job becomes important in Miles' "biography" of God, a silence that becomes deafening in the sombre realization that God apparently has nothing else of interest to say.[11] In the end Miles offers an elegant equivocation as to the tragic potential of the Tanakh (the Hebrew name for the Jewish Bible), ultimately affirming what is the fundamental thesis of my own study:

> If the Tanakh were tragedy, God, having learned the truth about himself through his relationship with mankind, above all his relationship with Job, would end in despair. But the Tanakh is not tragedy, and the Lord God does not end in despair. Tragedy has clarity and finality. The refusal of tragedy typically has neither. Tanakh refuses tragedy and ends as a result, in its own kind of muddle, but its protagonist ends alive, not dead. Taken as a whole, the Tanakh is a divine comedy but one that barely escapes tragedy.[12]

The issue that Miles raises and the very equivocation of his articulation vividly dramatize the tension between tragedy and comedy represented in Genesis and Job and by extension in the larger vision of the Bible whether in its Jewish or Christian form. This tension receives confirmation in the radical divisions among interpreters of Genesis and Job, two biblical books which serve in many profound respects as epitomes of the Bible. Thus we have already shown in our chapters on Genesis and Job how divided the commentators have been in assessing the two books' potential for comedy and tragedy. The majority of interpreters have usually set Genesis

---

Abraham, in the words of Kierkegaard, was 'the knight of faith,' Job a pawn. Abraham stayed silent in the face of his trial, Job rebelled, but still 'kept his innocence.' Abraham and Job are the poles in a person's being 'just' (*tsadik*) in the biblical sense of the word." Amos Funkenstein, *Perceptions of Jewish History* (Berkeley and Los Angeles: University of California Press, 1993), p. 64. Though one might argue with the oversimplified contrast between Abraham and Job in terms of the relative degree of their "faith," nonetheless Funkenstein has offered an illuminating contrast. In my judgment, the comic vision gives a fuller and richer portrayal of each patriarch with a more complicated and ambiguous characterization of each one's faith.

[11] Miles, *God: A Biography*, pp. 402–404.   [12] *Ibid.*, p. 404.

and Job in a tragic mode. Yet sensing a more dominant comic mood in these books remains a compelling possibility. In my judgment, the comic vision with its affirmation of life in the midst of death is ultimately more dominant, though tragedy retains its chilling threat. Hence I would characterize the Hebrew Bible as emerging finally as a comedy, a divine-human comedy where both creator and creatures are afflicted with contradiction and inner conflict, where both need often to muddle through to a happier end, yet where the biblical images of genuine tragedy are never fully eclipsed – let alone erased – even while they are encapsulated by the vision of comedy. Thus the "comedic intrusions" that Miles mentions must be viewed as more than intrusions;[13] rather they appear as dramatic and decisive interventions of a revolutionary comedy that revels in the desire and hope for a happier world, even when the threatening, terrifying possibility of death and despair remains. In the end, perhaps, Dante in his *Divine Comedy* represents arguably the most convincing adaptation of the Bible's ultimate vision, offering a more encompassing prospect than either Shakespeare's brooding evocation of the Bible's tragic sensibility as expressed so hauntingly in *Hamlet* or Milton's brilliant tragic adaptation of the Bible in *Paradise Lost*. But the faces of both tragedy and comedy linger in our mind's eye, evoking the full ambiguity of our human prospect.

Christopher Fry eloquently describes this intimate interplay between comic and tragic images in his memorable portrayal of the Janus-faced "person of Comedy" with its poignantly mixed features:

If I had to draw a picture of the person of Comedy it is so I should like to draw it: the tears of laughter running down the face, one hand still lying on the tragic page which so nearly contained the answer, the lips about to frame the great revelation, only to find it had gone as disconcertingly as a chair twitched away when we went to sit down. Comedy is an escape, not from truth but from despair: a narrow escape into faith.[14]

---

[13] *Ibid.*, p. 408.   [14] Fry, "Comedy," p. 15.

The escape clause that Fry describes must not be construed as mere escapism. Rather the comic vision contains a robust affirmation of life and revels in exuberance and excess. Its "escape into faith" reposes a fundamental trust in the gift of life, whatever "the slings and arrows of outrageous fortune." It shows how the comic eye can stare directly into the face of death and still see the surging powers of life and laughter.

"Our revels now are ended."

(SHAKESPEARE, *THE TEMPEST*)

Bibliography

Ackerman, James. "The Literary Context of the Moses Birth Story." In K. R. Gros Louis, *et al.*, eds., *Literary Interpretations of Biblical Narratives*. Nashville: Abingdon Press, 1974.

Adler, Rachel. "A Carnival at the Gates: Jonah and Laughter on Yom Kippur." Forthcoming in Judith A. Kates and Gail Twersky Reimer, eds., *Beginning Anew*. New York: Ballantine Books, 1997.

Alter, Robert. *The Art of Biblical Narrative*. New York: Basic Books, 1981.

The Art of Biblical Poetry. New York: Basic Books, 1985.

The World of Biblical Literature. New York: Basic Books, 1992.

Bakhtin, M. M. *The Dialogic Imagination: Four Essays*. Michael Holquist, ed. Trans. Caryl Emerson and Michael Holquist. Austin: University of Texas Press, 1981.

Rabelais and His World. Trans. Helene Iswolsky. Bloomington: Indiana University Press, 1984.

Bal, Mieke. *Lethal Love: Feminist Literary Readings of Biblical Love Stories*. Bloomington: Indiana University Press, 1987.

Barber, Chester J. *Shakespeare's Festive Comedy: A Study of Dramatic Form and Its Relation to Social Custom*. Princeton: Princeton University Press, 1959.

Barnes, Julian. *The History of the World in Ten and One-Half Chapters*. New York: Random House, 1990.

Barr, James. *The Garden of Eden and the Hope of Immortality*. Minneapolis: Fortress Press, 1993.

Baudelaire, Charles. "On the Essence of Laughter, and, in General, on the Comic in the Plastic Arts." In Robert W. Corrigan, ed., *Comedy: Meaning and Form*. San Francisco: Chandler Publishing Co., 1965, pp. 448–465.

Baumgartner, A. J. *L'Humour dans l'Ancien Testament*. Lausanne: Grayot, 1896.

Berg, Sandra Beth. *The Book of Esther. Society of Biblical Literature Dissertation Series* 44. Missoula: Scholars Press, 1979.

Berlin, Adele. "A Rejoinder to John A. Miles, Jr., with Some Observations on the Nature of Prophecy." *Jewish Quarterly Review* LXVI/4 (April, 1976), pp. 227–235.

Bermel, Albert. *Comic Agony: Mixed Impressions in the Modern Theatre.* Evanston: Northwestern University Press, 1993.

Bickerman, Elias. *Four Strange Books of the Bible: Jonah/Daniel/Koheleth/Esther.* New York: Schocken Books, 1967.

Bingham, Anne. "Ruse, Romance, and Resolution: The Comedy of Jacob." Unpublished essay. Claremont, CA: Pomona College, 1981.

Bjornson, Richard. *The Picaresque Hero in European Fiction.* Madison: The University of Wisconsin Press, 1977.

Blenkinsopp, Joseph. *A History of Prophecy in Israel: From the Settlement in the Land to the Hellenistic Period.* Philadelphia: The Westminster Press, 1983.

Boling, Robert B. *Judges: Introduction, Translation, and Commentary. The Anchor Bible.* New York: Doubleday and Company, 1975.

Bonhoeffer, Dietrich. *Creation and Fall: A Theological Interpretation of Genesis 1–3.* Trans. John C. Fletcher. London: SCM Press, 1959.

Branham, R. Bracht. "Authorizing Humor: Lucian's *Demonax* and Cynic Rhetoric." In Vernon K. Robbins, ed., *Semeia* 64 (1994), pp. 33–48.

Brenner, Athalya. "'Come Back, Come Back The Shulamite' (Song of Songs 7:1–10): A Parody of the *wasf* Genre." In Yehuda T. Radday and Athalya Brenner, eds., *On Humour and the Comic in the Hebrew Bible.* Sheffield: Almond Press, 1990, pp. 251–276.

"On the Semantic Field of Humour." *Ibid.,* pp. 39–58.

"Who's Afraid of Feminist Criticism? Who's Afraid of Biblical Humour? The Case of the Obtuse Foreign Ruler in the Hebrew Bible." *Journal for the Study of the Old Testament* 63 (1994), pp. 38–55.

Brenner, Athalya, ed. *A Feminist Companion to Exodus and Deuteronomy.* Sheffield: Sheffield Academic Press, 1994.

Brisman, Leslie. *The Voice of Jacob: On the Composition of Genesis.* Bloomington: Indiana University Press, 1990.

Brueggemann, Walter. "Pharaoh as Vassal: A Study of a Political Metaphor." *The Catholic Biblical Quarterly* 57 (1995), pp. 27–51. *Genesis.* Atlanta: John Knox Press, 1982.

Buber, Martin. *Moses: The Revelation and the Covenant.* New York: Harper & Row, 1958.

Buck-Morss, Susan. *The Dialectics of Seeing: Walter Benjamin and the Arcades Project.* Cambridge, MA: The MIT Press, 1989.

Carroll, R. P. "Strange Fire: Abstract of Presence Absent in the Text-Meditations on Exodus 3." *Journal for the Study of the Old Testament* 61 (1994), pp. 39–58.

Childs, Brevard S. *The Book of Exodus: A Critical, Theological Commentary.* Philadelphia: The Westminster Press, 1974.

Chotzner, J. *Hebrew Humor and Other Essays.* London: Methuen, 1905.

Clines, David J. A. *The Esther Scroll: The Story of the Story.* Sheffield: JSOT Press, 1984.

Job 1–20. Word Biblical Commentary 17. Dallas: Word Books, 1989.

What Does Eve Do to Help? and Other Readerly Questions to the Old Testament. Sheffield: Sheffield University Press, 1990.

Coats, George W. "Strife Without Reconciliation: A Narrative Theme in the Jacob Traditions." In R. Albertz, *et al.,* eds., *Werden und Wirken des Alten Testaments.* Goettingen: Vandenhoeck & Ruprecht, 1979.

From Canaan to Egypt: Structural and Theological Context for the Joseph Story. The Catholic Biblical Quarterly Monograph Series 4. Washington, DC: The Catholic Biblical Association of America, 1976.

Collins, John J. *Between Athens and Jerusalem: Jewish Identity in the Hellenistic Diaspora.* New York: Crossroad, 1983.

Cox, Harvey. *The Feast of Fools: A Theological Essay on Festivity and Fantasy.* Cambridge, MA: Harvard University Press, 1969.

Cox, Roger. "The Invented Self: An Essay on Comedy." *Soundings* 57 (1974), pp. 139–156.

Craig, Kenneth M. *A Poetics of Jonah: Art in the Service of Ideology.* Columbia: University of South Carolina, 1993.

Reading Esther: A Case for the Literary Carnivalesque. Louisville: Westminster/John Knox Press, 1995.

Cross, Frank M. *Canaanite Myth and Hebrew Epic: Essays in the History of the Religion of Israel.* Cambridge, MA: Harvard University Press, 1973.

Crouch, Walter B. "To Question an End, To End a Question: Opening the Closure of the Book of Jonah." *Journal for the Study of the Old Testament* 62 (1994), pp. 101–112.

Culler, Jonathan. "The Call of the Phoneme: Introduction." In Jonathan Culler, ed., *On Puns: The Foundation of Letters.* Oxford: Basil Blackwell, 1988, pp. 1–16.

Culley, Robert C. *Studies in the Structure of Hebrew Narrative. Semeia Supplements* 3. Philadelphia: Fortress Press, 1976.

Davidson, A. B. *The Book of Job.* Cambridge: Cambridge University Press, 1962.

Davidson, A. B. and C. H. Toy. "Job." *Encyclopaedia Britannica*

(1911). Reprinted in Ralph Hone, ed., *The Voice of the Whirlwind: The Book of Job.* San Francisco: Chandler Publishing Co., 1960.

Davies, Philip R. "Women, Men, Gods, Sex and Power: The Birth of a Biblical Myth." In Athalya Brenner, ed., *A Feminist Companion to Genesis.* Sheffield: Sheffield University Press, 1993.

Derrida, Jacques. *The Post Card: From Socrates to Freud and Beyond.* Trans. Alan Bass. Chicago: University of Chicago Press, 1987.

Dhorme, Eduard. *A Commentary on the Book of Job.* Trans. Harold Knight. Ontario: Nelson, 1967.

Douglas, Mary. "The Social Control of Cognition: Some Factors in Joke Perception." *Man,* n.s. III (1968).

Driver, S. R. *The Book of Exodus.* Cambridge: Cambridge University Press, 1953.

Durham, John I. *Exodus: Word Biblical Commentary* 3. Waco: Word Books, 1987.

Eskenazi, Tamara C. "Song of Songs as an Answer to the Book of Job." Unpublished paper presented at the Annual Meeting of the Society of Biblical Literature. San Francisco, 1981.

Exum, J. Cheryl. *Tragedy and Biblical Narrative: Arrows of the Almighty.* Cambridge: Cambridge University Press, 1992.

Exum, J. Cheryl, ed. *Tragedy and Comedy in the Bible. Semeia: An Experimental Journal for Biblical Criticism* 32 (1984).

Exum, J. Cheryl and Johanna W. H. Bos, eds. *Reasoning with the Foxes: Female Wit in a World of Male Power. Semeia: An Experimental Journal for Biblical Criticism* 42 (1988).

Exum, J. Cheryl and J. William Whedbee, "Isaac, Samson, and Saul: Reflections on the Comic and Tragic Visions." In J. Cheryl Exum, ed. *Tragedy and Comedy in the Bible. Semeia* 32 (1984), pp. 5–40.

Fisch, Harold. *Poetry with a Purpose: Biblical Poetics and Interpretation.* Bloomington: Indiana University Press, 1988.

Fischer, M. J. "Ethnicity and the Post-modern Arts of Memory." In J. Clifford and G. E. Marcs, eds., *Writing Culture: The Poetics and Politics of Ethnography.* Berkeley: University of California Press, 1986.

Fokkelman, J. P. "Genesis" and "Exodus." In Robert Alter and Frank Kermode, eds., *The Literary Guide to the Bible.* Cambridge, MA: Harvard University Press, 1987.

    Narrative Art in Genesis: Specimens of Stylistic and Structural Analysis. Sheffield: JSOT Press, 1991.

Foster, B. R. "Humor and Cuneiform Literature." *Journal of the Ancient Near Eastern Society of Columbia University* 6 (1974), pp. 69–86.

Fox, Everett. *These Are The Names: A New English Rendition of the Book of Exodus.* New York: Schocken Books, 1986.

Fox, Michael V. *Character and Ideology in the Book of Esther.* Columbia: University of South Carolina Press, 1991.

The Song of Songs and Ancient Egyptian Poetry. Madison: University of Wisconsin Press, 1985.

Fretheim, Terence E. *Exodus: Interpretation: A Commentary for Teaching and Preaching.* Louisville: John Knox Press, 1991.

Freud, Sigmund. *Civilization and Its Discontents.* Trans. and ed. James Strachey. New York: W. W. Norton & Co., 1961.

Fry, Christopher. "Comedy." In Robert W. Corrigan, ed., *Comedy: Meaning and Form.* San Francisco: Chandler Publishing Co., 1965, pp. 15–17.

Frye, Northrop. "The Argument of Comedy." In Paul Lauter, ed., *Theories of Comedy.* Garden City: Doubleday, 1964, pp. 450–460.

Anatomy of Criticism: Four Essays. New York: Atheneum, 1966.

Fables of Identity: Studies in Poetic Mythology. New York: Harcourt, Brace & World, 1963.

The Great Code: The Bible and Literature. New York: Harcourt Brace Jovanovich, 1982.

The Myth of Deliverance: Reflections on Shakespeare's Problem Comedies. Brighton: The Harvester Press, 1983.

A Natural Perspective: The Development of Shakespearian Comedy and Romance. New York: Harcourt, Brace & World, 1965.

Words of Power: Being a Second Study of the Bible and Literature. New York: Harcourt Brace Jovanovich, 1990.

Frye, Roland M. *The Reader's Bible: A Narrative.* Princeton: Princeton University Press, 1965.

Fullerton, Kemper. "Double Entendre in the First Speech of Eliphaz." *Journal of Biblical Literature* 53 (1934), pp. 321–349.

Funkenstein, Amos. *Perceptions of Jewish History.* Berkeley and Los Angeles: University of California Press, 1993.

Gardella, Peter. "Ego and Apocalypse in America." *Religious Studies Review* 21/3 (July, 1995), pp. 20.

Gerleman, Gillis. *Esther.* Neukirchen-Vluyn: Neukirchener Verlag, 1973.

Ruth. Das Hohelied. Biblischer Kommentar Altes Testament. Neukirchen-Vluyn: Neukirchener Verlag, 1965.

Studien zu Esther. Neukirchen-Vluyn: Neukirchener Verlag, 1966.

Good, Edwin M. "Job and the Literary Task: A Response." *Soundings* 56 (1973), pp. 471–475.

In Turns of the Tempest: A Reading of Job. Stanford: Stanford University Press, 1990.

Irony in the Old Testament. Philadelphia: Westminster Press, 1965.

Gottwald, Norman K. *The Hebrew Bible: A Socio-Literary Introduction.* Philadelphia: Fortress Press, 1985.

Gowan, Donald E. *Theology in Exodus: Biblical Theology in the Form of Commentary.* Louisville: Westminster/John Knox Press, 1994.

Grandsen, K. W. "Milton, Dryden, and the Comedy of the Fall." *Essays in Criticism* 26 (1976), pp. 116–133.

Greenstein, Edward L. "A Jewish Reading of Esther." In Jacob Neusner, Baruch A. Levine, and Ernest S. Frerichs, eds., *Judaic Perspectives on Ancient Israel.* Philadelphia: Fortress Press, 1987.

Gunkel, Hermann. *Genesis.* 6th ed. Goettingen: Vandenhoeck und Ruprecht, 1964.

Gunn, David M. and Danna Nolan Fewell. *Narrative in the Hebrew Bible.* Oxford: Oxford University Press, 1993.

Gutwirth, Marcel. *Laughing Matter: An Essay on the Comic.* Ithaca and London: Cornell University Press, 1993.

Habel, Norman C. *The Book of Job.* Philadelphia: Westminster Press, 1985.

Herion, Gary A. *et al.* "Humor and Wit." In David Noel Freedman, ed., *The Anchor Bible Dictionary.* New York: Doubleday, 1992, vol. III, pp. 325–333.

Holbert, John C. "'Deliverance Belongs to Yahweh!': Satire in the Book of Jonah." *Journal for the Study of the Old Testament* 21 (1981), pp. 59–81.

Humphreys, W. Lee. "A Life-style for the Diaspora: a Study of the Tales of Esther and Daniel." *Journal of Biblical Literature* 92 (1973), pp. 211–223.

The Tragic Vision and the Hebrew Tradition. Philadelphia: Fortress Press, 1985.

Hunter, Robert Grams. *Shakespeare and the Comedy of Forgiveness.* New York: Columbia University Press, 1965.

Hurston, Zora Neale. *Moses, Man of the Mountain.* New York: Harper & Row, 1991.

Hutcheon, Linda. *Irony's Edge: The Theory and Politics of Irony.* London and New York: Routledge, 1994.

Hyers, Conrad. *The Comic Vision and the Christian Faith: A Celebration of Life and Laughter.* New York: Pilgrim Press, 1981.

And God Created Laughter: The Bible as Divine Comedy. Atlanta: John Knox Press, 1987.

Isbell, Charles. "Exodus 1–2 in the Context of Exodus 1–14: Story Lines and Key Words." In David J. A. Clines, David M. Gunn, and Alan J. Hauser, eds., *Art and Meaning: Rhetoric in Biblical Literature. Journal for the Study of the Old Testament,* Supplement 19 (1982).

Jackson, Howard M. "The Shadow of Pharaoh, Your Lord, Falls upon You: Once Again *Wenamun 2.46.*" *Journal of Near Eastern Studies* 54 (1995), pp. 273–286.

Johnson, Samuel. *The Rambler* 125 (1751). In Paul Lauter, ed., *Theories of Comedy.* Garden City: Doubleday, 1964, pp. 253–258.

Johnson, Thomas, ed. *The Complete Poems of Emily Dickinson.* Boston: Little, Brown, & Co., 1960.

Jones, Bruce W. "Two Misconceptions about the Book of Esther." *Catholic Biblical Quarterly* 39 (1977), pp. 177–181.

Josipovici, Gabriel. *The Book of God: A Response to the Bible.* New Haven: Yale University Press, 1988.

Juhasz, Suzanne, Cristanne Miller, and Martha Nell Smith. *Comic Power in Emily Dickinson.* Austin: University of Texas Press, 1993.

Jung, Carl. *Answer to Job.* Cleveland: The World Publishing Co., 1960.

Kallen, H. M. *The Book of Job as a Greek Tragedy.* New York: Hill and Wang, 1959.

Kierkegaard, Soren. *Stages on Life's Way.* New York: Schocken Books, 1967.

Knierim, Rolf P. "The Composition of the Pentateuch." In Kent Harold Richards, ed., *Society of Biblical Literature Seminar Papers* 24 (1985), pp. 393–416.

The Task of Old Testament Theology: Method and Cases. Grand Rapids: Wm. B. Eerdmans Co., 1995.

Knight, A. F. and Friedemann W. Golka. *Revelation of God: A Commentary on the Books of The Song of Songs and Jonah.* Grand Rapids: Wm. B. Eerdmans Co., 1988.

Kort, Wesley A. *Story, Text, and Scripture: Literary Interests in Biblical Narrative.* University Park: The Pennsylvania University Press, 1988.

Kristeva, Julia. *Tales of Love.* Trans. Leon S. Roudiez. New York: Columbia University Press, 1987.

Landes, George M. "The Kerygma of the Book of Jonah." *Interpretation* 21 (January, 1967), pp. 3–31.

Landy, Francis. "Are We in the Place of Averroes? Response to the Articles of Exum and Whedbee, Buss, Gottwald, and Good." In J. Cheryl Exum, ed., *Tragedy and Comedy in the Bible: Semeia: An Experimental Journal for Biblical Criticism* 32 (1984), pp. 131–146.

"The Song of Songs." In Robert Alter and Frank Kermode, eds., *The Literary Guide to the Bible.* Cambridge, MA: Harvard University Press, 1987.

Paradoxes of Paradise. Sheffield: Almond Press, 1983.

Langer, Susanne. "The Rhythm of Comedy." In Robert W. Corrigan, ed. *Comedy: Meaning and Form.* San Francisco: Chandler Publishing Co., 1965, pp. 119–140.

Lautor, Paul, ed. *Themes of Comedy.* Garden City, NY: Doubleday and Co., 1964.

Levenson, Jon D. *The Death and Resurrection of the Beloved Son: The Transformation of Child Sacrifice in Judaism and Christianity.* New Haven: Yale University Press, 1992.

Lewalski, Barbara Kiefer. *Paradise Lost and the Rhetoric of Literary Forms.* Princeton: Princeton University Press, 1985.

Lohfink, Norbert. "Jona ging zur Stadt hinaus (Jon 4,5)." *Biblische Zeitschrift* 5 (1961), pp. 185–203.

Lowe, John. *Jump at the Sun: Zora Neale Hurston's Cosmic Comedy.* Chicago: University of Illinois Press, 1994.

Magonet, Jonathan. *Form and Meaning: Studies in Literary Techniques in the Book of Jonah.* Sheffield: The Almond Press, 1983.

A Rabbi's Bible. London: SCM Press, 1991.

Mann, Thomas. *Joseph und Seine Brüder.* Berlin: S. Fischer Verlag AG, 1975.

Marcus, David. *From Balaam to Jonah: Anti-prophetic Satire in the Hebrew Bible.* Atlanta: Scholars Press, 1995.

Matter, E. Ann. *The Voice of My Beloved: The Song of Songs in Western Medieval Christianity.* Philadelphia: University of Pennsylvania Press, 1990.

McAlpine, Thomas A. *Sleep, Divine and Human, in the Old Testament.* Sheffield: JSOT Press, 1987.

McEvenue, Sean. *Interpreting the Pentateuch.* Collegeville, MN: The Liturgical Press, 1990.

McLelland, J. C. *The Clown and the Crocodile.* Richmond: John Knox Press, 1970.

Medcalf, S. E. "Comedy." In R. J. Coggins and J. L. Houlden, eds., *A Dictionary of Biblical Interpretation.* London: SCM Press, 1990, pp. 128–129.

Meyers, Carol. *Discovering Eve: Ancient Israelite Woman in Context.* Oxford: Oxford University Press, 1988.

Miles, Jack. "Laughing at the Bible: Jonah as Parody." *Jewish Quarterly Review* 65 (1975), pp. 168–181.

God: A Biography. New York: Alfred A. Knopf, 1995.

Mitchell, Stephen. *The Book of Job.* San Francisco: North Point Press, 1987.

Murphy, Roland E. *The Song of Songs: A Commentary on the Book of Canticles or Song of Songs.* S. Dean McBride, Jr., ed. Minneapolis: Augsberg Press, 1990.

Napier, B. D. *Come Sweet Death: A Quintet from Genesis.* Philadelphia and Boston: United Church Press, 1967.

Niditch, Susan. "Genesis." In Carol A. Newsom and Sharon H. Ringe, eds., *The Women's Bible Commentary.* Louisville: Westminster/John Knox Press, 1992.

Underdogs and Tricksters: A Prelude to Biblical Folklore. San Francisco: Harper & Row, 1987.

O'Leary, Stephen D. *Arguing the Apocalypse: A Theory of Millennial Rhetoric.* New York: Oxford University Press, 1994.

Pardes, Ilana. *Countertraditions in the Bible: A Feminist Approach.* Cambridge, MA: Harvard University Press, 1992.

Phillips, John A. *Eve: The History of an Idea.* San Francisco: Harper & Row, 1984.

Polhemus, Robert M. *Comic Faith: The Great Tradition from Austen to Joyce.* Chicago: University of Chicago Press, 1980.

Polzin, Robert. "The Framework of the Book of Job." *Interpretation* 28 (1974), pp. 182–200.

Pope, Marvin. "Metastases in Canonical Shapes of the Super Song." In G. M. Tucker, D. G. Petersen, and R. R. Wilson, eds., *Canon, Theology, and Old Testament Interpretation.* Philadelphia: Fortress Press, 1988.

Job. The Anchor Bible. Garden City, NY: Doubleday & Co., 1965.

Song of Songs. The Anchor Bible. New York: Doubleday, 1977.

Powers, W. J. A. *Once Upon a Time: A Humorous Re-telling of the Genesis Stories.* Nashville: Abingdon Press, 1992.

Quinones, Richard J. *The Changes of Cain: Violence and the Lost Brother in Cain and Abel Literature.* Princeton: Princeton University Press, 1991.

Rad, Gerhard von. *Genesis: A Commentary.* Trans. John H. Marks. Philadelphia: The Westminster Press, 1956.

Old Testament Theology: Volume 1: The Theology of Israel's Historical Traditions. Trans. D. M. G. Stalker. New York: Harper and Bros., 1962.

The Problem of the Hexateuch and Other Essays. Trans. E. W. Trueman Dicken. New York: McGraw Hill Book Co., 1966.

Radday, Yehuda T. "Humour in Names." In Yehuda T. Radday and Athalya Brenner, eds., *On Humour and the Comic in the Hebrew Bible.* Sheffield: Sheffield Academic Press, 1990, pp. 86–89.

"On Missing the Humour in the Bible: An Introduction." *Ibid.,* pp. 21–38.

Radin, Paul. *The Trickster: A Study in American Indian Mythology.* New York: Schocken, 1972.

Rayner, Alice. *Comic Persuasion: Moral Structure in British Comedy from Shakespeare to Stoppard.* Berkeley: University of California Press, 1987.

Robertson, David. "The Book of Job: A Literary Study." *Soundings* 56 (1973), pp. 446–469.

The Old Testament and the Literary Critic. Philadelphia: Fortress Press, 1977.

Rose, Margaret A. *Parody: Ancient, Modern, and Post-Modern.* Cambridge: Cambridge University Press, 1993.

Rosenberg, David and Harold Bloom. *The Book of J.* New York: Grove Weidenfeld, 1990.

Rosenthal, Franz. *Humor in Early Islam.* Leiden: E. J. Brill, 1956.

Rowley, H. H. *Job.* Ontario: Nelson, 1970.

Russ, Daniel. "The Bible as Genesis of Comedy." In Louise Cowan, ed., *The Terrain of Comedy.* Dallas: The Institute of Humanities and Culture, 1984, pp. 40–59.

Russell, Jeffrey Burton. *Satan: The Early Christian Tradition.* Ithaca: Cornell University Press, 1981.

Saliers, Don. "Faith and the Comic Eye." *Andover Newton Quarterly* 13/4 (1973), pp. 259–276.

Sanders, Barry. *Sudden Glory: Laughter as Subversive History.* Boston: Beacon Press, 1995.

Sandmel, Samuel. *The Enjoyment of Scripture.* Oxford: Oxford University Press, 1972.

Sasson, Jack. "Esther." In Robert Alter and Frank Kermode, eds., *The Literary Guide to the Bible.* Cambridge, MA: Harvard University Press, 1987.

Jonah: A New Translation with Introduction, Commentary, and Interpretations. Anchor Bible. New York: Doubleday, 1990.

Schaeffer, Neil. *The Art of Laughter.* New York: Columbia University Press, 1981.

Shapiro, Amy. *The Myth of Job.* Unpublished Senior Thesis. Claremont, CA: Pomona College: Department of Religious Studies, 1975.

Simon, Deborah. "Unmasking the Masquerade: Doubt and Faith in Purim." Unpublished essay. Claremont CA: Pomona College, 1979.

Simon, Neil. *God's Favorite: A Comedy by Neil Simon.* New York: Random House, 1975.

Skehan, Patrick W. "I Will Speak Up." *Studies in Israelite Poetry and Wisdom. Catholic Biblical Quarterly Monograph Series 1.* Washington DC: Catholic Biblical Association, 1971.

Smith, Jonathan Z. *Map is Not Territory: Studies in the History of Religions.* Leiden: E. J. Brill, 1978.

Speiser, E. A. "The Case of the Obliging Servant." In J. J. Finkelstein and Moshe Greenberg, eds., *Oriental and Biblical Studies: Collected Writings of E. A. Speiser.* Philadelphia: University of Pennsylvania Press, 1967.

Steiner, George. *After Babel: Aspects of Language and Translation.* Oxford: Oxford University Press, 1975.

Sternberg, Meir. *The Poetics of Biblical Narrative: Ideological Literature and the Drama of Reading.* Bloomington: Indiana University Press, 1985.

Stinespring, W. F. "Humor." In George Arthur Buttrick, *et al.*, eds., *The Interpreter's Dictionary of the Bible.* New York: Abingdon Press, 1962, pp. 660–662.

Styan, J. L. *The Dark Comedy.* Cambridge: Cambridge University Press, 1968.

Swados, Elizabeth. "Job: He's a Clown." In Christina Buechmann and Celina Spiegel, eds., *Out of the Garden: Women Writers on the Bible.* New York: Fawcett Columbine, 1994, pp. 204–220.

Sypher, Wylie. "The Meanings of Comedy." In Wylie Sypher, ed., *Comedy: An Essay on Comedy, George Meredith and Laughter, Henri Bergson.* Garden City: Doubleday, 1956.

Terrien, Samuel. "The Yahweh Speeches and Job's Responses." *Review and Expositor* 58 (1971), pp. 497–509.

Thompson, Thomas L. *The Origin Tradition of Ancient Israel: I. The Literary Formation of Genesis and Exodus 1–23.* Sheffield: Sheffield Academic Press, 1987.

Trible, Phyllis. *God and the Rhetoric of Sexuality.* Philadelphia: Fortress Press, 1978.

Rhetorical Criticism: Context, Method, and the Book of Jonah. Minneapolis: Fortress Press, 1994.

Turner, L. A. "Lot as Jekyll and Hyde: A Reading of Genesis 18–19." In David J. A. Clines, Stephen E. Fowl, and Stanley E. Porter, eds., *The Bible in Three Dimensions: Essays in Celebration of Forty Years of Biblical Studies in the University of Sheffield.* Sheffield: Sheffield Academic Press, 1990.

Van de Walle, B. *L'Humour dans la Littérature et l'Art de l'Ancienne Egypte.* Leiden: E. J. Brill, 1969.

Van Seters, John. *The Life of Moses: The Yahwist as Historian in Exodus-Numbers.* Louisville: Westminster/John Knox Press, 1994.

Via, Dan O., Jr. *Kerygma and Comedy in the New Testament.* Philadelphia: Fortress Press, 1975.

Waskow, Arthur I. *Seasons of Our Joy: A Handbook of Jewish Festivals.* New York: Summit Books, 1982.

Westermann, Claus. *Genesis.* Neukirchen-Vluyn: Neukirchener Verlag, 1983.

Genesis: A Practical Commentary. Trans. David E. Green. Grand Rapids: Wm. B. Eerdmans Publishing Co., 1987.

Whedbee, J. William. "The Comedy of Job." *Semeia: An Experimental Journal for Biblical Criticism* 7 (1977), pp. 1–39.

"Jacob and the Comic Vision: The Adventures of a Rogue." *Bulletin of the Institute for Antiquity and Christianity* Vol. xv/2 (June, 1988), pp. 9–12.

"Paradox and Parody in the Song of Solomon: Towards a Comic Reading of the Most Sublime Song." In Athalya Brenner, ed., *A Feminist Companion to the Song of Songs.* Sheffield: Sheffield Academic Press, 1993.

Whitehead, A. N. *Dialogues.* Lucien Price, ed. Boston: Little and Brown, 1953.

Wiesel, Elie. *Sages and Dreamers: Portraits and Legends from the Jewish Tradition.* New York: Simon & Schuster, 1991.

Williams, James G. "'You Have Not Spoken Truth of Me': Mystery and Irony in Job." *Zeitschrift für die alttestamentliche Wissenschaft* 83 (1971), pp. 231–255.

Winterson, Jeanette. *Boating for Beginners.* London: Methuen London Ltd., 1985.

Wittgenstein, Ludwig. *Philosophical Investigations* (third edition). Trans. G. E. M. Anscombe. Englewood Cliffs, NJ: Prentice Hall, 1953.

Wolff, Hans Walter. *Obadiah and Jonah: A Commentary.* Trans. Margaret Kohl. Minneapolis: Augsburg Publishing House, 1986.

Zornberg, Avivah Gottlieb. *Genesis: The Beginning of Desire.* Philadelphia: The Jewish Publication Society, 1995.

Zuckerman, Bruce. *Job The Silent: A Study in Historical Counterpoint.* Oxford: Oxford University Press, 1991.

Index of authors

Index of biblical references

Index of topics